I0528479

www.ingramcontent.com/pod-product-compliance
Lightning Source LLC
Chambersburg PA
CBHW051320120626
46547CB00015B/2321

חמש מגילות

THE
ISRAEL
BIBLE

FIVE SCROLLS

EDITED BY

Rabbi Tuly Weisz

The Israel Bible: Five Scrolls

First Edition, 2021

The Israel Bible was produced by Israel365 in cooperation with Teach for Israel and is used with permission from Teach for Israel. All rights reserved. The English translation was adapted by Israel365 from the JPS Tanakh. Copyright © 1985 by the Jewish Publication Society. All rights reserved.

Cover image used under license from Shutterstock.com

ISBN 978-1-957109-42-8

A CIP catalogue record for this title is available from the British Library

The Israel Bible: Five Scrolls is a holy book that contains the name of God and should be treated with respect.

Table of Contents

Introduction

The Hebrew Bible is commonly known as the *Tanakh* which stands for *Torah* (the Five Books of Moses), *Neviim* (the Prophets) and *Ketuvim* (the Writings). The *Tanakh* consists of 24 books that are considered by Jews to be the word of God. While these books have been referred to as the "Old Testament," many Jews reject this label since it implies the replacement of the Hebrew Bible with something newer and prefer the more authentic Jewish name.

The *Tanakh* is not only the most important book known to man, it is God's word that is perfect and absolute. It is therefore a daunting undertaking to publish an edition of the *Tanakh*, and the responsibilities are awesome. There is no room for error or carelessness in dealing with the eternal word of God. Further, upon embarking on such a serious initiative, we ask ourselves if our efforts are gratuitous. Considering the many editions of the Bible in print, is there truly a need for yet another one?

While there are numerous Bibles in circulation today, its most central aspect – the Land of Israel – has often been overlooked. References to Israel appear on nearly every page, and the city of Jerusalem is specifically referred to hundreds of times throughout the Bible. The essential link between Israel and *Torah* is emphasized repeatedly in verses such as, "For instruction (*Torah*) shall come forth from *Tzion*, the word of *Hashem* from *Yerushalayim*" (Micah 4:2).

The miraculous return of the People of Israel to the Land of Israel in our own generation provides the perfect moment for a new volume to fill this void in biblical literature. *The Israel Bible* includes many special features elucidating God's focus on Israel throughout *Tanakh* and there are many additional, multimedia features available on our website **www.theisraelbible.com**.

Ordering and Presentation – In presenting *The Israel Bible*, our goal is to spread awareness of the biblical significance of the Land of Israel as well as the Jewish people's eternal connection to the land, based on the text of the *Tanakh*, the Hebrew Bible. We aim to honor "the God, the People and the Land of Israel" from an Orthodox Jewish perspective. To that end, *The Israel Bible* follows the traditional Jewish ordering of the books and the customary Hebrew division of chapters. Therefore, for example, we count 24 books of *Tanakh* with *Sefer Divrei Hayamim* (Chronicles) appearing last. It is our hope that our rich content will speak to all Jews and non-Jews who appreciate Israel as the God given land of the Jewish people.

English Translation – Throughout history, Jews have studied the Bible in Hebrew, as any form of translation would miss much of the nuance of the original holy tongue in which *Torah* has been transmitted since the days of Moses. However, as many Jews settled in America in the 19th Century, the need for an English translation became necessary. To be sure, there were already English translations prepared over the centuries by Christians, but in the words of the original editors of the Jewish Publication Society (JPS), "The Jew cannot afford to have his Bible translation prepared for him by others. He cannot have it as a gift, even as he cannot borrow his soul from others."

JPS set out in the late 1800s to publish an authoritative English translation "in the spirit of Jewish tradition." It was compiled over decades by some of the leading Jewish scholars of the time. They formed committees and subcommittees to compare existing English versions, considering medieval and modern Jewish commentators. The monumental JPS translation, originally published in 1917, has been updated in recent years, and *The Israel Bible* is proud to utilize the 1984 New Jewish Publication Society (NJPS) version with its modern, clear language, as well as its wide-ranging acceptance as an accurate and high-quality translation. We applied the NJPS translation verbatim, except for a select list of nouns which we replaced with their traditional Hebrew names. This is true even when we found the NJPS translation to be different than the popular translation of a word or phrase and when the NJPS switched the order of the text for the sake of clarity (see, for example, Ezekiel 24:22–24).

Hebrew Transliteration – To give our readers an authentic *Tanakh* experience, every verse that has commentary is transliterated from Hebrew into English. The Hebrew alphabet chart includes our standards for transliteration and pronunciation of Hebrew verses, enabling readers of *The Israel Bible* to decipher key biblical passages in the holy language. Readers can hear the entire Bible read in Hebrew on our website **www.theisraelbible.com**.

There are various standards when it comes to transliterating Hebrew words into English letters. While we have relied primarily on the classical Hebrew transliteration, we have occasionally deviated for the sake of simplicity, clarity and to reflect common usage.

In addition to whole verses, we have also transliterated many proper nouns in the English translation so that our readers can learn the names of key biblical figures and locations in their Hebrew form. As a rule, we chose to transliterate names of people that were central in the establishment and functioning of the nation of Israel, as well as significant places in the Holy Land. Therefore, regarding Adam's sons, for example, only *Shet* (Seth) is transliterated since it was from him that *Noach* (Noah), and ultimately *Avraham* (Abraham), descended. For this reason, there might be verses or sections of *The Israel Bible* that contains multiple names and only some of them are transliterated.

For the same reason, we have transliterated the names of the books of *Tanakh* when referring to them in our introductions and commentary. When referencing a specific chapter or verse, however, we use the English names of the books in our citations for clarity. We also transliterated ideas and concepts that are central to Judaism such as *Shabbat* (Sabbath), the names of the Jewish holidays and the *Beit Hamikdash* (Temple), as well as biblical measurements. Finally, the name of God is transliterated. Out of respect, Orthodox Jews generally refer to the Lord as *Hashem*, which literally means 'the Name.' Referring to God as *Hashem* reminds us that we feel close to Him but also recognize our distance at the same time. To stress this moniker, we transliterated both the Tetragrammaton as well as the name *Elohim* as *Hashem*.

Study Notes – Our unique commentary was compiled by Orthodox Jewish scholars who live in Israel. It is an anthology in the sense that most of the commentary is not original, but draws from traditional teachings of early Jewish Sages and modern rabbinic commentators. We also include quotations from individuals who have played a significant part in the past century of modern Israeli history including Israeli prime ministers, poets and military leaders.

Our commentary can be broken into four categories, three of which are identified by an icon at the beginning of the study note:

 Israel lessons are indicated with an icon bearing the map of Israel and focus on the Land of Israel and the modern State of Israel.

 Jewish lessons are indicated with a *Torah* scroll and teach a concept in Judaism or a classic idea from rabbinic thought.

 Hebrew lessons are represented by an icon bearing the letter *aleph* and focus on the meaning of a Hebrew word or phrase.

All other comments are considered general comments and are not assigned an icon.

Supplemental Material – In addition to our unique translation and original commentary, *The Israel Bible* offers supplementary material to enrich the learning experience of our readers. Before every book of *Tanakh,* we provide an introduction, as well as information, generally in the form of a map, a chart or a list, which is central to the specific book.

Maps – As the purpose of *The Israel Bible* is to highlight the biblical significance of the Land of Israel, significant time was spent researching and preparing maps to bring the physical contours of the holy land to life with great accuracy. However, since there is a lack of information regarding the precise locations of certain ancient cities, some of the places on our maps are approximate or subject to debate. In these cases, we followed the opinion that we are most comfortable with, but acknowledge that there is room for disagreement. We continue to produce new maps, which are available on our website **www.theisraelbible.com/maps**.

Torah **Readings** – The *Torah* is not just a work that is studied privately, it is also read out loud in synagogue. Every *Shabbat* and holiday a portion of the *Torah* is read, as well as a related section from *Neviim,* the prophets, called the *haftarah.* We included the blessings recited before and after the reading of the *Torah,* a list of the weekly *Torah* portions and their corresponding *haftarot,* and a chart of the *Torah* readings for special days with their corresponding *haftarot.* Readers can always find the current week's *Torah* portion by visiting **www.theisraelbible.com/weekly-torah-portion**. In this volume, we indicate where a new *Torah* portion begins by highlighting the Hebrew verse number with a gray box so readers can follow along with the communal *Torah* readings. Furthermore, we have included prayers for the State of Israel and the soldiers of the Israel Defense Forces (IDF) that are generally recited following the *Torah* reading in synagogue. It is our constant prayer that God watch over the State of Israel and the members of the IDF, who defend Israel every hour of every day.

In 1948, the State of Israel was created providing a modern answer to Isaiah's ancient question, "Is a nation born all at once?" (Isaiah 66:8). *The Israel Bible* was first published in the 70th year of God's miraculous restoration of the People of Israel to the Land of Israel. Jewish wisdom teaches that 70 is a significant number: *Moshe* (Moses) translated the *Torah* into 70 languages for all 70 nations of the world. From our very origins, the Jewish people were meant to be a light unto the 70 nations, spreading God's truth to the masses.

In the seven decades since the modern rebirth of the State of Israel, God's plan has been unfolding with unprecedented speed, dramatic highs and heartbreaking lows. Never has Israel been at the forefront of the world's attention as it is in our generation. Efforts to vilify the Jewish State seem to spread every day across the globe. At the same time, so does the growing movement of millions of non-Jewish biblical Zionists who stand with the nation of Israel as an expression of their commitment to God's word. As we seek to understand the clash of these two conflicting worldviews, the need for *The Israel Bible* has never been so important.

Standing on the great shoulders of those who came before us and emanating from the land that has always served as the birthplace for the Bible, we conclude with a heartfelt prayer: May the Almighty bless our efforts in offering this *Tanakh* to influence the hearts, minds and actions of its readers. In this way, it is our hope to spread God's name so that the publication of *The Israel Bible* brings us one step closer to the final redemption of Israel and the entire world.

Rabbi Tuly Weisz
Editor, *The Israel Bible*

Foreword

The mandate to study God's word daily is interestingly not found in the Five Books of Moses (Pentateuch), but rather in the first book of our prophetic writings: "Let not this Book of the Teaching cease from your lips, but recite it day and night, so that you may observe faithfully all that is written in it. Only then will you prosper in your undertakings and only then will you be successful" (Joshua 1:8). Charged with bringing the Israelites into the land covenantally promised to Abraham, Isaac and Jacob, God ensures Joshua of His protection if the nation observes His ways as dictated in the Divine constitution known as the *Torah*.

In Jewish tradition, Joshua (1:8) is directly linked with Deuteronomy (11:14), "You shall gather in your new grain and wine, and oil."[1] Our Sages deduced from this scriptural combination the importance of merging *Torah* study with a profession. Completely dedicating oneself to the study of *Torah* without having the financial means to sustain this lifestyle can lead one to eventually straying from observance of God's will. Poverty and crime can have an intimate relationship.

We must also be careful that our work does not affect our daily study of Scripture. The addiction of becoming a workaholic and not making *Torah* study a priority can also lead one into temptations that can violate our personal relationship with Him as well as our fellow human beings. The goal is to achieve a healthy balance between our study of God's word and our daily work.

The Deuteronomic verse quoted above is part of the second section of the Shema[2] that discusses the concept of reward and punishment. Sanctifying God by fulfilling His commandments results in the Land of Israel practically benefitting from rains that occur in the right season and reaping the abundance from the fields. However, if the nation follows pagan gods and practices, the consequences are devastating – famine and death. The Land of Israel is intrinsically linked with the keeping of the *Torah*. Covenant Land comes with covenant responsibility.

---

1   Talmud Bavli Berachot 35b
2   Consisting of three sections within the Five Books of Moses (Deut. 6:4–8; 11:13–22 and Numbers 15:37–42), the *Shema* is proclamation of accepting God's Kingdom in our lives, loyalty to His commandments and remembering His redemptive act of liberating us from Egypt. Jews recite the *Shema* twice a day as stated in Deut. 6:7.

Born into slavery, Joshua is now leading His people into the Promised Land. More than 500 years separates him from his ancestral forefather Abraham. The historical narratives that took place between Abraham leaving everything behind to follow God in Genesis 12 and the death of Moses in the last chapter of Deuteronomy are filled with intrigue, suspense, joy, sorrow and hope. What began as a family is now a nation actualizing its mission to be a kingdom of priests to the world. However, for the Israelites to succeed in the Land of Israel, they must see the *Torah* as the only compass to direct their lives.

The biblical episodes after our first entry into the land are well known. Our ancestors' triumphs and sins are all on public record. We learned the harsh reality of Leviticus (18:28) "So let not the land spew you out for defiling it as it spewed out the nation that came before you." Twice, we lost the privilege to be stewards of the Land of Israel and to fulfill our nation state mandate to be a light to the world. However, when the annals of history were ready to archive the Jewish people after the Holocaust, God kept His covenantal promise and gathered us from the four corners of the globe to come home. The year 1948 was a game changer. Biblical prophecies were and are being realized. We are now living in the birth pangs of the messianic era.

In our morning prayers, we recite a series of blessings over the *Torah* that include petitioning God to have a sweet tooth for His word, to study it without any ulterior motive and to have Him to teach it to us. They are some congregations that invoke the following liturgical prayer after the completion of these blessings: *May the Torah be my faith and El Shaddai my help. Blessed be the name of His glorious kingdom forever and all time.*

According to Jewish tradition, the neglect of not blessing the *Torah* before engaging in its study was one of the reasons for the destruction of the Temple.[3] This is deduced from the redundancy of words in Jeremiah (9:12) that talks about Israel not following God: " . . . Because they forsook the teaching I had set before them. They did not obey Me and they did not follow it [did not make a blessing before studying it]." Our inability to properly cherish God's greatest gift to the world, the *Torah*, led to our eventual exile from our land.

On Israel's Independence Day, Jews around the world recite Psalms 113–118 to express our gratitude to God for His Divine hand in helping establish the State of Israel. We have learned from our past and realize the privilege to see firsthand the land, people and *Torah* operating all together in our generation.

---

3   Babylonian Talmud Nedarim 81a

When Rabbi Tuly Weisz approached me about his intent to publish *The Israel Bible* that would highlight commentary about the special relationship between the land and people, I saw this project as another way to publicly demonstrate our appreciation to God for having the State of Israel. In addition, it is another educational tool to ensure biblical literacy. If we are to truly enjoy the Land of Israel, it is incumbent upon us to continually study the *Torah*. Isaiah once prophesied that the Jewish people would return to Zion with songs, "crowned with everlasting joy" (35:10). *The Israel Bible* provides us the lyrical content to express our joy in living in the land that God calls holy.

Rabbi Shlomo Riskin
Chief Rabbi of Efrat
Founder of the Center for Jewish-Christian
Understanding & Cooperation (cjcuc)

Megillat Shir Hashirim
The Scroll of Song of Songs

Introduction and commentary by Batya Markowitz

At first glance, *Megillat Shir Hashirim* (Song of Songs) is a poignant love song between the *dod*, 'lover,' and his *re'aya*, 'beloved,' relating a lengthy dialogue between the couple. However, if it was only a simple love song, it would not be part of *Tanakh*. The canonization of the book indicates that it contains a much deeper meaning; it expresses a dialogue between *Hashem* and His people that spans history.

The *Mishna* records a debate among the Sages regarding whether or not *Megillat Shir Hashirim* should be included in the corpus of *Tanakh*. Rabbi Akiva declares that is it not only worthy of being part of the canon; it is actually holier than any of the other books in the Bible. In his words, "All the writings are holy, but *Shir Hashirim* is the holy of holies." What makes *Megillat Shir Hashirim* so special is precisely the fact that it speaks of the relationship and love between the Children of Israel and the Creator.

According to the interpretation of the classic commentaries, *Megillat Shir Hashirim* alludes to the Exodus, the time the Israelites spent traveling in the desert, the first and second Temple periods and the wandering of the Jews throughout the exile. The high points of history are remembered longingly, both by God and by His people in exile, distanced from their homeland and their connection with *Hashem*. Traditionally, *Megillat Shir Hashirim* is read publicly during the holiday of *Pesach*, since that is the time when God's love for the People of Israel was made manifest with outright miracles, and when the relationship between *Hashem* and His people began.

In chronicling the history of the relationship between God and the Children of Israel, *Megillat Shir Hashirim* is replete with imagery taken from the breathtaking landscape of *Eretz Yisrael*. The metaphors are based on its natural phenomena, its plants and wildlife. References are made to the gazelle and the deer, the horse, doves, ravens, pigeons, foxes, lions and leopards. Specific places are mentioned, such as *Ein Gedi*, the mountains of *Gilad*, *Snir* and *Chermon*, as well as other hills, deserts, streams and vineyards – all of which are integral parts of Israel's landscape. Furthermore, there are twenty-three types of plants mentioned in *Shir Hashirim*, including various spices, roses, nuts, apples and the classic "milk and honey" for which the land is well-known. Additionally, most of the seven species unique to Israel are mentioned in *Shir Hashirim*. Our commentary highlights the similarities between some of these fruits and the People of Israel.

While *Shir Hashirim* is mainly the dialogue between the lover (*Hashem*), and His beloved people, at times the book turns to "the daughters of *Yerushalayim*," which is understood as a reference to the other nations of the world. These nations are called "daughters of *Yerushalayim*" because eventually, all of mankind will come to recognize Jerusalem as the center of the world.

The book ends with a plea from the female: "Hurry, my beloved, swift as a gazelle or a young stag, to the hills of spices!" Though by the conclusion of *Megillat Shir Hashirim* the lovers have not yet managed to fulfill their desire to reunite, they continue to yearn for the fulfillment of this dream. Understood on a deeper level, this expresses the cry of the Jewish people asking that *Hashem* speedily redeem them from their lengthy exile, and bring them back to *Eretz Yisrael* and *Yerushalayim*.

Map of Places in *Shir Hashirim*

1. **Carmel** (Song of Songs 7:6) is a coastal mountain range in northern Israel that stretches from the Mediterranean Sea southeast. Mount Carmel is famous for being the mountain on which *Eliyahu* the prophet confronted the prophets of Baal (I Kings 18).

2. **Chermon** (Song of Songs 4:8) is a mountain range at the southern end of the Anti-Lebanon mountain range, whose southern slope extends into the northern Golan Heights. This slope is the highest point in the Land of Israel, soaring 2,300 meters above sea level.

3. **Damascus** (Song of Songs 7:5), a city at the foot of the *Chermon* mountain range.

4. **Ein Gedi** (Song of Songs 1:14), an oasis in the desert, is located on the western shores of the Dead Sea.

5. **Heshbon** (Song of Songs 7:5) was a city in the territory of *Reuven*. It was situated next to a river and had very nice pools of water.

6. **Yerushalayim** (Song of Songs 6:4) is the modern-day capital of the State of Israel and the ancestral capital of the Jewish people. In addition to this reference to the city of Jerusalem, Song of Songs also makes mention of the "daughters of Jerusalem" in a number of places (1:5, 2:7, 3:5, 3:10, 5:8, 5:16, 8:4).

7. **Lebanon** (Song of Songs 7:5), a reference to the mountains of Lebanon which could be seen above the houses and towers of Damascus. The Mount Lebanon range extends along the entire country parallel to the Mediterranean coast.

8. **Mount Gilad** (Song of Songs 4:1) is located on the east side of the Jordan River, and was known in biblical times as an excellent spot for grazing

9. **Tirzah** (Song of Songs 6:4) was the capital of the northern kingdom of Israel during the reigns of *Basha, Elah, Zimri* and *Omri*.

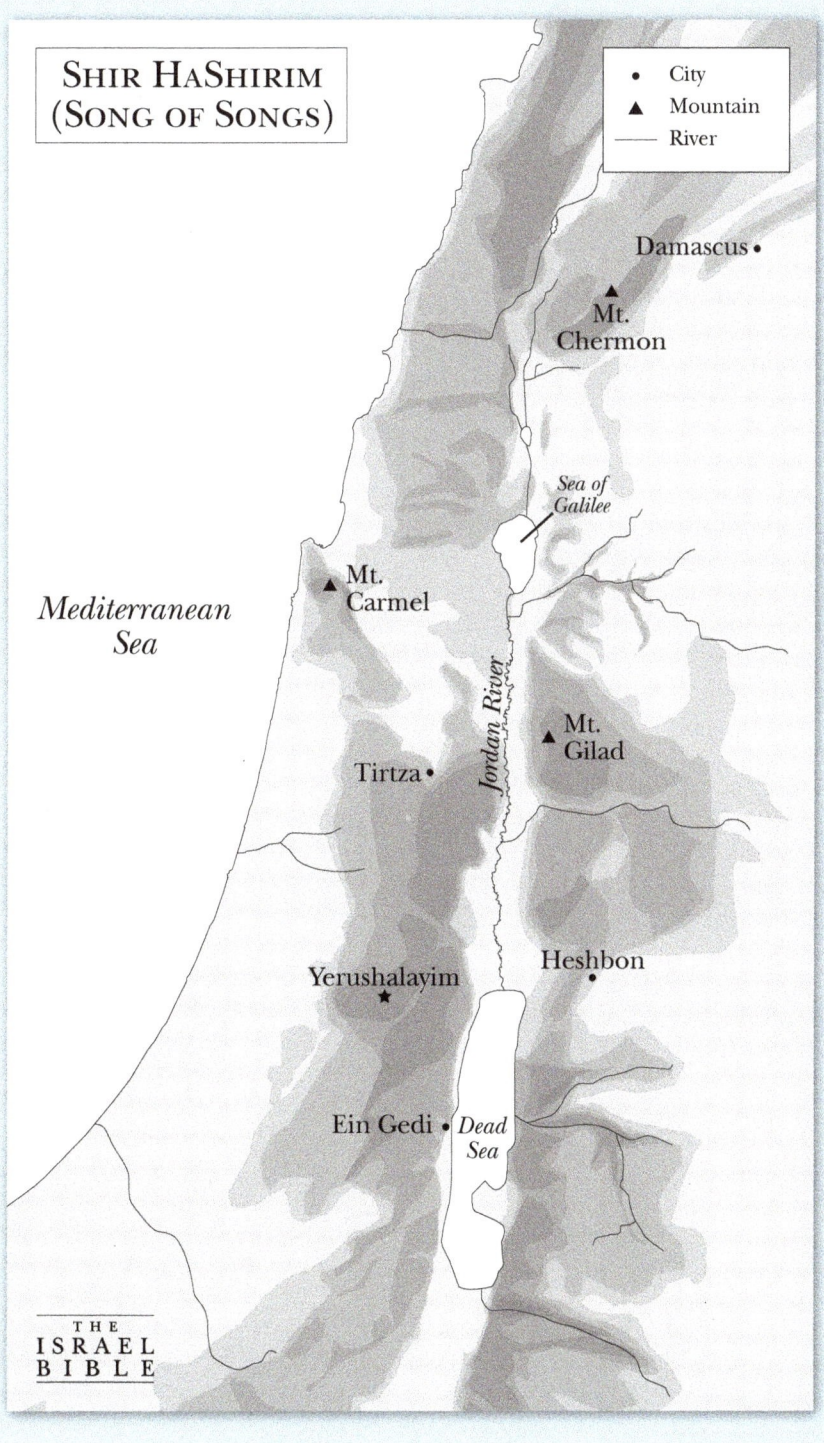

SHIR HASHIRIM
(SONG OF SONGS)

● City
▲ Mountain
— River

Damascus ●

▲ Mt.
Chermon

Sea of Galilee

Mediterranean Sea

▲ Mt.
Carmel

Jordan River

▲ Mt.
Gilad

Tirtza ●

Heshbon ●

Yerushalayim
★

Ein Gedi ● *Dead Sea*

THE
ISRAEL
BIBLE

1 ¹ The Song of Songs, by *Shlomo*.

א שִׁיר הַשִּׁירִים אֲשֶׁר לִשְׁלֹמֹה:

² Oh, give me of the kisses of your mouth, For your love is more delightful than wine.

ב יִשָּׁקֵנִי מִנְּשִׁיקוֹת פִּיהוּ כִּי־טוֹבִים דֹּדֶיךָ מִיָּיִן:

³ Your ointments yield a sweet fragrance, Your name is like finest oil – Therefore do maidens love you.

ג לְרֵיחַ שְׁמָנֶיךָ טוֹבִים שֶׁמֶן תּוּרַק שְׁמֶךָ עַל־כֵּן עֲלָמוֹת אֲהֵבוּךָ:

⁴ Draw me after you, let us run! The king has brought me to his chambers. Let us delight and rejoice in your love, Savoring it more than wine – Like new wine they love you!

ד מָשְׁכֵנִי אַחֲרֶיךָ נָּרוּצָה הֱבִיאַנִי הַמֶּלֶךְ חֲדָרָיו נָגִילָה וְנִשְׂמְחָה בָּךְ נַזְכִּירָה דֹדֶיךָ מִיַּיִן מֵישָׁרִים אֲהֵבוּךָ:

⁵ I am dark, but comely, O daughters of *Yerushalayim* – Like the tents of Kedar, Like the pavilions of *Shlomo*.

ה שְׁחוֹרָה אֲנִי וְנָאוָה בְּנוֹת יְרוּשָׁלָ͏ִם כְּאָהֳלֵי קֵדָר כִּירִיעוֹת שְׁלֹמֹה:

⁶ Don't stare at me because I am swarthy, Because the sun has gazed upon me. My mother's sons quarreled with me, They made me guard the vineyards; My own vineyard I did not guard.

ו אַל־תִּרְאוּנִי שֶׁאֲנִי שְׁחַרְחֹרֶת שֶׁשֱּׁזָפַתְנִי הַשָּׁמֶשׁ בְּנֵי אִמִּי נִחֲרוּ־בִי שָׂמֻנִי נֹטֵרָה אֶת־הַכְּרָמִים כַּרְמִי שֶׁלִּי לֹא נָטָרְתִּי:

⁷ Tell me, you whom I love so well; Where do you pasture your sheep? Where do you rest them at noon? Let me not be as one who strays Beside the flocks of your fellows.

ז הַגִּידָה לִּי שֶׁאָהֲבָה נַפְשִׁי אֵיכָה תִרְעֶה אֵיכָה תַּרְבִּיץ בַּצָּהֳרָיִם שַׁלָּמָה אֶהְיֶה כְּעֹטְיָה עַל עֶדְרֵי חֲבֵרֶיךָ:

⁸ If you do not know, O fairest of women, Go follow the tracks of the sheep, And graze your kids By the tents of the shepherds.

ח אִם־לֹא תֵדְעִי לָךְ הַיָּפָה בַּנָּשִׁים צְאִי־לָךְ בְּעִקְבֵי הַצֹּאן וּרְעִי אֶת־גְּדִיֹּתַיִךְ עַל מִשְׁכְּנוֹת הָרֹעִים:

⁹ I have likened you, my darling, To a mare in Pharaoh's chariots:

ט לְסֻסָתִי בְּרִכְבֵי פַרְעֹה דִּמִּיתִיךְ רַעְיָתִי:

¹⁰ Your cheeks are comely with plaited wreaths, Your neck with strings of jewels.

י נָאווּ לְחָיַיִךְ בַּתֹּרִים צַוָּארֵךְ בַּחֲרוּזִים:

¹¹ We will add wreaths of gold To your spangles of silver.

יא תּוֹרֵי זָהָב נַעֲשֶׂה־לָּךְ עִם נְקֻדּוֹת הַכָּסֶף:

¹² While the king was on his couch, My nard gave forth its fragrance.

יב עַד־שֶׁהַמֶּלֶךְ בִּמְסִבּוֹ נִרְדִּי נָתַן רֵיחוֹ:

¹³ My beloved to me is a bag of myrrh Lodged between my breasts.

יג צְרוֹר הַמֹּר דּוֹדִי לִי בֵּין שָׁדַי יָלִין:

¹⁴ My beloved to me is a spray of henna blooms From the vineyards of *Ein Gedi*.

יד אֶשְׁכֹּל הַכֹּפֶר דּוֹדִי לִי בְּכַרְמֵי עֵין גֶּדִי:

esh-KOL ha-KO-fer do-DEE lee b'-khar-MAY ayn GE-dee

Ein Gedi waterfalls

1:14 A spray of henna blooms from the vineyards of *Ein Gedi* *Ein Gedi* is located on the western shores of the Dead Sea. It7 is a lush oasis to this day, providing an abundance of water in a hot climate, surrounded in all directions by arid desert regions. According to the *Vilna Gaon*, this verse hints to the days of

¹⁵ Ah, you are fair, my darling, Ah, you are fair, With your dove-like eyes!

טו הִנָּךְ יָפָה רַעְיָתִי הִנָּךְ יָפָה עֵינַיִךְ יוֹנִים:

¹⁶ And you, my beloved, are handsome, Beautiful indeed! Our couch is in a bower;

טז הִנְּךָ יָפֶה דוֹדִי אַף נָעִים אַף־עַרְשֵׂנוּ רַעֲנָנָה:

¹⁷ Cedars are the beams of our house, Cypresses the rafters.

יז קֹרוֹת בָּתֵּינוּ אֲרָזִים רחיטנו [רַהִיטֵנוּ] בְּרוֹתִים:

2 ¹ I am a rose of *Sharon*, A lily of the valleys.

ב א אֲנִי חֲבַצֶּלֶת הַשָּׁרוֹן שׁוֹשַׁנַּת הָעֲמָקִים:

² Like a lily among thorns, So is my darling among the maidens.

ב כְּשׁוֹשַׁנָּה בֵּין הַחוֹחִים כֵּן רַעְיָתִי בֵּין הַבָּנוֹת:

³ Like an apple tree among trees of the forest, So is my beloved among the youths. I delight to sit in his shade, And his fruit is sweet to my mouth.

ג כְּתַפּוּחַ בַּעֲצֵי הַיַּעַר כֵּן דּוֹדִי בֵּין הַבָּנִים בְּצִלּוֹ חִמַּדְתִּי וְיָשַׁבְתִּי וּפִרְיוֹ מָתוֹק לְחִכִּי:

⁴ He brought me to the banquet room And his banner of love was over me.

ד הֱבִיאַנִי אֶל־בֵּית הַיַּיִן וְדִגְלוֹ עָלַי אַהֲבָה:

⁵ "Sustain me with raisin cakes, Refresh me with apples, For I am faint with love."

ה סַמְּכוּנִי בָּאֲשִׁישׁוֹת רַפְּדוּנִי בַּתַּפּוּחִים כִּי־חוֹלַת אַהֲבָה אָנִי:

⁶ His left hand was under my head, His right arm embraced me.

ו שְׂמֹאלוֹ תַּחַת לְרֹאשִׁי וִימִינוֹ תְּחַבְּקֵנִי:

⁷ I adjure you, O maidens of *Yerushalayim*, By gazelles or by hinds of the field: Do not wake or rouse Love until it please!

ז הִשְׁבַּעְתִּי אֶתְכֶם בְּנוֹת יְרוּשָׁלַם בִּצְבָאוֹת אוֹ בְּאַיְלוֹת הַשָּׂדֶה אִם־תָּעִירוּ וְאִם־תְּעוֹרְרוּ אֶת־הָאַהֲבָה עַד שֶׁתֶּחְפָּץ:

⁸ Hark! My beloved! There he comes, Leaping over mountains, Bounding over hills.

ח קוֹל דּוֹדִי הִנֵּה־זֶה בָּא מְדַלֵּג עַל־הֶהָרִים מְקַפֵּץ עַל־הַגְּבָעוֹת:

⁹ My beloved is like a gazelle Or like a young stag. There he stands behind our wall, Gazing through the window, Peering through the lattice.

ט דּוֹמֶה דוֹדִי לִצְבִי אוֹ לְעֹפֶר הָאַיָּלִים הִנֵּה־זֶה עוֹמֵד אַחַר כָּתְלֵנוּ מַשְׁגִּיחַ מִן־הַחַלֹּנוֹת מֵצִיץ מִן־הַחֲרַכִּים:

¹⁰ My beloved spoke thus to me, "Arise, my darling; My fair one, come away!

י עָנָה דוֹדִי וְאָמַר לִי קוּמִי לָךְ רַעְיָתִי יָפָתִי וּלְכִי־לָךְ:

¹¹ For now the winter is past, The rains are over and gone.

יא כִּי־הִנֵּה הַסְּתָו [הַסְּתָיו] עָבָר הַגֶּשֶׁם חָלַף הָלַךְ לוֹ:

¹² The blossoms have appeared in the land, The time of pruning has come; The song of the turtledove Is heard in our land.

יב הַנִּצָּנִים נִרְאוּ בָאָרֶץ עֵת הַזָּמִיר הִגִּיעַ וְקוֹל הַתּוֹר נִשְׁמַע בְּאַרְצֵנוּ:

Yehoshua, when the Children of Israel entered *Eretz Yisrael*. Located near the Jordan river, *Ein Gedi* is near the border that the Israelites crossed upon entering the land. Just as the henna tree was a permanent fixture of this region,

Hashem's presence became a permanent fixture on earth when the People of Israel entered the Land of Israel as a nation for the first time.

13 The green figs form on the fig tree, The vines in blossom give off fragrance. Arise, my darling; My fair one, come away!

יג הַתְּאֵנָה חָנְטָה פַגֶּיהָ וְהַגְּפָנִים סְמָדַר נָתְנוּ רֵיחַ קוּמִי לְכִי [לָךְ] רַעְיָתִי יָפָתִי וּלְכִי־לָךְ:

*ha-t'-ay-NAH kha-n'-TAH fa-GE-ha v'-ha-g'-fa-NEEM s'-ma-DAR
na-t'-NU RAY-akh KU-mee LAKH ra-ya-TEE ya-fa-TEE ul-khee LAKH*

14 "O my dove, in the cranny of the rocks, Hidden by the cliff, Let me see your face, Let me hear your voice; For your voice is sweet And your face is comely."

יד יוֹנָתִי בְּחַגְוֵי הַסֶּלַע בְּסֵתֶר הַמַּדְרֵגָה הַרְאִינִי אֶת־מַרְאַיִךְ הַשְׁמִיעִנִי אֶת־קוֹלֵךְ כִּי־קוֹלֵךְ עָרֵב וּמַרְאֵיךְ נָאוֶה:

15 Catch us the foxes, The little foxes That ruin the vineyards – For our vineyard is in blossom.

טו אֶחֱזוּ־לָנוּ שׁוּעָלִים שׁוּעָלִים קְטַנִּים מְחַבְּלִים כְּרָמִים וּכְרָמֵינוּ סְמָדַר:

16 My beloved is mine And I am his Who browses among the lilies.

טז דּוֹדִי לִי וַאֲנִי לוֹ הָרֹעֶה בַּשׁוֹשַׁנִּים:

17 When the day blows gently And the shadows flee, Set out, my beloved, Swift as a gazelle Or a young stag, For the hills of spices!

יז עַד שֶׁיָּפוּחַ הַיּוֹם וְנָסוּ הַצְּלָלִים סֹב דְּמֵה־לְךָ דוֹדִי לִצְבִי אוֹ לְעֹפֶר הָאַיָּלִים עַל־הָרֵי בָתֶר:

3 1 Upon my couch at night I sought the one I love – I sought, but found him not.

ג א עַל־מִשְׁכָּבִי בַּלֵּילוֹת בִּקַּשְׁתִּי אֵת שֶׁאָהֲבָה נַפְשִׁי בִּקַּשְׁתִּיו וְלֹא מְצָאתִיו:

2 "I must rise and roam the town, Through the streets and through the squares; I must seek the one I love." I sought but found him not.

ב אָקוּמָה נָּא וַאֲסוֹבְבָה בָעִיר בַּשְּׁוָקִים וּבָרְחֹבוֹת אֲבַקְשָׁה אֵת שֶׁאָהֲבָה נַפְשִׁי בִּקַּשְׁתִּיו וְלֹא מְצָאתִיו:

3 I met the watchmen Who patrol the town. "Have you seen the one I love?"

ג מְצָאוּנִי הַשֹּׁמְרִים הַסֹּבְבִים בָּעִיר אֵת שֶׁאָהֲבָה נַפְשִׁי רְאִיתֶם:

4 Scarcely had I passed them When I found the one I love. I held him fast, I would not let him go Till I brought him to my mother's house, To the chamber of her who conceived me

ד כִּמְעַט שֶׁעָבַרְתִּי מֵהֶם עַד שֶׁמָּצָאתִי אֵת שֶׁאָהֲבָה נַפְשִׁי אֲחַזְתִּיו וְלֹא אַרְפֶּנּוּ עַד־שֶׁהֲבֵיאתִיו אֶל־בֵּית אִמִּי וְאֶל־חֶדֶר הוֹרָתִי:

5 I adjure you, O maidens of *Yerushalayim*, By gazelles or by hinds of the field: Do not wake or rouse Love until it please!

ה הִשְׁבַּעְתִּי אֶתְכֶם בְּנוֹת יְרוּשָׁלַם בִּצְבָאוֹת אוֹ בְּאַיְלוֹת הַשָּׂדֶה אִם־תָּעִירוּ וְאִם־תְּעוֹרְרוּ אֶת־הָאַהֲבָה עַד שֶׁתֶּחְפָּץ:

6 Who is she that comes up from the desert Like columns of smoke, In clouds of myrrh and frankincense, Of all the powders of the merchant?

ו מִי זֹאת עֹלָה מִן־הַמִּדְבָּר כְּתִימְרוֹת עָשָׁן מְקֻטֶּרֶת מוֹר וּלְבוֹנָה מִכֹּל אַבְקַת רוֹכֵל:

2:13 The vines in blossom give off fragrance
Grapes, like each of the other seven special agricultural species for which the Land of Israel is praised (Deuteronomy 8:8), are a symbol of the People of Israel. The Sages teach that the vine is the weakest and lowliest of trees, lacking even a trunk. To produce wine, which is served at royal banquets, grapes are crushed underfoot. Similarly, the Jewish people are a small, modest nation. Often, they are crushed and trampled by others, but ultimately they will be raised to royalty. Additionally, the largest grapes hang at the bottom of the cluster, similar to the greatest leaders such as *Moshe* who carried himself with great humility (Numbers 12:3).

A grape vine in *Kfar Tabor*, Israel

7 There is *Shlomo*'s couch, Encircled by sixty warriors Of the warriors of *Yisrael*,

ז הִנֵּה מִטָּתוֹ שֶׁלִּשְׁלֹמֹה שִׁשִּׁים גִּבֹּרִים סָבִיב לָהּ מִגִּבֹּרֵי יִשְׂרָאֵל:

8 All of them trained in warfare, Skilled in battle, Each with sword on thigh Because of terror by night.

ח כֻּלָּם אֲחֻזֵי חֶרֶב מְלֻמְּדֵי מִלְחָמָה אִישׁ חַרְבּוֹ עַל־יְרֵכוֹ מִפַּחַד בַּלֵּילוֹת:

9 King *Shlomo* made him a palanquin Of wood from Lebanon.

ט אַפִּרְיוֹן עָשָׂה לוֹ הַמֶּלֶךְ שְׁלֹמֹה מֵעֲצֵי הַלְּבָנוֹן:

10 He made its posts of silver, Its back of gold, Its seat of purple wool. Within, it was decked with love By the maidens of *Yerushalayim*.

י עַמּוּדָיו עָשָׂה כֶסֶף רְפִידָתוֹ זָהָב מֶרְכָּבוֹ אַרְגָּמָן תּוֹכוֹ רָצוּף אַהֲבָה מִבְּנוֹת יְרוּשָׁלָ͏ִם:

a-mu-DAV a-SAH KHE-sef r'-fee-da-TO za-HAV mer-ka-VO ar-ga-MAN to-KHO ra-TZUF a-ha-VAH mi-b'-NOT y'-ru-sha-LA-im

11 O maidens of *Tzion*, go forth And gaze upon King *Shlomo* Wearing the crown that his mother Gave him on his wedding day, On his day of bliss.

יא צְאֶינָה וּרְאֶינָה בְּנוֹת צִיּוֹן בַּמֶּלֶךְ שְׁלֹמֹה בָּעֲטָרָה שֶׁעִטְּרָה־לּוֹ אִמּוֹ בְּיוֹם חֲתֻנָּתוֹ וּבְיוֹם שִׂמְחַת לִבּוֹ:

4 1 Ah, you are fair, my darling, Ah, you are fair. Your eyes are like doves Behind your veil. Your hair is like a flock of goats Streaming down Mount *Gilad*.

ד א הִנָּךְ יָפָה רַעְיָתִי הִנָּךְ יָפָה עֵינַיִךְ יוֹנִים מִבַּעַד לְצַמָּתֵךְ שַׂעְרֵךְ כְּעֵדֶר הָעִזִּים שֶׁגָּלְשׁוּ מֵהַר גִּלְעָד:

2 Your teeth are like a flock of ewes Climbing up from the washing pool; All of them bear twins, And not one loses her young.

ב שִׁנַּיִךְ כְּעֵדֶר הַקְּצוּבוֹת שֶׁעָלוּ מִן־הָרַחְצָה שֶׁכֻּלָּם מַתְאִימוֹת וְשַׁכֻּלָה אֵין בָּהֶם:

3 Your lips are like a crimson thread, Your mouth is lovely. Your brow behind your veil [Gleams] like a pomegranate split open.

ג כְּחוּט הַשָּׁנִי שִׂפְתֹתַיִךְ וּמִדְבָּרֵיךְ נָאוֶה כְּפֶלַח הָרִמּוֹן רַקָּתֵךְ מִבַּעַד לְצַמָּתֵךְ:

4 Your neck is like the Tower of *David*, Built to hold weapons, Hung with a thousand shields – All the quivers of warriors.

ד כְּמִגְדַּל דָּוִיד צַוָּארֵךְ בָּנוּי לְתַלְפִּיּוֹת אֶלֶף הַמָּגֵן תָּלוּי עָלָיו כֹּל שִׁלְטֵי הַגִּבֹּרִים:

5 Your breasts are like two fawns, Twins of a gazelle, Browsing among the lilies.

ה שְׁנֵי שָׁדַיִךְ כִּשְׁנֵי עֲפָרִים תְּאוֹמֵי צְבִיָּה הָרוֹעִים בַּשּׁוֹשַׁנִּים:

6 When the day blows gently And the shadows flee, I will betake me to the mount of myrrh, To the hill of frankincense.

ו עַד שֶׁיָּפוּחַ הַיּוֹם וְנָסוּ הַצְּלָלִים אֵלֶךְ לִי אֶל־הַר הַמּוֹר וְאֶל־גִּבְעַת הַלְּבוֹנָה:

7 Every part of you is fair, my darling, There is no blemish in you

ז כֻּלָּךְ יָפָה רַעְיָתִי וּמוּם אֵין בָּךְ:

Song of Songs

3:10 By the maidens of *Yerushalayim* In a number of places throughout *Shir Hashirim* in addition to this verse, the "maidens" or "daughters" of *Yerushalayim* represent the nations of the world (see 1:5, 2:7, 3:5, 5:8, 8:4). The medieval commentator *Rashi* explains that this is because in the future, *Yerushalayim* will be the metropolis of all countries, and all people will accept its centrality. Though the nations of the world will one day accept *Yerushalayim* as their political and religious capital, the Jewish people have always seen it as their eternal capital, providing inspiration and the means for fulfilling their spiritual needs even when they were in exile.

Yerushalayim

8 From Lebanon come with me; From Lebanon, my bride, with me! Trip down from Amana's peak, From the peak of Senir and *Chermon*, From the dens of lions, From the hills of leopards.

ח אִתִּי מִלְּבָנוֹן כַּלָּה אִתִּי מִלְּבָנוֹן תָּבוֹאִי תָּשׁוּרִי מֵרֹאשׁ אֲמָנָה מֵרֹאשׁ שְׂנִיר וְחֶרְמוֹן מִמְּעֹנוֹת אֲרָיוֹת מֵהַרְרֵי נְמֵרִים:

9 You have captured my heart, My own, my bride, You have captured my heart With one [glance] of your eyes, With one coil of your necklace.

ט לִבַּבְתִּנִי אֲחֹתִי כַלָּה לִבַּבְתִּנִי באחד [בְּאַחַת] מֵעֵינַיִךְ בְּאַחַד עֲנָק מִצַּוְּרֹנָיִךְ:

10 How sweet is your love, My own, my bride! How much more delightful your love than wine, Your ointments more fragrant Than any spice!

י מַה־יָּפוּ דֹדַיִךְ אֲחֹתִי כַלָּה מַה־טֹּבוּ דֹדַיִךְ מִיַּיִן וְרֵיחַ שְׁמָנַיִךְ מִכָּל־בְּשָׂמִים:

11 Sweetness drops From your lips, O bride; Honey and milk Are under your tongue And the scent of your robes Is like the scent of Lebanon.

יא נֹפֶת תִּטֹּפְנָה שִׂפְתוֹתַיִךְ כַּלָּה דְּבַשׁ וְחָלָב תַּחַת לְשׁוֹנֵךְ וְרֵיחַ שַׂלְמֹתַיִךְ כְּרֵיחַ לְבָנוֹן:

12 A garden locked Is my own, my bride, A fountain locked, A sealed-up spring.

יב גַּן נָעוּל אֲחֹתִי כַלָּה גַּל נָעוּל מַעְיָן חָתוּם:

13 Your limbs are an orchard of pomegranates And of all luscious fruits, Of henna and of nard –

יג שְׁלָחַיִךְ פַּרְדֵּס רִמּוֹנִים עִם פְּרִי מְגָדִים כְּפָרִים עִם־נְרָדִים:

sh'-la-KHA-yikh par-DAYS ri-mo-NEEM IM p'-REE
m'-ga-DEEM k'-fa-REEM im n'-ra-DEEM

14 Nard and saffron, Fragrant reed and cinnamon, With all aromatic woods, Myrrh and aloes – All the choice perfumes.

יד נֵרְדְּ וְכַרְכֹּם קָנֶה וְקִנָּמוֹן עִם כָּל־עֲצֵי לְבוֹנָה מֹר וַאֲהָלוֹת עִם כָּל־רָאשֵׁי בְשָׂמִים:

15 You are] a garden spring, A well of fresh water, A rill of Lebanon.

טו מַעְיַן גַּנִּים בְּאֵר מַיִם חַיִּים וְנֹזְלִים מִן־לְבָנוֹן:

16 Awake, O north wind, Come, O south wind! Blow upon my garden, That its perfume may spread. Let my beloved come to his garden And enjoy its luscious fruits!

טז עוּרִי צָפוֹן וּבוֹאִי תֵימָן הָפִיחִי גַנִּי יִזְּלוּ בְשָׂמָיו יָבֹא דוֹדִי לְגַנּוֹ וְיֹאכַל פְּרִי מְגָדָיו:

4:13 An orchard of pomegranates The pomegranate is one of the seven special agricultural species of the Land of Israel (Deuteronomy 8:8). It has always been a symbol of beauty. Its unique shape is a favorite design element, appearing on the priestly garments and on the pillars at the entrance to the *Beit Hamikdash* in *Yerushalayim*, as well as in many forms of artwork to this day. At its crown, the pomegranate has a six-pointed star, which makes it the only place the *Magen David*, 'star of David,' appears in nature. According to Jewish teachings, the numerous seeds in the pomegranate represent the 613 biblical commandments of the *Torah*. On the Jewish New Year, *Rosh Hashana*, Jews say a special prayer over the beautiful fruit, "May our good deeds be as numerous as the seeds of a pomegranate."

Pomegranates in *Beit Dagan*

5 **¹** I have come to my garden, My own, my bride; I have plucked my myrrh and spice, Eaten my honey and honeycomb, Drunk my wine and my milk. Eat, lovers, and drink: Drink deep of love!

ה **א** בָּאתִי לְגַנִּי אֲחֹתִי כַלָּה אָרִיתִי מוֹרִי עִם־בְּשָׂמִי אָכַלְתִּי יַעְרִי עִם־דִּבְשִׁי שָׁתִיתִי יֵינִי עִם־חֲלָבִי אִכְלוּ רֵעִים שְׁתוּ וְשִׁכְרוּ דּוֹדִים:

> BA-tee l'-ga-NEE a-kho-TEE kha-LAH a-REE-tee mo-REE im
> b'-sa-MEE a-KHAL-tee ya-REE im div-SHEE sha-TEE-tee yay-NEE
> im kha-la-VEE ikh-LU ray-EEM sh'-TU v'-shikh-RU do-DEEM

² I was asleep, But my heart was wakeful. Hark, my beloved knocks! "Let me in, my own, My darling, my faultless dove! For my head is drenched with dew, My locks with the damp of night."

ב אֲנִי יְשֵׁנָה וְלִבִּי עֵר קוֹל דּוֹדִי דוֹפֵק פִּתְחִי־לִי אֲחֹתִי רַעְיָתִי יוֹנָתִי תַמָּתִי שֶׁרֹאשִׁי נִמְלָא־טָל קְוֻּצּוֹתַי רְסִיסֵי לָיְלָה:

> a-NEE y'-shay-NAH v'-li-BEE ayr KOL do-DEE do-FAYK
> pit-khee LEE a-kho-TEE ra-ya-TEE yo-na-TEE ta-ma-TEE
> she-ro-SHEE nim-la TAL k'-vu-tzo-TAI r'-see-SAY LAI-lah

³ I had taken off my robe – Was I to don it again? I had bathed my feet – Was I to soil them again?

ג פָּשַׁטְתִּי אֶת־כֻּתָּנְתִּי אֵיכָכָה אֶלְבָּשֶׁנָּה רָחַצְתִּי אֶת־רַגְלַי אֵיכָכָה אֲטַנְּפֵם:

⁴ My beloved took his hand off the latch, And my heart was stirred for him.

ד דּוֹדִי שָׁלַח יָדוֹ מִן־הַחֹר וּמֵעַי הָמוּ עָלָיו:

⁵ I rose to let in my beloved; My hands dripped myrrh – My fingers, flowing myrrh – Upon the handles of the bolt.

ה קַמְתִּי אֲנִי לִפְתֹּחַ לְדוֹדִי וְיָדַי נָטְפוּ־מוֹר וְאֶצְבְּעֹתַי מוֹר עֹבֵר עַל כַּפּוֹת הַמַּנְעוּל:

⁶ I opened the door for my beloved, But my beloved had turned and gone. I was faint because of what he said. I sought, but found him not; I called, but he did not answer.

ו פָּתַחְתִּי אֲנִי לְדוֹדִי וְדוֹדִי חָמַק עָבָר נַפְשִׁי יָצְאָה בְדַבְּרוֹ בִּקַּשְׁתִּיהוּ וְלֹא מְצָאתִיהוּ קְרָאתִיו וְלֹא עָנָנִי:

⁷ I met the watchmen Who patrol the town; They struck me, they bruised me. The guards of the walls Stripped me of my mantle.

ז מְצָאֻנִי הַשֹּׁמְרִים הַסֹּבְבִים בָּעִיר הִכּוּנִי פְצָעוּנִי נָשְׂאוּ אֶת־רְדִידִי מֵעָלַי שֹׁמְרֵי הַחֹמוֹת:

⁸ I adjure you, O maidens of *Yerushalayim*! If you meet my beloved, tell him this: That I am faint with love.

ח הִשְׁבַּעְתִּי אֶתְכֶם בְּנוֹת יְרוּשָׁלָ͏ִם אִם־תִּמְצְאוּ אֶת־דּוֹדִי מַה־תַּגִּידוּ לוֹ שֶׁחוֹלַת אַהֲבָה אָנִי:

Song of Songs

5:1 I have come to my garden According to *Metzudat David*, this verse is a metaphor for *Hashem* entering the *Beit Hamikdash* that the people built for Him, and accepting the sacrifices they offer to Him. The garden is a reference to the Temple and the gathering of myrrh and spice to the acceptance of the incense offering that is brought in His honor. God metaphorically "eats" and "drinks" the offerings and libations, by means of a fire that descends from Heaven to consume them. Finally, He calls upon his "friends," the loyal priests, to partake in their share of the offerings. The use of a garden as the image to represent the *Beit Hamikdash* paints a picture of beauty and harmony which befits the meeting place of God and mankind on earth.

5:2 Hark, my beloved knocks! The words: "My beloved knocks," in Hebrew *kol dodi dofek* (קוֹל דּוֹדִי דוֹפֵק), form the title and theme of Rabbi Joseph B. Soloveitchik's classic essay on religious Zionism. In this essay, Rabbi Soloveitchik highlights the miraculous events surrounding the establishment of the State of Israel and posits that God "knocked" six times to get our attention. He points to military successes, political opportunities, the theological awakening of the Christian world and other developments as contemporary signs that *Hashem* is beckoning the Jewish people to return to the Land of Israel. Rabbi Soloveichik cautions that we must respond quickly to these knocks, unlike the beloved who hesitates in this chapter, and later regrets her lost opportunity.

Rabbi Joseph
B. Soloveitchik
(1903–1993)

9 How is your beloved better than another, O fairest of women? How is your beloved better than another That you adjure us so?

ט מַה־דּוֹדֵךְ מִדּוֹד הַיָּפָה בַּנָּשִׁים מַה־דּוֹדֵךְ מִדּוֹד שֶׁכָּכָה הִשְׁבַּעְתָּנוּ:

10 My beloved is clear-skinned and ruddy, Preeminent among ten thousand.

י דּוֹדִי צַח וְאָדוֹם דָּגוּל מֵרְבָבָה:

11 His head is finest gold, His locks are curled And black as a raven.

יא רֹאשׁוֹ כֶּתֶם פָּז קְוֻצּוֹתָיו תַּלְתַּלִּים שְׁחֹרוֹת כָּעוֹרֵב:

12 His eyes are like doves By watercourses, Bathed in milk, Set by a brimming pool.

יב עֵינָיו כְּיוֹנִים עַל־אֲפִיקֵי מָיִם רֹחֲצוֹת בֶּחָלָב יֹשְׁבוֹת עַל־מִלֵּאת:

13 His cheeks are like beds of spices, Banks of perfume His lips are like lilies; They drip flowing myrrh.

יג לְחָיָו כַּעֲרוּגַת הַבֹּשֶׂם מִגְדְּלוֹת מֶרְקָחִים שִׂפְתוֹתָיו שׁוֹשַׁנִּים נֹטְפוֹת מוֹר עֹבֵר:

14 His hands are rods of gold, Studded with beryl; His belly a tablet of ivory, Adorned with sapphires.

יד יָדָיו גְּלִילֵי זָהָב מְמֻלָּאִים בַּתַּרְשִׁישׁ מֵעָיו עֶשֶׁת שֵׁן מְעֻלֶּפֶת סַפִּירִים:

15 His legs are like marble pillars Set in sockets of fine gold. He is majestic as Lebanon, Stately as the cedars.

טו שׁוֹקָיו עַמּוּדֵי שֵׁשׁ מְיֻסָּדִים עַל־אַדְנֵי־פָז מַרְאֵהוּ כַּלְּבָנוֹן בָּחוּר כָּאֲרָזִים:

16 His mouth is delicious And all of him is delightful. Such is my beloved, Such is my darling, O maidens of *Yerushalayim*!

טז חִכּוֹ מַמְתַקִּים וְכֻלּוֹ מַחֲמַדִּים זֶה דוֹדִי וְזֶה רֵעִי בְּנוֹת יְרוּשָׁלָם:

6 1 "Whither has your beloved gone, O fairest of women? Whither has your beloved turned? Let us seek him with you."

א אָנָה הָלַךְ דּוֹדֵךְ הַיָּפָה בַּנָּשִׁים אָנָה פָּנָה דוֹדֵךְ וּנְבַקְשֶׁנּוּ עִמָּךְ:

2 My beloved has gone down to his garden, To the beds of spices, To browse in the gardens And to pick lilies.

ב דּוֹדִי יָרַד לְגַנּוֹ לַעֲרוּגוֹת הַבֹּשֶׂם לִרְעוֹת בַּגַּנִּים וְלִלְקֹט שׁוֹשַׁנִּים:

3 I am my beloved's And my beloved is mine; He browses among the lilies.

ג אֲנִי לְדוֹדִי וְדוֹדִי לִי הָרֹעֶה בַּשׁוֹשַׁנִּים:

4 You are beautiful, my darling, as *Tirtza*, Comely as *Yerushalayim*, Awesome as bannered hosts.

ד יָפָה אַתְּ רַעְיָתִי כְּתִרְצָה נָאוָה כִּירוּשָׁלָם אֲיֻמָּה כַּנִּדְגָּלוֹת:

ya-FAH AT ra-ya-TEE k'-tir-TZAH na-VAH
kee-ru-sha-LA-im a-yu-MAH ka-nid-ga-LOT

5 Turn your eyes away from me, For they overwhelm me! Your hair is like a flock of goats Streaming down from *Gilad*.

ה הָסֵבִּי עֵינַיִךְ מִנֶּגְדִּי שֶׁהֵם הִרְהִיבֻנִי שַׂעְרֵךְ כְּעֵדֶר הָעִזִּים שֶׁגָּלְשׁוּ מִן־הַגִּלְעָד:

Dramatic sunset over *Yerushalayim*

תרצה
ירושלים

6:4 You are beautiful, my darling, as *Tirtza*, comely as *Yerusha-layim* *Tirtza* was an important city of the northern kingdom of *Yisrael*, which served as its capital during the reigns of the kings *Baasha, Elah, Zimri* and *Omri* (see I Kings 14:17). *Yerusha-layim*, of course, was the capital of the kingdom of *Ye-huda*. On a simple level, the lover says that his beloved is

as beautiful as these capitals; that she is like a queen befitting the royal cities. On a deeper level, Rabbi Amos Hakham notes that the name *Tirza* (תרצה) is related to the word *ratza* (רצה), 'desire,' and the name *Yerushalayim* (ירושלים) is derived from the word *shalem* (שלם), meaning 'complete.' Hence, this verse also alludes to the fact that *Hashem* finds His people both 'desirable' and 'complete.'

Song of Songs

6 Your teeth are like a flock of ewes Climbing up from the washing pool; All of them bear twins, And not one loses her young.	ו שִׁנַּיִךְ כְּעֵדֶר הָרְחֵלִים שֶׁעָלוּ מִן־הָרַחְצָה שֶׁכֻּלָּם מַתְאִימוֹת וְשַׁכֻּלָה אֵין בָּהֶם:
7 Your brow behind your veil [Gleams] like a pomegranate split open.	ז כְּפֶלַח הָרִמּוֹן רַקָּתֵךְ מִבַּעַד לְצַמָּתֵךְ:
8 There are sixty queens, And eighty concubines, And damsels without number.	ח שִׁשִּׁים הֵמָּה מְלָכוֹת וּשְׁמֹנִים פִּילַגְשִׁים וַעֲלָמוֹת אֵין מִסְפָּר:
9 Only one is my dove, My perfect one, The only one of her mother, The delight of her who bore her. Maidens see and acclaim her; Queens and concubines, and praise her.	ט אַחַת הִיא יוֹנָתִי תַמָּתִי אַחַת הִיא לְאִמָּהּ בָּרָה הִיא לְיוֹלַדְתָּהּ רָאוּהָ בָנוֹת וַיְאַשְּׁרוּהָ מְלָכוֹת וּפִילַגְשִׁים וַיְהַלְלוּהָ:
10 Who is she that shines through like the dawn, Beautiful as the moon, Radiant as the sun Awesome as bannered hosts?	י מִי־זֹאת הַנִּשְׁקָפָה כְּמוֹ־שָׁחַר יָפָה כַלְּבָנָה בָּרָה כַּחַמָּה אֲיֻמָּה כַּנִּדְגָּלוֹת:
11 I went down to the nut grove To see the budding of the vale; To see if the vines had blossomed, If the pomegranates were in bloom.	יא אֶל־גִּנַּת אֱגוֹז יָרַדְתִּי לִרְאוֹת בְּאִבֵּי הַנָּחַל לִרְאוֹת הֲפָרְחָה הַגֶּפֶן הֵנֵצוּ הָרִמֹּנִים:
12 Before I knew it, My desire set me Mid the chariots of Ammi-nadib.	יב לֹא יָדַעְתִּי נַפְשִׁי שָׂמַתְנִי מַרְכְּבוֹת עַמִּי־נָדִיב:
7 1 Turn back, turn back, O maid of Shulem! Turn back, turn back, That we may gaze upon you. "Why will you gaze at the Shulammite In the Mahanaim dance?"	**ז** א שׁוּבִי שׁוּבִי הַשּׁוּלַמִּית שׁוּבִי שׁוּבִי וְנֶחֱזֶה־בָּךְ מַה־תֶּחֱזוּ בַּשּׁוּלַמִּית כִּמְחֹלַת הַמַּחֲנָיִם:
2 How lovely are your feet in sandals, O daughter of nobles! Your rounded thighs are like jewels, The work of a master's hand.	ב מַה־יָּפוּ פְעָמַיִךְ בַּנְּעָלִים בַּת־נָדִיב חַמּוּקֵי יְרֵכַיִךְ כְּמוֹ חֲלָאִים מַעֲשֵׂה יְדֵי אָמָּן:
3 Your navel is like a round goblet – Let mixed wine not be lacking! – Your belly like a heap of wheat Hedged about with lilies.	ג שָׁרְרֵךְ אַגַּן הַסַּהַר אַל־יֶחְסַר הַמָּזֶג בִּטְנֵךְ עֲרֵמַת חִטִּים סוּגָה בַּשּׁוֹשַׁנִּים:
4 Your breasts are like two fawns, Twins of a gazelle.	ד שְׁנֵי שָׁדַיִךְ כִּשְׁנֵי עֳפָרִים תָּאֳמֵי צְבִיָּה:
5 Your neck is like a tower of ivory, Your eyes like pools in Heshbon By the gate of Bath-rabbim, Your nose like the Lebanon tower That faces toward Damascus.	ה צַוָּארֵךְ כְּמִגְדַּל הַשֵּׁן עֵינַיִךְ בְּרֵכוֹת בְּחֶשְׁבּוֹן עַל־שַׁעַר בַּת־רַבִּים אַפֵּךְ כְּמִגְדַּל הַלְּבָנוֹן צוֹפֶה פְּנֵי דַמָּשֶׂק:
6 The head upon you is like crimson wool, The locks of your head are like purple – A king is held captive in the tresses.	ו רֹאשֵׁךְ עָלַיִךְ כַּכַּרְמֶל וְדַלַּת רֹאשֵׁךְ כָּאַרְגָּמָן מֶלֶךְ אָסוּר בָּרְהָטִים:
7 How fair you are, how beautiful! O Love, with all its rapture!	ז מַה־יָּפִית וּמַה־נָּעַמְתְּ אַהֲבָה בַּתַּעֲנוּגִים:

12

8 Your stately form is like the palm, Your breasts are like clusters.

ח זֹאת קוֹמָתֵךְ דָּמְתָה לְתָמָר וְשָׁדַיִךְ לְאַשְׁכֹּלוֹת:

ZOT ko-ma-TAYKH da-m'-TAH l'-ta-MAR v'-sha-DA-yikh l'-ash-ko-LOT

9 I say: Let me climb the palm, Let me take hold of its branches; Let your breasts be like clusters of grapes, Your breath like the fragrance of apples,

ט אָמַרְתִּי אֶעֱלֶה בְתָמָר אֹחֲזָה בְּסַנְסִנָּיו וְיִהְיוּ־נָא שָׁדַיִךְ כְּאֶשְׁכְּלוֹת הַגֶּפֶן וְרֵיחַ אַפֵּךְ כַּתַּפּוּחִים:

10 And your mouth like choicest wine. "Let it flow to my beloved as new wine Gliding over the lips of sleepers."

י וְחִכֵּךְ כְּיֵין הַטּוֹב הוֹלֵךְ לְדוֹדִי לְמֵישָׁרִים דּוֹבֵב שִׂפְתֵי יְשֵׁנִים:

11 I am my beloved's, And his desire is for me.

יא אֲנִי לְדוֹדִי וְעָלַי תְּשׁוּקָתוֹ:

12 Come, my beloved, Let us go into the open; Let us lodge among the henna shrubs.

יב לְכָה דוֹדִי נֵצֵא הַשָּׂדֶה נָלִינָה בַּכְּפָרִים:

13 Let us go early to the vineyards; Let us see if the vine has flowered, If its blossoms have opened, If the pomegranates are in bloom. There I will give my love to you.

יג נַשְׁכִּימָה לַכְּרָמִים נִרְאֶה אִם פָּרְחָה הַגֶּפֶן פִּתַּח הַסְּמָדַר הֵנֵצוּ הָרִמּוֹנִים שָׁם אֶתֵּן אֶת־דֹּדַי לָךְ:

14 The mandrakes yield their fragrance, At our doors are all choice fruits; Both freshly picked and long-stored Have I kept, my beloved, for you.

יד הַדּוּדָאִים נָתְנוּ־רֵיחַ וְעַל־פְּתָחֵינוּ כָּל־מְגָדִים חֲדָשִׁים גַּם־יְשָׁנִים דּוֹדִי צָפַנְתִּי לָךְ:

8 1 If only it could be as with a brother, As if you had nursed at my mother's breast: Then I could kiss you When I met you in the street, And no one would despise me.

ח א מִי יִתֶּנְךָ כְּאָח לִי יוֹנֵק שְׁדֵי אִמִּי אֶמְצָאֲךָ בַחוּץ אֶשָּׁקְךָ גַּם לֹא־יָבוּזוּ לִי:

2 I would lead you, I would bring you To the house of my mother, Of her who taught me – I would let you drink of the spiced wine, Of my pomegranate juice.

ב אֶנְהָגֲךָ אֲבִיאֲךָ אֶל־בֵּית אִמִּי תְּלַמְּדֵנִי אַשְׁקְךָ מִיַּיִן הָרֶקַח מֵעֲסִיס רִמֹּנִי:

3 His left hand was under my head, His right hand caressed me.

ג שְׂמֹאלוֹ תַּחַת רֹאשִׁי וִימִינוֹ תְּחַבְּקֵנִי:

4 I adjure you, O maidens of *Yerushalayim*: Do not wake or rouse Love until it please!

ד הִשְׁבַּעְתִּי אֶתְכֶם בְּנוֹת יְרוּשָׁלִָם מַה־תָּעִירוּ וּמַה־תְּעֹרְרוּ אֶת־הָאַהֲבָה עַד שֶׁתֶּחְפָּץ:

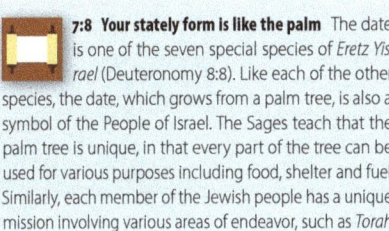

7:8 Your stately form is like the palm The date is one of the seven special species of *Eretz Yisrael* (Deuteronomy 8:8). Like each of the other species, the date, which grows from a palm tree, is also a symbol of the People of Israel. The Sages teach that the palm tree is unique, in that every part of the tree can be used for various purposes including food, shelter and fuel. Similarly, each member of the Jewish people has a unique mission involving various areas of endeavor, such as *Torah* study, charity and other good deeds. However, the date only has one pit, illustrating that while each individual has a separate mission, the nation has but one heart united by the common goal of fulfilling *Hashem's* will in this world.

Date palms in Northern Israel

5 Who is she that comes up from the desert, Leaning upon her beloved? Under the apple tree I roused you; It was there your mother conceived you, There she who bore you conceived you.

ה מִי זֹאת עֹלָה מִן־הַמִּדְבָּר מִתְרַפֶּקֶת עַל־דּוֹדָהּ תַּחַת הַתַּפּוּחַ עוֹרַרְתִּיךָ שָׁמָּה חִבְּלַתְךָ אִמֶּךָ שָׁמָּה חִבְּלָה יְלָדַתְךָ:

6 Let me be a seal upon your heart, Like the seal upon your hand. For love is fierce as death, Passion is mighty as Sheol; Its darts are darts of fire, A blazing flame.

ו שִׂימֵנִי כַחוֹתָם עַל־לִבֶּךָ כַּחוֹתָם עַל־זְרוֹעֶךָ כִּי־עַזָּה כַמָּוֶת אַהֲבָה קָשָׁה כִשְׁאוֹל קִנְאָה רְשָׁפֶיהָ רִשְׁפֵּי אֵשׁ שַׁלְהֶבֶתְיָה:

7 Vast floods cannot quench love, Nor rivers drown it. If a man offered all his wealth for love, He would be laughed to scorn.

ז מַיִם רַבִּים לֹא יוּכְלוּ לְכַבּוֹת אֶת־הָאַהֲבָה וּנְהָרוֹת לֹא יִשְׁטְפוּהָ אִם־יִתֵּן אִישׁ אֶת־כָּל־הוֹן בֵּיתוֹ בָּאַהֲבָה בּוֹז יָבוּזוּ לוֹ:

8 "We have a little sister, Whose breasts are not yet formed. What shall we do for our sister When she is spoken for?

ח אָחוֹת לָנוּ קְטַנָּה וְשָׁדַיִם אֵין לָהּ מַה־נַּעֲשֶׂה לַאֲחֹתֵנוּ בַּיּוֹם שֶׁיְּדֻבַּר־בָּהּ:

9 If she be a wall, We will build upon it a silver battlement; If she be a door, We will panel it in cedar."

ט אִם־חוֹמָה הִיא נִבְנֶה עָלֶיהָ טִירַת כָּסֶף וְאִם־דֶּלֶת הִיא נָצוּר עָלֶיהָ לוּחַ אָרֶז:

10 I am a wall, My breasts are like towers. So I became in his eyes As one who finds favor.

י אֲנִי חוֹמָה וְשָׁדַי כַּמִּגְדָּלוֹת אָז הָיִיתִי בְעֵינָיו כְּמוֹצְאֵת שָׁלוֹם:

11 *Shlomo* had a vineyard In Baal-hamon. He had to post guards in the vineyard: A man would give for its fruit A thousand pieces of silver.

יא כֶּרֶם הָיָה לִשְׁלֹמֹה בְּבַעַל הָמוֹן נָתַן אֶת־הַכֶּרֶם לַנֹּטְרִים אִישׁ יָבִא בְּפִרְיוֹ אֶלֶף כָּסֶף:

12 I have my very own vineyard: You may have the thousand, O *Shlomo*, And the guards of the fruit two hundred!

יב כַּרְמִי שֶׁלִּי לְפָנָי הָאֶלֶף לְךָ שְׁלֹמֹה וּמָאתַיִם לְנֹטְרִים אֶת־פִּרְיוֹ:

13 O you who linger in the garden, A lover is listening; Let me hear your voice.

יג הַיּוֹשֶׁבֶת בַּגַּנִּים חֲבֵרִים מַקְשִׁיבִים לְקוֹלֵךְ הַשְׁמִיעִינִי:

14 "Hurry, my beloved, Swift as a gazelle or a young stag, To the hills of spices!"

יד בְּרַח דּוֹדִי וּדְמֵה־לְךָ לִצְבִי אוֹ לְעֹפֶר הָאַיָּלִים עַל הָרֵי בְשָׂמִים:

b'-RAKH do-DEE ud-MAY l'-KHA litz-VEE O l'-O-fer
ha-a-ya-LEEM AL ha-RAY v'-sa-MEEM

Song of Songs

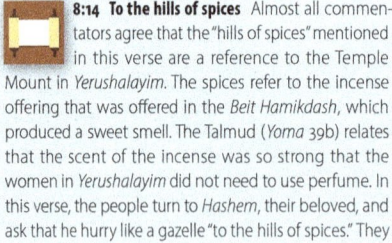

8:14 To the hills of spices Almost all commentators agree that the "hills of spices" mentioned in this verse are a reference to the Temple Mount in *Yerushalayim*. The spices refer to the incense offering that was offered in the *Beit Hamikdash*, which produced a sweet smell. The Talmud (*Yoma* 39b) relates that the scent of the incense was so strong that the women in *Yerushalayim* did not need to use perfume. In this verse, the people turn to *Hashem*, their beloved, and ask that he hurry like a gazelle "to the hills of spices." They wish to be redeemed quickly from their bitter exile. They beg for God to return them to the Land of Israel, and for His presence to also return to the Holy Land and to the *Beit Hamikdash* in *Yerushalayim*.

The Temple Mount in *Yerushalayim*

Megillat Rut
The Scroll of Ruth

Introduction and commentary by Rabbi Tuly Weisz

To most Jews, *Megillat Rut* (Ruth) immediately conjures up thoughts and memories of the holiday of *Shavuot*, when it is read publicly in synagogue.

Shavuot is one of the three central pilgrimage festivals and, according to Jewish tradition, is the day when the Children of Israel experienced revelation and received the *Torah* from *Hashem* at Mount Sinai. At first glance, it seems puzzling that, of all the books in the holy Bible, we specifically read *Megillat Rut* on the day that commemorates the giving of the *Torah*.

The giving of the *Torah* was the single most important moment in the history of civilization – not only for Jews, but for all of mankind. Long ago, the Sages wondered why, if the *Torah* is so holy, it wasn't given in the Holy Land? Why was the *Torah* given in a barren desert instead?

The ancient rabbis explained that since Israel is the Jewish homeland, had the *Torah* been given in there it would have belonged exclusively to the Jewish people. Instead, therefore, *Hashem* chose to transmit His moral code on a barren mountain in the ownerless wilderness, to emphasize that His Word is for everyone equally, because His instructions are the key to universal redemption.

In *Megillat Rut* we read about the Moabite princess *Rut* who forges her own path to Mount Sinai through her relationship with her mother-in-law *Naomi*. *Rut* is associated with the holiday of *Shavuot* because, with great self-sacrifice, she finds her way to the ultimate truth of the *Torah*. As she movingly declares to *Naomi*, "your people shall be my people, and your God my God" (Ruth 1:16).

This redemptive experience leads *Rut* to become the matriarch of King *David*'s royal lineage, and the ultimate ancestress of the *Mashiach*, who will bring the whole world to recognize *Hashem* and the *Torah* He gave on Mount Sinai on the holiday of *Shavuot*.

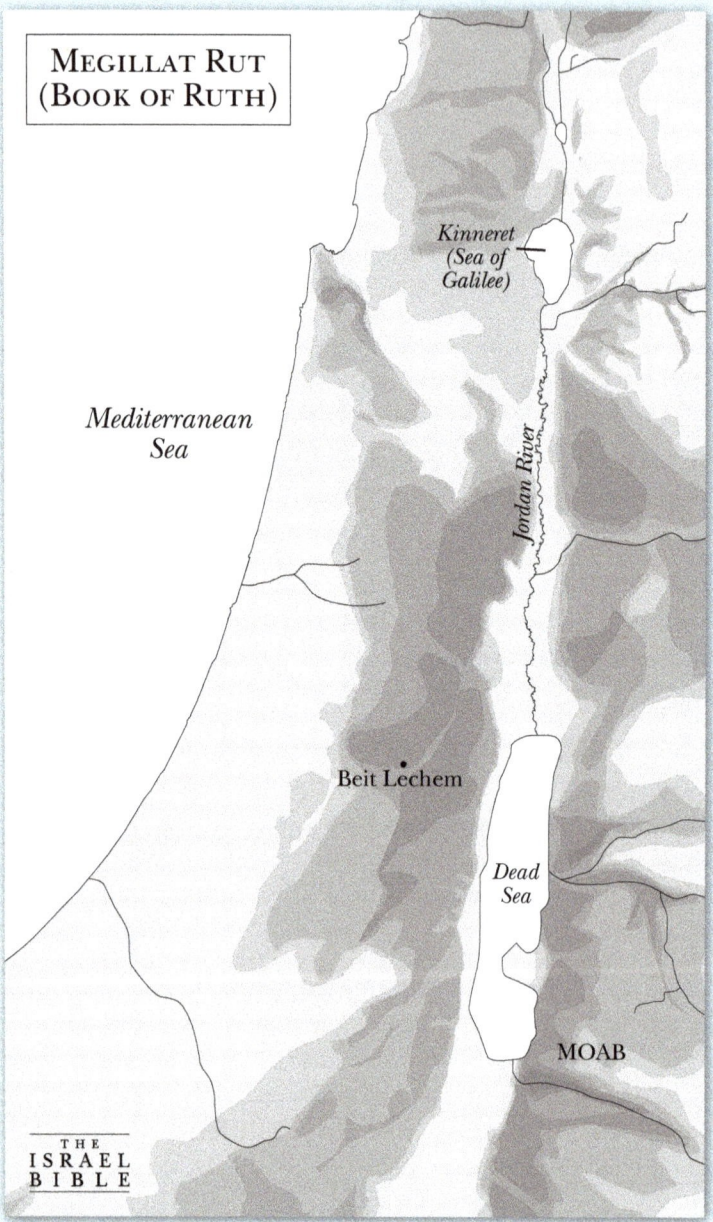

MEGILLAT RUT
(BOOK OF RUTH)

*Kinneret
(Sea of
Galilee)*

*Mediterranean
Sea*

Jordan River

Beit Lechem

*Dead
Sea*

MOAB

THE
ISRAEL
BIBLE

1. **Beit Lechem** – Part of the area of the tribe of *Yehuda*, it is the place where most of the events in the Book of Ruth transpire.

2. **Moab** – *Elimelech* escapes famine in Israel by bringing his family to Moab on the east side of the Jordan River (Ruth 1:1). In Moab, his children marry Moabite women, most notably *Rut*, who becomes the mother of Jewish royalty. *Elimelech* and his sons die in Moab.

1 ¹ In the days when the chieftains ruled, there was a famine in the land; and a man of *Beit Lechem* in *Yehuda*, with his wife and two sons, went to reside in the country of Moab.

א וַיְהִי בִּימֵי שְׁפֹט הַשֹּׁפְטִים וַיְהִי רָעָב בָּאָרֶץ וַיֵּלֶךְ אִישׁ מִבֵּית לֶחֶם יְהוּדָה לָגוּר בִּשְׂדֵי מוֹאָב הוּא וְאִשְׁתּוֹ וּשְׁנֵי בָנָיו:

² The man's name was *Elimelech*, his wife's name was *Naomi*, and his two sons were named *Machlon* and *Kilyon* – Ephrathites of *Beit Lechem* in *Yehuda*. They came to the country of Moab and remained there.

ב וְשֵׁם הָאִישׁ אֱלִימֶלֶךְ וְשֵׁם אִשְׁתּוֹ נָעֳמִי וְשֵׁם שְׁנֵי־בָנָיו מַחְלוֹן וְכִלְיוֹן אֶפְרָתִים מִבֵּית לֶחֶם יְהוּדָה וַיָּבֹאוּ שְׂדֵי־מוֹאָב וַיִּהְיוּ־שָׁם:

³ *Elimelech*, *Naomi*'s husband, died; and she was left with her two sons.

ג וַיָּמָת אֱלִימֶלֶךְ אִישׁ נָעֳמִי וַתִּשָּׁאֵר הִיא וּשְׁנֵי בָנֶיהָ:

⁴ They married Moabite women, one named Orpah and the other *Rut*, and they lived there about ten years.

ד וַיִּשְׂאוּ לָהֶם נָשִׁים מֹאֲבִיּוֹת שֵׁם הָאַחַת עָרְפָּה וְשֵׁם הַשֵּׁנִית רוּת וַיֵּשְׁבוּ שָׁם כְּעֶשֶׂר שָׁנִים:

⁵ Then those two – *Machlon* and *Kilyon* – also died; so the woman was left without her two sons and without her husband.

ה וַיָּמוּתוּ גַם־שְׁנֵיהֶם מַחְלוֹן וְכִלְיוֹן וַתִּשָּׁאֵר הָאִשָּׁה מִשְּׁנֵי יְלָדֶיהָ וּמֵאִישָׁהּ:

va-ya-MU-tu gam sh'-nay-HEM makh-LON v'-khil-YON va-ti-sha-AYR ha-i-SHAH mi-sh'-NAY y'-la-DE-ha u-may-ee-SHAH

⁶ She started out with her daughters-in-law to return from the country of Moab; for in the country of Moab she had heard that *Hashem* had taken note of His people and given them food.

ו וַתָּקָם הִיא וְכַלֹּתֶיהָ וַתָּשָׁב מִשְּׂדֵי מוֹאָב כִּי שָׁמְעָה בִּשְׂדֵה מוֹאָב כִּי־פָקַד יְהֹוָה אֶת־עַמּוֹ לָתֵת לָהֶם לָחֶם:

⁷ Accompanied by her two daughters-in-law, she left the place where she had been living; and they set out on the road back to the land of *Yehuda*.

ז וַתֵּצֵא מִן־הַמָּקוֹם אֲשֶׁר הָיְתָה־שָּׁמָּה וּשְׁתֵּי כַלֹּתֶיהָ עִמָּהּ וַתֵּלַכְנָה בַדֶּרֶךְ לָשׁוּב אֶל־אֶרֶץ יְהוּדָה:

⁸ But *Naomi* said to her two daughters-in-law, "Turn back, each of you to her mother's house. May *Hashem* deal kindly with you, as you have dealt with the dead and with me!

ח וַתֹּאמֶר נָעֳמִי לִשְׁתֵּי כַלֹּתֶיהָ לֵכְנָה שֹּׁבְנָה אִשָּׁה לְבֵית אִמָּהּ יעשה [יַעַשׂ] יְהֹוָה עִמָּכֶם חֶסֶד כַּאֲשֶׁר עֲשִׂיתֶם עִם־הַמֵּתִים וְעִמָּדִי:

⁹ May *Hashem* grant that each of you find security in the house of a husband!" And she kissed them farewell. They broke into weeping

ט יִתֵּן יְהֹוָה לָכֶם וּמְצֶאןָ מְנוּחָה אִשָּׁה בֵּית אִישָׁהּ וַתִּשַּׁק לָהֶן וַתִּשֶּׂאנָה קוֹלָן וַתִּבְכֶּינָה:

¹⁰ and said to her, "No, we will return with you to your people."

י וַתֹּאמַרְנָה־לָּהּ כִּי־אִתָּךְ נָשׁוּב לְעַמֵּךְ:

1:5 So the woman was left without her two sons and without her husband The Sages teach that *Machlon*, *Kilyon* and their father *Elimelech* were all leaders of their generation, yet the text is silent regarding the reason for their untimely deaths. According to *Rashi*, their punishment was the result of the grave sin of abandoning the Land of Israel during a famine. Their actions greatly demoralized the struggling nation. This first lesson of *Megillat Rut* contains a valuable message for us today. We must not to turn our backs on the Promised Land, especially in her time of need.

Rabbi Tuly Weisz provides financial and emotional support to Beit Meir residents after an arson attack

17

¹¹ But *Naomi* replied, "Turn back, my daughters! Why should you go with me? Have I any more sons in my body who might be husbands for you?

יא וַתֹּאמֶר נָעֳמִי שֹׁבְנָה בְנֹתַי לָמָּה תֵלַכְנָה עִמִּי הַעוֹד־לִי בָנִים בְּמֵעַי וְהָיוּ לָכֶם לַאֲנָשִׁים:

¹² Turn back, my daughters, for I am too old to be married. Even if I thought there was hope for me, even if I were married tonight and I also bore sons,

יב שֹׁבְנָה בְנֹתַי לֵכְןָ כִּי זָקַנְתִּי מִהְיוֹת לְאִישׁ כִּי אָמַרְתִּי יֶשׁ־לִי תִקְוָה גַּם הָיִיתִי הַלַּיְלָה לְאִישׁ וְגַם יָלַדְתִּי בָנִים:

¹³ should you wait for them to grow up? Should you on their account debar yourselves from marriage? Oh no, my daughters! My lot is far more bitter than yours, for the hand of *Hashem* has struck out against me."

יג הֲלָהֵן תְּשַׂבֵּרְנָה עַד אֲשֶׁר יִגְדָּלוּ הֲלָהֵן תֵּעָגֵנָה לְבִלְתִּי הֱיוֹת לְאִישׁ אַל בְּנֹתַי כִּי־מַר־לִי מְאֹד מִכֶּם כִּי־יָצְאָה בִי יַד־יְהֹוָה:

¹⁴ They broke into weeping again, and Orpah kissed her mother-in-law farewell. But *Rut* clung to her.

יד וַתִּשֶּׂנָה קוֹלָן וַתִּבְכֶּינָה עוֹד וַתִּשַּׁק עׇרְפָּה לַחֲמוֹתָהּ וְרוּת דָּבְקָה בָּהּ:

¹⁵ So she said, "See, your sister-in-law has returned to her people and her gods. Go follow your sister-in-law."

טו וַתֹּאמֶר הִנֵּה שָׁבָה יְבִמְתֵּךְ אֶל־עַמָּהּ וְאֶל־אֱלֹהֶיהָ שׁוּבִי אַחֲרֵי יְבִמְתֵּךְ:

¹⁶ But *Rut* replied, "Do not urge me to leave you, to turn back and not follow you. For wherever you go, I will go; wherever you lodge, I will lodge; your people shall be my people, and your God my God.

טז וַתֹּאמֶר רוּת אַל־תִּפְגְּעִי־בִי לְעׇזְבֵךְ לָשׁוּב מֵאַחֲרָיִךְ כִּי אֶל־אֲשֶׁר תֵּלְכִי אֵלֵךְ וּבַאֲשֶׁר תָּלִינִי אָלִין עַמֵּךְ עַמִּי וֵאלֹהַיִךְ אֱלֹהָי:

> *va-TO-mer Ruth al tif-g'-ee VEE l'-oz-VAYKH la-SHUV may-a-kha-RA-yikh KEE el a-SHER tay-l'-KHEE ay-LAYKH u-va-a-SHER ta-LEE-nee a-LEEN a-MAYKH a-MEE vay-lo-HA-yikh e-lo-HAI*

¹⁷ Where you die, I will die, and there I will be buried. Thus and more may *Hashem* do to me if anything but death parts me from you."

יז בַּאֲשֶׁר תָּמוּתִי אָמוּת וְשָׁם אֶקָּבֵר כֹּה יַעֲשֶׂה יְהֹוָה לִי וְכֹה יֹסִיף כִּי הַמָּוֶת יַפְרִיד בֵּינִי וּבֵינֵךְ:

¹⁸ When [*Naomi*] saw how determined she was to go with her, she ceased to argue with her;

יח וַתֵּרֶא כִּי־מִתְאַמֶּצֶת הִיא לָלֶכֶת אִתָּהּ וַתֶּחְדַּל לְדַבֵּר אֵלֶיהָ:

¹⁹ and the two went on until they reached *Beit Lechem*. When they arrived in *Beit Lechem*, the whole city buzzed with excitement over them. The women said, "Can this be *Naomi*?"

יט וַתֵּלַכְנָה שְׁתֵּיהֶם עַד־בֹּאָנָה בֵּית לָחֶם וַיְהִי כְּבֹאָנָה בֵּית לֶחֶם וַתֵּהֹם כָּל־הָעִיר עֲלֵיהֶן וַתֹּאמַרְנָה הֲזֹאת נָעֳמִי:

²⁰ "Do not call me *Naomi*," she replied. "Call me *Mara*, for *Shaddai* has made my lot very bitter.

כ וַתֹּאמֶר אֲלֵיהֶן אַל־תִּקְרֶאנָה לִי נָעֳמִי קְרֶאןָ לִי מָרָא כִּי־הֵמַר שַׁדַּי לִי מְאֹד:

1:16 Your people shall be my people, and your God my God
After *Naomi* begs her daughters-in-law not to follow her back to *Eretz Yisrael* and gives them compelling reasons to leave her, Orpah does what most people would do. She takes the easy way out, returns to her father's house and goes off to live a life of anonymity. *Rut*, on the other hand, answers the call in one of the most beautiful statements of faith and allegiance in the entire Bible. Her words and actions set her on the path of royalty, and have inspired the faithful for hundreds of years. *Rut* demonstrates for all time what it means to cast one's lot with the People of Israel, the Land of Israel and the God of Israel. For *Rut's* sacrifice, she was rewarded by becoming the matriarch of the Davidic dynasty, and the ancestress of the *Mashiach*.

Rabbi Tuly Weisz with Christian tourists at the Western Wall

²¹ I went away full, and *Hashem* has brought me back empty. How can you call me *Naomi*, when *Hashem* has dealt harshly with me, when *Shaddai* has brought misfortune upon me!"

כא אֲנִי מְלֵאָה הָלַכְתִּי וְרֵיקָם הֱשִׁיבַנִי יְהֹוָה לָמָּה תִקְרֶאנָה לִי נָעֳמִי וַיהֹוָה עָנָה בִי וְשַׁדַּי הֵרַע לִי:

²² Thus *Naomi* returned from the country of Moab; she returned with her daughter-in-law *Rut* the Moabite. They arrived in *Beit Lechem* at the beginning of the barley harvest.

כב וַתָּשָׁב נָעֳמִי וְרוּת הַמּוֹאֲבִיָּה כַלָּתָהּ עִמָּהּ הַשָּׁבָה מִשְּׂדֵי מוֹאָב וְהֵמָּה בָּאוּ בֵּית לֶחֶם בִּתְחִלַּת קְצִיר שְׂעֹרִים:

2 ¹ Now *Naomi* had a kinsman on her husband's side, a man of substance, of the family of *Elimelech*, whose name was *Boaz*.

ב א וּלְנָעֳמִי מידע [מוֹדָע] לְאִישָׁהּ אִישׁ גִּבּוֹר חַיִל מִמִּשְׁפַּחַת אֱלִימֶלֶךְ וּשְׁמוֹ בֹּעַז:

² *Rut* the Moabite said to *Naomi*, "I would like to go to the fields and glean among the ears of grain, behind someone who may show me kindness." "Yes, daughter, go," she replied;

ב וַתֹּאמֶר רוּת הַמּוֹאֲבִיָּה אֶל־נָעֳמִי אֵלְכָה־נָּא הַשָּׂדֶה וַאֲלַקֳטָה בַשִּׁבֳּלִים אַחַר אֲשֶׁר אֶמְצָא־חֵן בְּעֵינָיו וַתֹּאמֶר לָהּ לְכִי בִתִּי:

³ and off she went. She came and gleaned in a field, behind the reapers; and, as luck would have it, it was the piece of land belonging to *Boaz*, who was of *Elimelech*'s family.

ג וַתֵּלֶךְ וַתָּבוֹא וַתְּלַקֵּט בַּשָּׂדֶה אַחֲרֵי הַקֹּצְרִים וַיִּקֶר מִקְרֶהָ חֶלְקַת הַשָּׂדֶה לְבֹעַז אֲשֶׁר מִמִּשְׁפַּחַת אֱלִימֶלֶךְ:

⁴ Presently *Boaz* arrived from *Beit Lechem*. He greeted the reapers, "*Hashem* be with you!" And they responded, "*Hashem* bless you!"

ד וְהִנֵּה־בֹעַז בָּא מִבֵּית לֶחֶם וַיֹּאמֶר לַקּוֹצְרִים יְהֹוָה עִמָּכֶם וַיֹּאמְרוּ לוֹ יְבָרֶכְךָ יְהֹוָה:

v'-hi-nay VO-az BA mi-BAYT LE-khem va-YO-mer la-ko-tz'-REEM a-do-NAI i-ma-KHEM va-YO-m'-ru LO y'-va-re-kh'-KHA a-do-NAI

⁵ *Boaz* said to the servant who was in charge of the reapers, "Whose girl is that?"

ה וַיֹּאמֶר בֹּעַז לְנַעֲרוֹ הַנִּצָּב עַל־הַקּוֹצְרִים לְמִי הַנַּעֲרָה הַזֹּאת:

⁶ The servant in charge of the reapers replied, "She is a Moabite girl who came back with *Naomi* from the country of Moab.

ו וַיַּעַן הַנַּעַר הַנִּצָּב עַל־הַקּוֹצְרִים וַיֹּאמַר נַעֲרָה מוֹאֲבִיָּה הִיא הַשָּׁבָה עִם־נָעֳמִי מִשְּׂדֵה מוֹאָב:

⁷ She said, 'Please let me glean and gather among the sheaves behind the reapers.' She has been on her feet ever since she came this morning. She has rested but little in the hut."

ז וַתֹּאמֶר אֲלַקֳטָה־נָּא וְאָסַפְתִּי בָעֳמָרִים אַחֲרֵי הַקּוֹצְרִים וַתָּבוֹא וַתַּעֲמוֹד מֵאָז הַבֹּקֶר וְעַד־עַתָּה זֶה שִׁבְתָּהּ הַבַּיִת מְעָט:

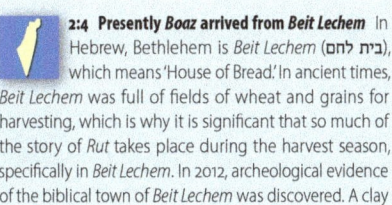

2:4 Presently *Boaz* arrived from *Beit Lechem* In Hebrew, Bethlehem is *Beit Lechem* (בית לחם), which means 'House of Bread.' In ancient times, *Beit Lechem* was full of fields of wheat and grains for harvesting, which is why it is significant that so much of the story of *Rut* takes place during the harvest season, specifically in *Beit Lechem*. In 2012, archeological evidence of the biblical town of *Beit Lechem* was discovered. A clay seal was uncovered in the City of David in Jerusalem, with the inscription "from *Beit Lechem* to the king," presumably sealing a package containing a tax payment in the seventh or eighth century BCE.

Clay seal bearing the name *Beit Lechem*

<table>
<tr>
<td>

8 *Boaz* said to *Rut*, "Listen to me, daughter. Don't go to glean in another field. Don't go elsewhere, but stay here close to my girls.

9 Keep your eyes on the field they are reaping, and follow them. I have ordered the men not to molest you. And when you are thirsty, go to the jars and drink some of [the water] that the men have drawn."

10 She prostrated herself with her face to the ground, and said to him, "Why are you so kind as to single me out, when I am a foreigner?"

11 *Boaz* said in reply, "I have been told of all that you did for your mother-in-law after the death of your husband, how you left your father and mother and the land of your birth and came to a people you had not known before.

12 May *Hashem* reward your deeds. May you have a full recompense from *Hashem*, the God of *Yisrael*, under whose wings you have sought refuge!"

13 She answered, "You are most kind, my lord, to comfort me and to speak gently to your maidservant – though I am not so much as one of your maidservants."

14 At mealtime, *Boaz* said to her, "Come over here and partake of the meal, and dip your morsel in the vinegar." So she sat down beside the reapers. He handed her roasted grain, and she ate her fill and had some left over.

15 When she got up again to glean, *Boaz* gave orders to his workers, "You are not only to let her glean among the sheaves, without interference,

16 but you must also pull some [stalks] out of the heaps and leave them for her to glean, and not scold her."

17 She gleaned in the field until evening. Then she beat out what she had gleaned – it was about an *'efah* of barley –

</td>
<td dir="rtl">

ח וַיֹּאמֶר בֹּעַז אֶל־רוּת הֲלוֹא שָׁמַעַתְּ בִּתִּי אַל־תֵּלְכִי לִלְקֹט בְּשָׂדֶה אַחֵר וְגַם לֹא תַעֲבוּרִי מִזֶּה וְכֹה תִדְבָּקִין עִם־נַעֲרֹתָי:

ט עֵינַיִךְ בַּשָּׂדֶה אֲשֶׁר־יִקְצֹרוּן וְהָלַכְתְּ אַחֲרֵיהֶן הֲלוֹא צִוִּיתִי אֶת־הַנְּעָרִים לְבִלְתִּי נָגְעֵךְ וְצָמִת וְהָלַכְתְּ אֶל־הַכֵּלִים וְשָׁתִית מֵאֲשֶׁר יִשְׁאֲבוּן הַנְּעָרִים:

י וַתִּפֹּל עַל־פָּנֶיהָ וַתִּשְׁתַּחוּ אָרְצָה וַתֹּאמֶר אֵלָיו מַדּוּעַ מָצָאתִי חֵן בְּעֵינֶיךָ לְהַכִּירֵנִי וְאָנֹכִי נָכְרִיָּה:

יא וַיַּעַן בֹּעַז וַיֹּאמֶר לָהּ הֻגֵּד הֻגַּד לִי כֹּל אֲשֶׁר־עָשִׂית אֶת־חֲמוֹתֵךְ אַחֲרֵי מוֹת אִישֵׁךְ וַתַּעַזְבִי אָבִיךְ וְאִמֵּךְ וְאֶרֶץ מוֹלַדְתֵּךְ וַתֵּלְכִי אֶל־עַם אֲשֶׁר לֹא־יָדַעַתְּ תְּמוֹל שִׁלְשׁוֹם:

יב יְשַׁלֵּם יְהוָה פָּעֳלֵךְ וּתְהִי מַשְׂכֻּרְתֵּךְ שְׁלֵמָה מֵעִם יְהוָה אֱלֹהֵי יִשְׂרָאֵל אֲשֶׁר־בָּאת לַחֲסוֹת תַּחַת־כְּנָפָיו:

יג וַתֹּאמֶר אֶמְצָא־חֵן בְּעֵינֶיךָ אֲדֹנִי כִּי נִחַמְתָּנִי וְכִי דִבַּרְתָּ עַל־לֵב שִׁפְחָתֶךָ וְאָנֹכִי לֹא אֶהְיֶה כְּאַחַת שִׁפְחֹתֶיךָ:

יד וַיֹּאמֶר לָהּ בֹעַז לְעֵת הָאֹכֶל גֹּשִׁי הֲלֹם וְאָכַלְתְּ מִן־הַלֶּחֶם וְטָבַלְתְּ פִּתֵּךְ בַּחֹמֶץ וַתֵּשֶׁב מִצַּד הַקּוֹצְרִים וַיִּצְבָּט־לָהּ קָלִי וַתֹּאכַל וַתִּשְׂבַּע וַתֹּתַר:

טו וַתָּקָם לְלַקֵּט וַיְצַו בֹּעַז אֶת־נְעָרָיו לֵאמֹר גַּם בֵּין הָעֳמָרִים תְּלַקֵּט וְלֹא תַכְלִימוּהָ:

טז וְגַם שֹׁל־תָּשֹׁלּוּ לָהּ מִן־הַצְּבָתִים וַעֲזַבְתֶּם וְלִקְּטָה וְלֹא תִגְעֲרוּ־בָהּ:

יז וַתְּלַקֵּט בַּשָּׂדֶה עַד־הָעָרֶב וַתַּחְבֹּט אֵת אֲשֶׁר־לִקֵּטָה וַיְהִי כְּאֵיפָה שְׂעֹרִים:

</td>
</tr>
</table>

*va-t'-la-KAYT ba-sa-DEH ad ha-A-rev va-takh-BOT AYT
a-sher li-KAY-tah vai-HEE k'-ay-FAH s'-o-REEM*

Barley in the Western Negev

2:17 It was about an *efah* of barley Barley, the second of the special agricultural products of the Land of Israel (Deuteronomy 8:8), looks similar to wheat but is a smaller grain, and is surrounded by long, hair-like strands. This explains its Hebrew name *se'orah* (שעורה), which

שעורה

Ruth

¹⁸ and carried it back with her to the town. When her mother-in-law saw what she had gleaned, and when she also took out and gave her what she had left over after eating her fill,

יח וַתִּשָּׂא וַתָּבוֹא הָעִיר וַתֵּרֶא חֲמוֹתָהּ אֵת אֲשֶׁר־לִקֵּטָה וַתּוֹצֵא וַתִּתֶּן־לָהּ אֵת אֲשֶׁר־הוֹתִרָה מִשָּׂבְעָהּ:

¹⁹ her mother-in-law asked her, "Where did you glean today? Where did you work? Blessed be he who took such generous notice of you!" So she told her mother-in-law whom she had worked with, saying, "The name of the man with whom I worked today is *Boaz*."

יט וַתֹּאמֶר לָהּ חֲמוֹתָהּ אֵיפֹה לִקַּטְתְּ הַיּוֹם וְאָנָה עָשִׂית יְהִי מַכִּירֵךְ בָּרוּךְ וַתַּגֵּד לַחֲמוֹתָהּ אֵת אֲשֶׁר־עָשְׂתָה עִמּוֹ וַתֹּאמֶר שֵׁם הָאִישׁ אֲשֶׁר עָשִׂיתִי עִמּוֹ הַיּוֹם בֹּעַז:

²⁰ *Naomi* said to her daughter-in-law, "Blessed be he of *Hashem*, who has not failed in His kindness to the living or to the dead! For," *Naomi* explained to her daughter-in-law, "the man is related to us; he is one of our redeeming kinsmen."

כ וַתֹּאמֶר נָעֳמִי לְכַלָּתָהּ בָּרוּךְ הוּא לַיהֹוָה אֲשֶׁר לֹא־עָזַב חַסְדּוֹ אֶת־הַחַיִּים וְאֶת־הַמֵּתִים וַתֹּאמֶר לָהּ נָעֳמִי קָרוֹב לָנוּ הָאִישׁ מִגֹּאֲלֵנוּ הוּא:

²¹ *Rut* the Moabite said, "He even told me, 'Stay close by my workers until all my harvest is finished.'"

כא וַתֹּאמֶר רוּת הַמּוֹאֲבִיָּה גַּם כִּי־אָמַר אֵלַי עִם־הַנְּעָרִים אֲשֶׁר־לִי תִּדְבָּקִין עַד אִם־כִּלּוּ אֵת כָּל־הַקָּצִיר אֲשֶׁר־לִי:

²² And *Naomi* answered her daughter-in-law *Rut*, "It is best, daughter, that you go out with his girls, and not be annoyed in some other field."

כב וַתֹּאמֶר נָעֳמִי אֶל־רוּת כַּלָּתָהּ טוֹב בִּתִּי כִּי תֵצְאִי עִם־נַעֲרוֹתָיו וְלֹא יִפְגְּעוּ־בָךְ בְּשָׂדֶה אַחֵר:

²³ So she stayed close to the maidservants of *Boaz*, and gleaned until the barley harvest and the wheat harvest were finished. Then she stayed at home with her mother-in-law.

כג וַתִּדְבַּק בְּנַעֲרוֹת בֹּעַז לְלַקֵּט עַד־כְּלוֹת קְצִיר־הַשְּׂעֹרִים וּקְצִיר הַחִטִּים וַתֵּשֶׁב אֶת־חֲמוֹתָהּ:

va-tid-BAK b'-na-a-ROT BO-az l'-la-KAYT ad k'-LOT k'-tzeer ha-s'-o-REEM uk-TZEER ha-khi-TEEM va-TAY-shev et kha-mo-TAH

3 ¹ *Naomi*, her mother-in-law, said to her, "Daughter, I must seek a home for you, where you may be happy.

ג א וַתֹּאמֶר לָהּ נָעֳמִי חֲמוֹתָהּ בִּתִּי הֲלֹא אֲבַקֶּשׁ־לָךְ מָנוֹחַ אֲשֶׁר יִיטַב־לָךְ:

² Now there is our kinsman *Boaz*, whose girls you were close to. He will be winnowing barley on the threshing floor tonight.

ב וְעַתָּה הֲלֹא בֹעַז מֹדַעְתָּנוּ אֲשֶׁר הָיִית אֶת־נַעֲרוֹתָיו הִנֵּה־הוּא זֹרֶה אֶת־גֹּרֶן הַשְּׂעֹרִים הַלָּיְלָה:

Old City of *Yerushalayim* with wild barley and oats in the foreground

comes from the word *sei'ar* (שיער), meaning 'hair'. Additionally, barley requires less water and ripens earlier than wheat. In the Bible, the barley harvest signifies the beginning of spring, and barley would be brought to the *Beit Hamikdash* in *Yerushalayim* as part of the offerings of the holiday of *Pesach*. The barley offering in the Temple was a joyous ceremony that teaches us the importance of dedicating a portion of our crops to our Creator before we eat from them ourselves.

2:23 Until the barley harvest and the wheat harvest were finished One reason that *Megillat Rut* is read on the holiday of *Shavuot*, also known as the Feast of Weeks or Pentecost, is that the story took place during the barley and wheat harvest. *Shavuot* is referred to as the "Feast of the Harvest" (Exodus 23:16). It is the festival which began the season for Jewish farmers to make a pilgrimage to *Yerushalayim* to offer their first fruit and grain in the *Beit Hamikdash*, and when an offering of two loaves of bread was brought from the newly harvested wheat crop.

³ So bathe, anoint yourself, dress up, and go down to the threshing floor. But do not disclose yourself to the man until he has finished eating and drinking.

ג וְרָחַצְתְּ וָסַכְתְּ וְשַׂמְתְּ שִׂמְלֹתַךְ [שִׂמְלֹתַיִךְ] עָלַיִךְ וירדתי [וְיָרַדְתְּ] הַגֹּרֶן אַל־תִּוָּדְעִי לָאִישׁ עַד כַּלֹּתוֹ לֶאֱכֹל וְלִשְׁתּוֹת:

⁴ When he lies down, note the place where he lies down, and go over and uncover his feet and lie down. He will tell you what you are to do."

ד וִיהִי בְשָׁכְבוֹ וְיָדַעַתְּ אֶת־הַמָּקוֹם אֲשֶׁר יִשְׁכַּב־שָׁם וּבָאת וְגִלִּית מַרְגְּלֹתָיו ושכבתי [וְשָׁכָבְתְּ] וְהוּא יַגִּיד לָךְ אֵת אֲשֶׁר תַּעֲשִׂין:

⁵ She replied, "I will do everything you tell me."

ה וַתֹּאמֶר אֵלֶיהָ כֹּל אֲשֶׁר־תֹּאמְרִי [אֵלַי] אֶעֱשֶׂה:

⁶ She went down to the threshing floor and did just as her mother-in-law had instructed her.

ו וַתֵּרֶד הַגֹּרֶן וַתַּעַשׂ כְּכֹל אֲשֶׁר־צִוַּתָּה חֲמוֹתָהּ:

⁷ *Boaz* ate and drank, and in a cheerful mood went to lie down beside the grainpile. Then she went over stealthily and uncovered his feet and lay down.

ז וַיֹּאכַל בֹּעַז וַיֵּשְׁתְּ וַיִּיטַב לִבּוֹ וַיָּבֹא לִשְׁכַּב בִּקְצֵה הָעֲרֵמָה וַתָּבֹא בַלָּט וַתְּגַל מַרְגְּלֹתָיו וַתִּשְׁכָּב:

⁸ In the middle of the night, the man gave a start and pulled back – there was a woman lying at his feet!

ח וַיְהִי בַּחֲצִי הַלַּיְלָה וַיֶּחֱרַד הָאִישׁ וַיִּלָּפֵת וְהִנֵּה אִשָּׁה שֹׁכֶבֶת מַרְגְּלֹתָיו:

⁹ "Who are you?" he asked. And she replied, "I am your handmaid *Rut*. Spread your robe over your handmaid, for you are a redeeming kinsman."

ט וַיֹּאמֶר מִי־אָתְּ וַתֹּאמֶר אָנֹכִי רוּת אֲמָתֶךָ וּפָרַשְׂתָּ כְנָפֶךָ עַל־אֲמָתְךָ כִּי גֹאֵל אָתָּה:

va-YO-mer mee AT va-TO-mer a-no-KHEE RUT a-ma-TE-kha
u-fa-ras-TA kh'-na-FE-kha al a-ma-t'-KHA KEE go-AYL A-tah

¹⁰ He exclaimed, "Be blessed of *Hashem*, daughter! Your latest deed of loyalty is greater than the first, in that you have not turned to younger men, whether poor or rich.

י וַיֹּאמֶר בְּרוּכָה אַתְּ לַיהוָה בִּתִּי הֵיטַבְתְּ חַסְדֵּךְ הָאַחֲרוֹן מִן־הָרִאשׁוֹן לְבִלְתִּי־לֶכֶת אַחֲרֵי הַבַּחוּרִים אִם־דַּל וְאִם־עָשִׁיר:

¹¹ And now, daughter, have no fear. I will do in your behalf whatever you ask, for all the elders of my town know what a fine woman you are.

יא וְעַתָּה בִּתִּי אַל־תִּירְאִי כֹּל אֲשֶׁר־תֹּאמְרִי אֶעֱשֶׂה־לָּךְ כִּי יוֹדֵעַ כָּל־שַׁעַר עַמִּי כִּי אֵשֶׁת חַיִל אָתְּ:

¹² But while it is true I am a redeeming kinsman, there is another redeemer closer than I.

יב וְעַתָּה כִּי אָמְנָם כִּי אִם גֹאֵל אָנֹכִי וְגַם יֵשׁ גֹּאֵל קָרוֹב מִמֶּנִּי:

Ruth

Siblings at the beach

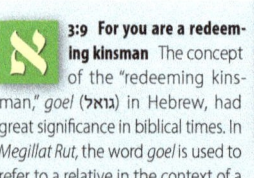
3:9 For you are a redeeming kinsman The concept of the "redeeming kins-man," *goel* (גואל) in Hebrew, had great significance in biblical times. In *Megillat Rut*, the word *goel* is used to refer to a relative in the context of a levirate marriage, which occurs when a man dies without children. In such a case, his brother is supposed to marry his widow and perpetuate the name of the deceased. In the *Tanakh*, the term *goel* is also used in another context.

Vayikra (25:25) says "his nearest re-deemer shall come," referring to someone so deeply in debt that he is forced to sell his property until his closest relative comes to bail him out. Once again, a person's redeemer is his closest relative. *Hashem* has many names in the Bible, one of which is Redeemer, as in the "Redeemer of *Yisrael*" (Isaiah 49:7). By referring to God as our Redeemer, we are stating that He is even closer to us than any of our nearest relations.

גֹּאֵל

13 Stay for the night. Then in the morning, if he will act as a redeemer, good! let him redeem. But if he does not want to act as redeemer for you, I will do so myself, as *Hashem* lives! Lie down until morning."

יג לִינִי הַלַּיְלָה וְהָיָה בַבֹּקֶר אִם־יִגְאָלֵךְ טוֹב יִגְאָל וְאִם־לֹא יַחְפֹּץ לְגָאֳלֵךְ וּגְאַלְתִּיךְ אָנֹכִי חַי־יְהוָֹה שִׁכְבִי עַד־הַבֹּקֶר:

14 So she lay at his feet until dawn. She rose before one person could distinguish another, for he thought, "Let it not be known that the woman came to the threshing floor."

יד וַתִּשְׁכַּב מַרְגְּלוֹתוֹ [מַרְגְּלוֹתָיו] עַד־הַבֹּקֶר וַתָּקָם בְּטֶרֶום [בְּטֶרֶם] יַכִּיר אִישׁ אֶת־רֵעֵהוּ וַיֹּאמֶר אַל־יִוָּדַע כִּי־בָאָה הָאִשָּׁה הַגֹּרֶן:

15 And he said, "Hold out the shawl you are wearing." She held it while he measured out six measures of barley, and he put it on her back. When she got back to the town,

טו וַיֹּאמֶר הָבִי הַמִּטְפַּחַת אֲשֶׁר־עָלַיִךְ וְאֶחֳזִי־בָהּ וַתֹּאחֶז בָּהּ וַיָּמָד שֵׁשׁ־שְׂעֹרִים וַיָּשֶׁת עָלֶיהָ וַיָּבֹא הָעִיר:

16 she came to her mother-in-law, who asked, "How is it with you, daughter?" She told her all that the man had done for her;

טז וַתָּבוֹא אֶל־חֲמוֹתָהּ וַתֹּאמֶר מִי־אַתְּ בִּתִּי וַתַּגֶּד־לָהּ אֵת כָּל־אֲשֶׁר עָשָׂה־לָהּ הָאִישׁ:

17 and she added, "He gave me these six measures of barley, saying to me, 'Do not go back to your mother-in-law empty-handed.'"

יז וַתֹּאמֶר שֵׁשׁ־הַשְּׂעֹרִים הָאֵלֶּה נָתַן לִי כִּי אָמַר [אֵלַי] אַל־תָּבוֹאִי רֵיקָם אֶל־חֲמוֹתֵךְ:

18 And *Naomi* said, "Stay here, daughter, till you learn how the matter turns out. For the man will not rest, but will settle the matter today."

יח וַתֹּאמֶר שְׁבִי בִתִּי עַד אֲשֶׁר תֵּדְעִין אֵיךְ יִפֹּל דָּבָר כִּי לֹא יִשְׁקֹט הָאִישׁ כִּי־אִם־כִּלָּה הַדָּבָר הַיּוֹם:

4 1 Meanwhile, *Boaz* had gone to the gate and sat down there. And now the redeemer whom *Boaz* had mentioned passed by. He called, "Come over and sit down here, So-and-so!" And he came over and sat down.

ד א וּבֹעַז עָלָה הַשַּׁעַר וַיֵּשֶׁב שָׁם וְהִנֵּה הַגֹּאֵל עֹבֵר אֲשֶׁר דִּבֶּר־בֹּעַז וַיֹּאמֶר סוּרָה שְׁבָה־פֹּה פְּלֹנִי אַלְמֹנִי וַיָּסַר וַיֵּשֵׁב:

2 Then [*Boaz*] took ten elders of the town and said, "Be seated here"; and they sat down.

ב וַיִּקַּח עֲשָׂרָה אֲנָשִׁים מִזִּקְנֵי הָעִיר וַיֹּאמֶר שְׁבוּ־פֹה וַיֵּשֵׁבוּ:

3 He said to the redeemer, "*Naomi*, now returned from the country of Moab, must sell the piece of land which belonged to our kinsman *Elimelech*.

ג וַיֹּאמֶר לַגֹּאֵל חֶלְקַת הַשָּׂדֶה אֲשֶׁר לְאָחִינוּ לֶאֱלִימֶלֶךְ מָכְרָה נָעֳמִי הַשָּׁבָה מִשְּׂדֵה מוֹאָב:

4 I thought I should disclose the matter to you and say: Acquire it in the presence of those seated here and in the presence of the elders of my people. If you are willing to redeem it, redeem! But if you will not redeem, tell me, that I may know. For there is no one to redeem but you, and I come after you." "I am willing to redeem it," he replied.

ד וַאֲנִי אָמַרְתִּי אֶגְלֶה אָזְנְךָ לֵאמֹר קְנֵה נֶגֶד הַיֹּשְׁבִים וְנֶגֶד זִקְנֵי עַמִּי אִם־תִּגְאַל גְּאָל וְאִם־לֹא יִגְאַל הַגִּידָה לִּי וְאֵדַע [וְאֵדְעָה] כִּי אֵין זוּלָתְךָ לִגְאוֹל וְאָנֹכִי אַחֲרֶיךָ וַיֹּאמֶר אָנֹכִי אֶגְאָל:

5 *Boaz* continued, "When you acquire the property from *Naomi* and from *Rut* the Moabite, you must also acquire the wife of the deceased, so as to perpetuate the name of the deceased upon his estate."

ה וַיֹּאמֶר בֹּעַז בְּיוֹם־קְנוֹתְךָ הַשָּׂדֶה מִיַּד נָעֳמִי וּמֵאֵת רוּת הַמּוֹאֲבִיָּה אֵשֶׁת־הַמֵּת קָנִיתִי [קָנִיתָה] לְהָקִים שֵׁם־הַמֵּת עַל־נַחֲלָתוֹ:

23

6 The redeemer replied, "Then I cannot redeem it for myself, lest I impair my own estate. You take over my right of redemption, for I am unable to exercise it."

ו וַיֹּ֣אמֶר הַגֹּאֵ֗ל לֹ֤א אוּכַל֙ לִגְאָול־[לִגְאָל־] לִ֔י פֶּן־אַשְׁחִ֖ית אֶת־נַחֲלָתִ֑י גְּאַל־לְךָ֤ אַתָּה֙ אֶת־גְּאֻלָּתִ֔י כִּ֥י לֹא־אוּכַ֖ל לִגְאֹֽל:

7 Now this was formerly done in *Yisrael* in cases of redemption or exchange: to validate any transaction, one man would take off his sandal and hand it to the other. Such was the practice in *Yisrael*.

ז וְזֹאת֩ לְפָנִ֨ים בְּיִשְׂרָאֵ֜ל עַל־הַגְּאוּלָּ֤ה וְעַל־הַתְּמוּרָה֙ לְקַיֵּ֣ם כָּל־דָּבָ֔ר שָׁלַ֥ף אִ֛ישׁ נַעֲל֖וֹ וְנָתַ֣ן לְרֵעֵ֑הוּ וְזֹ֥את הַתְּעוּדָ֖ה בְּיִשְׂרָאֵֽל:

8 So when the redeemer said to *Boaz*, "Acquire for yourself," he drew off his sandal.

ח וַיֹּ֧אמֶר הַגֹּאֵ֛ל לְבֹ֖עַז קְנֵה־לָ֑ךְ וַיִּשְׁלֹ֖ף נַעֲלֽוֹ:

9 And *Boaz* said to the elders and to the rest of the people, "You are witnesses today that I am acquiring from *Naomi* all that belonged to *Elimelech* and all that belonged to *Kilyon* and *Machlon*.

ט וַיֹּאמֶר֩ בֹּ֨עַז לַזְּקֵנִ֜ים וְכָל־הָעָ֣ם עֵדִ֣ים אַתֶּ֣ם הַיּ֗וֹם כִּ֤י קָנִ֨יתִי֙ אֶת־כָּל־אֲשֶׁ֣ר לֶאֱלִימֶ֔לֶךְ וְאֵ֛ת כָּל־אֲשֶׁ֥ר לְכִלְי֖וֹן וּמַחְל֑וֹן מִיַּ֖ד נָעֳמִֽי:

10 I am also acquiring *Rut* the Moabite, the wife of *Machlon*, as my wife, so as to perpetuate the name of the deceased upon his estate, that the name of the deceased may not disappear from among his kinsmen and from the gate of his home town. You are witnesses today."

י וְגַ֣ם אֶת־ר֣וּת הַמֹּאֲבִיָּה֩ אֵ֨שֶׁת מַחְל֜וֹן קָנִ֧יתִי לִ֣י לְאִשָּׁ֗ה לְהָקִ֤ים שֵׁם־הַמֵּת֙ עַל־נַחֲלָת֔וֹ וְלֹא־יִכָּרֵ֧ת שֵׁם־הַמֵּ֛ת מֵעִ֥ם אֶחָ֖יו וּמִשַּׁ֣עַר מְקוֹמ֑וֹ עֵדִ֥ים אַתֶּ֖ם הַיּֽוֹם:

11 All the people at the gate and the elders answered, "We are. May *Hashem* make the woman who is coming into your house like *Rachel* and *Leah*, both of whom built up the House of *Yisrael*! Prosper in *Efrat* and perpetuate your name in *Beit Lechem*!

יא וַיֹּ֨אמְר֜וּ כָּל־הָעָ֧ם אֲשֶׁר־בַּשַּׁ֛עַר וְהַזְּקֵנִ֖ים עֵדִ֑ים יִתֵּן֩ יְהֹוָ֨ה אֶֽת־הָאִשָּׁ֜ה הַבָּאָ֣ה אֶל־בֵּיתֶ֗ךָ כְּרָחֵ֤ל ׀ וּכְלֵאָה֙ אֲשֶׁ֨ר בָּנ֤וּ שְׁתֵּיהֶם֙ אֶת־בֵּ֣ית יִשְׂרָאֵ֔ל וַעֲשֵׂה־חַ֣יִל בְּאֶפְרָ֔תָה וּקְרָא־שֵׁ֖ם בְּבֵ֥ית לָֽחֶם:

12 And may your house be like the house of *Peretz* whom *Tamar* bore to *Yehuda* – through the offspring which *Hashem* will give you by this young woman."

יב וִיהִ֤י בֵֽיתְךָ֙ כְּבֵ֣ית פֶּ֔רֶץ אֲשֶׁר־יָלְדָ֥ה תָמָ֖ר לִֽיהוּדָ֑ה מִן־הַזֶּ֗רַע אֲשֶׁ֨ר יִתֵּ֤ן יְהֹוָה֙ לְךָ֔ מִן־הַֽנַּעֲרָ֖ה הַזֹּֽאת:

13 So *Boaz* married *Rut*; she became his wife, and he cohabited with her. *Hashem* let her conceive, and she bore a son.

יג וַיִּקַּ֨ח בֹּ֤עַז אֶת־רוּת֙ וַתְּהִי־ל֣וֹ לְאִשָּׁ֔ה וַיָּבֹ֖א אֵלֶ֑יהָ וַיִּתֵּ֨ן יְהֹוָ֥ה לָ֛הּ הֵרָי֖וֹן וַתֵּ֥לֶד בֵּֽן:

14 And the women said to *Naomi*, "Blessed be *Hashem*, who has not withheld a redeemer from you today! May his name be perpetuated in *Yisrael*!

יד וַתֹּאמַ֤רְנָה הַנָּשִׁים֙ אֶֽל־נָ֣עֳמִ֔י בָּר֣וּךְ יְהֹוָ֔ה אֲשֶׁ֠ר לֹ֣א הִשְׁבִּ֥ית לָ֛ךְ גֹּאֵ֖ל הַיּ֑וֹם וְיִקָּרֵ֥א שְׁמ֖וֹ בְּיִשְׂרָאֵֽל:

15 He will renew your life and sustain your old age; for he is born of your daughter-in-law, who loves you and is better to you than seven sons."

טו וְהָ֤יָה לָךְ֙ לְמֵשִׁ֣יב נֶ֔פֶשׁ וּלְכַלְכֵּ֖ל אֶת־שֵׂיבָתֵ֑ךְ כִּ֣י כַלָּתֵ֤ךְ אֲשֶׁר־אֲהֵבַ֨תֶךְ֙ יְלָדַ֔תּוּ אֲשֶׁר־הִיא֙ ט֣וֹבָה לָ֔ךְ מִשִּׁבְעָ֖ה בָּנִֽים:

16 *Naomi* took the child and held it to her bosom. She became its foster mother,

טז וַתִּקַּ֨ח נָעֳמִ֤י אֶת־הַיֶּ֨לֶד֙ וַתְּשִׁתֵ֣הוּ בְחֵיקָ֔הּ וַתְּהִי־ל֖וֹ לְאֹמֶֽנֶת:

¹⁷ and the women neighbors gave him a name, saying, "A son is born to *Naomi*!" They named him *Oved*; he was the father of *Yishai*, father of *David*.

יז וַתִּקְרֶאנָה לוֹ הַשְּׁכֵנוֹת שֵׁם לֵאמֹר יֻלַּד־בֵּן לְנָעֳמִי וַתִּקְרֶאנָה שְׁמוֹ עוֹבֵד הוּא אֲבִי־יִשַׁי אֲבִי דָוִד:

¹⁸ This is the line of *Peretz*: *Peretz* begot *Chetzron*,

יח וְאֵלֶּה תּוֹלְדוֹת פָּרֶץ פֶּרֶץ הוֹלִיד אֶת־חֶצְרוֹן:

¹⁹ *Chetzron* begot *Ram*, *Ram* begot *Aminadav*,

יט וְחֶצְרוֹן הוֹלִיד אֶת־רָם וְרָם הוֹלִיד אֶת־עַמִּינָדָב:

²⁰ *Aminadav* begot *Nachshon*, *Nachshon* begot *Salma*,

כ וְעַמִּינָדָב הוֹלִיד אֶת־נַחְשׁוֹן וְנַחְשׁוֹן הוֹלִיד אֶת־שַׂלְמָה:

²¹ *Salma* begot *Boaz*, *Boaz* begot *Oved*,

כא וְשַׂלְמוֹן הוֹלִיד אֶת־בֹּעַז וּבֹעַז הוֹלִיד אֶת־עוֹבֵד:

²² *Oved* begot *Yishai*, and *Yishai* begot *David*.

כב וְעֹבֵד הוֹלִיד אֶת־יִשַׁי וְיִשַׁי הוֹלִיד אֶת־דָּוִד:

v'-o-VAYD ho-LEED et yi-SHAI v'-yi-SHAI ho-LEED et da-VID

4:22 And *Yishai* begot *David* *Megillat Rut* ends by emphasizing *Rut's* great reward for her selfless dedication to her mother-in-law and her late husband. She gives birth to a child who becomes the grandfather of King *David*, making *Rut* the ancestress of the Davidic dynasty as well as its future descendant, the *Mashiach*. Most other nations would have chosen a king with a perfect pedigree and impeccable lineage, yet King *David* descends from a Moabite convert. The lesson of King *David's* humble origins is a powerful one. *Rut* teaches us that salvation and redemption can come from unlikely sources. No matter what our background is, we all have the ability to play a great role in history and make a difference in the world if we align ourselves with the God of Israel, the People of Israel and the Land of Israel.

Statue of King *David* in *Yerushalayim*

Megillat Eicha
The Scroll of Lamentations

Introduction and commentary by Rabbi Noam Shapiro

In *Megillat Eicha* (Lamentations) the prophet *Yirmiyahu* records his impressions of the destruction of *Yerushalayim* and the first *Beit Hamikdash*, and the exile of the Jews from the Land of Israel. It is a very emotional book in which the prophet expresses feelings of intense loneliness, a sense of utter abandonment, desolation, desecration of that which was sacred, pain and suffering. There are times when *Yirmiyahu* even seems to challenge *Hashem* for allowing this to happen, yet the book also contains elements of prayer, faith and hope.

How did it happen? What led to the great destruction of the Holy Land and the exile of the Jews? Throughout the Bible, the Jews are told that *Eretz Yisrael* is their eternal inheritance, but that living in the land is dependent upon following God and His *Torah*. The prophets warn again and again that continuing to sin, abandoning *Hashem*, and treating others inappropriately will lead to destruction and exile. Ultimately, that is what happened. However, *Yirmiyahu* also reminds us that *Hashem* did not abandon His people and His land, even though He destroyed the place where they connect to Him most. Their new challenge is to find *Hashem* and rebuild their connection with Him, even in exile.

Amidst the mourning, sorrow and misery of *Megillat Eicha*, there are elements of faith and optimism. In the middle of chapter 3, the prophet declares "The kindness of *Hashem* has not ended, His mercies are not spent" (3:22). He continues a little further in the chapter: "For *Hashem* does not reject forever, but first afflicts, then pardons in His abundant kindness. For He does not willfully bring grief or affliction to man" (3:31–33). *Yirmiyahu* reminds us that destruction and exile from the Land of Israel is not an indication of a divorce between *Hashem* and His nation. Rather, the exile is meant to serve a rehabilitative function. It is meant to trigger introspection, evaluation of our behavior and relationship with *Hashem*, and to lead us to recommit ourselves to God and to each other. Indeed, *Yirmiyahu* himself composes a letter to the exiles in which he gives them the guidelines for surviving in exile, and promises redemption if they call out to *Hashem* (Jeremiah 28).

Similarly, the Talmud (*Makkot* 24b) relates that a number of leading Sages were visiting *Yerushalayim* following the destruction of the *Beit Hamikdash*, and they came upon the ruins of the Temple Mount. Seeing a jackal scamper across the holiest site in the world, three of the four rabbis started to cry. The great Rabbi Akiva, on the other hand, began to laugh joyously. Shocked, the others asked him to explain his behavior. Rabbi Akiva replied that if the prophecies of destruction have so clearly been fulfilled, we can be certain that the promises of redemption will also be fulfilled. *Megillat Eicha*, therefore, calls on us to "search and examine our ways, and turn back to *Hashem*" (3:40). It ends with a call to the Lord to fulfill those prophecies of redemption and "renew our days as of old" (5:21).

The Talmud (*Taanit* 30b) teaches that those who participate in mourning for the destruction of *Yerushalayim* will merit to participate in rejoicing over its rebuilding. Throughout the cycle of life, Jews express sorrow for the fact that the *Beit Hamikdash* is no longer with us, and that as a result, God's presence is more distant. For this reason, a glass is broken at Jewish weddings, to remember *Yerushalayim* even at the happiest of occasions. And once a year, on the ninth of the Hebrew month of *Av*, the mourning for *Yerushalayim* is particularly vivid. For more than twenty-four hours it is forbidden to eat or drink; Jews sit on the floor as an expression of mourning, and recall the events surrounding the destruction by reciting *Megillat Eicha* and other prayers of lament, as if the tragedy had just happened. In this way, it is possible to come to grips with what has been lost. *Megillat Eicha* is the text that best expresses our broken hearts as we call out again and again, *Eicha* (איכה), 'alas,' or 'how [did this happen].'

For almost two thousand years, Jews have mourned over the destruction of *Yerushalayim* and the *Beit Hamikdash*. In modern times, we have begun to experience the rebirth of the Land of Israel and the Holy City. May we merit to quickly see *Hashem*'s comfort and the fulfillment of the rest of the redemption, through the coming of the *Mashiach* and the building of the third *Beit Hamikdash*.

Chart of Israel's Exiles, Persecutions and Wars

Megillat Eicha laments the destruction of *Yerushalayim* and the *Beit Hamikdash*, as well as the exile of the Jews from the Land of Israel at the hands of Nebuchadnezzar king of Babylon. This first exile of the Jews happened in stages, and is just one example of the many exiles, expulsions and persecutions of the Jewish people throughout history. The following is a partial list of persecutions and exiles of the Jewish people in the Land of Israel, as well as modern Israel's wars.

Event	Description	Perpetrator	Date	King of Israel/ Prime Minister	Relevant Verses
First stage of the exile of *Yisrael*	The Israelite populations of the Galilee, Gilad and the eastern side of the Jordan River are taken into exile.	Tiglath-Pileser king of Assyria	734 BCE	*Pekach*	II Kings 15:29, I Chronicles 5:26
Complete exile of the ten tribes of *Yisrael*	The remaining members of the ten tribes of *Yisrael* are exiled and scattered. Other populations are brought into the land to replace them.	Sennacherib king of Assyria	722 BCE	*Hoshea son of Eila*	II Kings 17:6, II Kings 18:9–12
First stage of the exile of *Yehuda*	The youths of the royal family are taken to Babylon	Nebuchadnezzar king of Babylon	604 BCE	*Yehoyakim*	Daniel 1:1–6
Second stage of the exile of *Yehuda* – Exile of the artisans and craftsmen	The king, the royal family, royal officials, warriors, artisans, and other distinguished people from *Yerushalayim* and *Yehuda* are exiled to Babylon	Nebuchadnezzar king of Babylon	597 BCE	*Yehoyachin*	II Kings 24:8–17
Third stage of the exile of *Yehuda*/ Destruction of *Yerushalayim* and the *Beit Hamikdash*	The *Beit Hamikdash* is destroyed and all the remaining inhabitants of *Yehuda* and *Yerushalayim*, aside from the poorest people, are exiled to Babylon	Nebuchadnezzar king of Babylon	586 BCE	*Tzidkiyahu*	II Kings 25:8–21, II Chronicles 36:15–20
Religious persecution by the Syrian-Greeks	The Jews in Israel are forbidden from *Torah* study and Jewish practice and the *Beit Hamikdash* is defiled. Those who continue to practice Judaism are killed.	Antiochus Epiphanes, king of the Seleucids (Syrian-Greek empire)	168–165 BCE		
Destruction of *Yerushalayim* and the Second *Beit Hamikdash*	The city of *Yerushalayim* is captured and the *Beit Hamikdash* is destroyed. Nearly one million Jews are killed in *Yerushalayim* alone and 100,000 taken captive	Titus of Rome	70 CE		
Bar Kochba Revolt	As a result of Bar Kochba's rebellion against the Romans, hundreds of thousands of Jews are slaughtered. Jews are banned from entering the city of *Yerushalayim* from the end of the Bar Kochba Revolt until the capture of *Yerushalayim* by the Muslims in 638 CE. Israel is renamed Syria Palaestina.	Hadrian, emperor of Rome	135 CE		

Event	Description	Perpetrator	Date	King of Israel/ Prime Minister	Relevant Verses
Chevron attacks	At the beginning of the Ottoman rule, the Sultan's deputy armies attack the Jews of *Chevron*. They are beaten, raped and murdered, and their homes and businesses are looted and pillaged. Jews do not return to *Chevron* for another 15 years.	Murad Bey, deputy of the Sultan from Jerusalem	1517 CE		
Tzfat Arab Pogrom	A 33 day pogrom against the Jews of *Tzfat* as part of the general rebellion against governor Muhammed Ali. Jews are raped and murdered, and their homes, synagogues and businesses are destroyed and looted.	Mobs of peasants	1834 CE		
Arab riots	At the encouragement of Haj Amin el-Husseini, Arabs begin rioting and carrying out murderous attacks against Jews throughout the Land of Israel, especially in the North, in *Yerushalayim* and in *Yaffo* and its environs.	Arab rioters encouraged by Haj Amin el-Husseini	1920– 1921		
Jihad against the Jews – *Chevron* Massacre and *Tzfat* Massacre	Accusing the Jews of trying to take over Muslim holy sites, especially the Temple Mount, Haj Amin el-Husseini calls for jihad against the Jews. Incitement spreads throughout the Land of Israel, especially in *Yerushalayim* and *Chevron*. The Jews of *Yerushalayim* suffer numerous attacks, and the Jewish community of *Chevron* is destroyed. One week later, the same thing happens to the Jews of *Tzfat*.	Arab rioters encouraged by Haj Amin el-Husseini	1929		
War of Independence	The Israeli War of Independence takes place along the entire border of the country. Israel fights against Lebanon and Syria in the north, Iraq and Jordan in the east, Egypt, assisted by Sudan, in the south, and Palestinians and Arab volunteers inside the country. Israel emerges victorious, defeating the invading Arab forces and capturing 5,000 square kilometers more than what was initially allocated by the United Nations. However, the Jews lose access to the eastern part of *Yerushalayim*, including the Western Wall and the Temple Mount, until 1967.	Egypt Transjordan Iraq Syria Lebanon	1947– 1949	David Ben-Gurion	
Sinai War	The Sinai War, or Sinai Campaign, is fought to end terrorist infiltrations and attacks in Israel, and to break the Egyptian blockade of *Eilat*. Israel's attack on Egypt is successful and Israel takes control of the Gaza Strip and the Sinai Peninsula before being pressured to give the Sinai Peninsula back to the Egyptians.	Egypt	1956	David Ben-Gurion	

Event	Description	Perpetrator	Date	King of Israel/ Prime Minister	Relevant Verses
Six-Day War	The Six-Day War begins in response to Egypt's mobilization of forces in the Sinai Peninsula, expelling of the UN forces and signing an agreement with Jordan. Israel launches a surprise attack which demolishes the Egyptian air force while it is still on the ground. In just six days, the IDF overruns the entire Sinai peninsula, takes the West Bank of the Jordan River, captures a great part of the Golan Heights, and regains control of the Old City of *Yerushalayim* and its Western Wall.	Egypt Syria Jordan Iraq Lebanon	1967	Levi Eshkol	
War of Attrition	The War of Attrition refers to the continuous, static fighting along the ceasefire borders of the Six-Day War, focused around the Bar Lev line on the Suez Canal. The fighting is initiated by Egypt in the hopes of regaining control of the Sinai Peninsula, lost to Israel in the Six-Day War. The war ends with a ceasefire in August 1970.	Egypt	1968– 1970	Golda Meir	
Yom Kippur War	The Yom Kippur War begins with an attack by a coalition of Arab forces, led by Egypt and Syria, in both the Sinai Peninsula and the Golan Heights. The attack is carried out on *Yom Kippur*, the holiest day on the Jewish calendar, and takes Israel by surprise. While Egypt and Syria make significant initial gains, the IDF pushes them back. Within a few days, the Israeli army has crossed the Suez Canal into Egypt and are within artillery range of the airfields outside the Syrian capital of Damascus. The war ends by a ceasefire on October 25th.	Egypt Syria Jordan Iraq	1973	Golda Meir	
First Lebanon War	The First Lebanon War is Israel's response to continuous attacks on northern Israel carried out by Palestinian terror organizations in Lebanon. The war begins after an assassination attempt against Israel's ambassador to the United Kingdom, Shlomo Argov. As a result of the war, the Palestinian Liberation Organization (PLO) is expelled from Lebanon and an Israeli Security Zone is created in Southern Lebanon.	PLO	1982	Menachem Begin	
Second Lebanon War	The Second Lebanon War begins in response to the abduction of two Israeli soldiers by the Hezbollah terror organization. It lasts just over a month and results in the pacification of Southern Lebanon and a weakening of the Hezbollah terror group.	Hezbollah	2006	Ehud Olmert	

Event	Description	Perpetrator	Date	King of Israel/ Prime Minister	Relevant Verses
Operation Protective Edge	Operation Protective Edge begins in response to increased rocket fire by the Hamas terror organization from the Gaza Strip into Israel, following the abduction and murder of three Israeli teens. The operation begins with Israeli airstrikes into Gaza which are followed by a ground invasion aimed at destroying Hamas terror tunnels leading into Israel. As a result of the war, the Hamas terror organization is weakened and many of their tunnels are destroyed.	Hamas	2014	Benjamin Netanyahu	

1 ¹ Alas! Lonely sits the city Once great with people! She that was great among nations Is become like a widow; The princess among states Is become a thrall.

א אֵיכָה ׀ יָשְׁבָה בָדָד הָעִיר רַבָּתִי עָם הָיְתָה כְּאַלְמָנָה רַבָּתִי בַגּוֹיִם שָׂרָתִי בַּמְּדִינוֹת הָיְתָה לָמַס:

² Bitterly she weeps in the night, Her cheek wet with tears. There is none to comfort her Of all her friends. All her allies have betrayed her; They have become her foes.

ב בָּכוֹ תִבְכֶּה בַּלַּיְלָה וְדִמְעָתָהּ עַל לֶחֱיָהּ אֵין לָהּ מְנַחֵם מִכָּל אֹהֲבֶיהָ כָּל רֵעֶיהָ בָּגְדוּ בָהּ הָיוּ לָהּ לְאֹיְבִים:

ba-KHO tiv-KEH ba-LAI-lah v'-dim-a-TAH AL le-khe-YAH
ayn LAH m'-na-KHAYM mi-kol o-ha-VE-ha kol ray-E-ha
BA-g'-du VAH ha-YU LAH l'-o-y'-VEEM

³ *Yehuda* has gone into exile Because of misery and harsh oppression; When she settled among the nations, She found no rest; All her pursuers overtook her In the narrow places.

ג גָּלְתָה יְהוּדָה מֵעֹנִי וּמֵרֹב עֲבֹדָה הִיא יָשְׁבָה בַגּוֹיִם לֹא מָצְאָה מָנוֹחַ כָּל רֹדְפֶיהָ הִשִּׂיגוּהָ בֵּין הַמְּצָרִים:

⁴ *Tzion*'s roads are in mourning, Empty of festival pilgrims; All her gates are deserted. Her *Kohanim* sigh, Her maidens are unhappy – She is utterly disconsolate!

ד דַּרְכֵי צִיּוֹן אֲבֵלוֹת מִבְּלִי בָּאֵי מוֹעֵד כָּל שְׁעָרֶיהָ שׁוֹמֵמִין כֹּהֲנֶיהָ נֶאֱנָחִים בְּתוּלֹתֶיהָ נּוּגוֹת וְהִיא מַר לָהּ:

⁵ Her enemies are now the masters, Her foes are at ease, Because *Hashem* has afflicted her For her many transgressions; Her infants have gone into captivity Before the enemy.

ה הָיוּ צָרֶיהָ לְרֹאשׁ אֹיְבֶיהָ שָׁלוּ כִּי יְהֹוָה הוֹגָהּ עַל רֹב פְּשָׁעֶיהָ עוֹלָלֶיהָ הָלְכוּ שְׁבִי לִפְנֵי צָר:

⁶ Gone from Fair *Tzion* are all That were her glory; Her leaders were like stags That found no pasture; They could only walk feebly Before the pursuer.

ו וַיֵּצֵא מִן בַּת־[מִבַּת־] צִיּוֹן כָּל הֲדָרָהּ הָיוּ שָׂרֶיהָ כְּאַיָּלִים לֹא מָצְאוּ מִרְעֶה וַיֵּלְכוּ בְלֹא כֹחַ לִפְנֵי רוֹדֵף:

⁷ All the precious things she had In the days of old *Yerushalayim* recalled In her days of woe and sorrow, When her people fell by enemy hands With none to help her; When enemies looked on and gloated Over her downfall.

ז זָכְרָה יְרוּשָׁלַ͏ִם יְמֵי עָנְיָהּ וּמְרוּדֶיהָ כֹּל מַחֲמֻדֶיהָ אֲשֶׁר הָיוּ מִימֵי קֶדֶם בִּנְפֹל עַמָּהּ בְּיַד צָר וְאֵין עוֹזֵר לָהּ רָאוּהָ צָרִים שָׂחֲקוּ עַל מִשְׁבַּתֶּהָ:

1:2 All her allies have betrayed her; They have become her foes Jewish history has demonstrated time and time again just how drastically friends can indeed turn into enemies. Ever since the biblical account of Pharaoh inviting *Yosef*'s family down to Egypt, which eventually led to the bitter enslavement of the Israelites, we have seen one host country after another turn against her Jewish subjects. In the last century, for example, Jews were active contributors in all realms of European society: Politicians, academics, doctors, lawyers, artists, and more. It was thus all the more devastating when, in 1935, with Adolf Hitler's power steadily growing, the Nuremberg Laws were passed. These laws called for clear genetic definitions regarding who is a Jew, and all those defined as Jews were denied the right to German citizenship, demonstrating how dramatically a friend can turn into an enemy! In contrast, Israel's Law of Return was modified in 1970 to include anyone who would have been defined as a Jew under the Nuremberg Laws. According to the current law, anyone born a Jew, a child of a Jew or grandchild of a Jew, and their spouses, all have the right to attain citizenship in the State of Israel if they so desire.

The Law of Return

8 *Yerushalayim* has greatly sinned, Therefore she is become a mockery. All who admired her despise her, For they have seen her disgraced; And she can only sigh And shrink back.

ח חֵטְא חָטְאָה יְרוּשָׁלַ͏ִם עַל־כֵּן לְנִידָה הָיָתָה כָּל־מְכַבְּדֶיהָ הִזִּילוּהָ כִּי־רָאוּ עֶרְוָתָהּ גַּם־הִיא נֶאֶנְחָה וַתָּשָׁב אָחוֹר:

9 Her uncleanness clings to her skirts. She gave no thought to her future; She has sunk appallingly, With none to comfort her. – See, *Hashem*, my misery; How the enemy jeers!

ט טֻמְאָתָהּ בְּשׁוּלֶיהָ לֹא זָכְרָה אַחֲרִיתָהּ וַתֵּרֶד פְּלָאִים אֵין מְנַחֵם לָהּ רְאֵה יְהֹוָה אֶת־עָנְיִי כִּי הִגְדִּיל אוֹיֵב:

10 The foe has laid hands On everything dear to her. She has seen her Sanctuary Invaded by nations Which You have denied admission Into Your community.

י יָדוֹ פָּרַשׂ צָר עַל כָּל־מַחֲמַדֶּיהָ כִּי־רָאֲתָה גוֹיִם בָּאוּ מִקְדָּשָׁהּ אֲשֶׁר צִוִּיתָה לֹא־יָבֹאוּ בַקָּהָל לָךְ:

11 All her inhabitants sigh, As they search for bread; They have bartered their treasures for food, To keep themselves alive. – See, *Hashem*, and behold, How abject I have become!

יא כָּל־עַמָּהּ נֶאֱנָחִים מְבַקְשִׁים לֶחֶם נָתְנוּ מַחֲמַדֵּיהֶם [מַחֲמַדֵּיהֶם] בְּאֹכֶל לְהָשִׁיב נָפֶשׁ רְאֵה יְהֹוָה וְהַבִּיטָה כִּי הָיִיתִי זוֹלֵלָה:

12 May it never befall you, All who pass along the road – Look about and see: Is there any agony like mine, Which was dealt out to me When *Hashem* afflicted me On His day of wrath?

יב לוֹא אֲלֵיכֶם כָּל־עֹבְרֵי דֶרֶךְ הַבִּיטוּ וּרְאוּ אִם־יֵשׁ מַכְאוֹב כְּמַכְאֹבִי אֲשֶׁר עוֹלַל לִי אֲשֶׁר הוֹגָה יְהֹוָה בְּיוֹם חֲרוֹן אַפּוֹ:

13 From above He sent a fire Down into my bones. He spread a net for my feet, He hurled me backward; He has left me forlorn, In constant misery.

יג מִמָּרוֹם שָׁלַח־אֵשׁ בְּעַצְמֹתַי וַיִּרְדֶּנָּה פָּרַשׂ רֶשֶׁת לְרַגְלַי הֱשִׁיבַנִי אָחוֹר נְתָנַנִי שֹׁמֵמָה כָּל־הַיּוֹם דָּוָה:

14 The yoke of my offenses is bound fast, Lashed tight by His hand; Imposed upon my neck, It saps my strength; *Hashem* has delivered me into the hands Of those I cannot withstand.

יד נִשְׂקַד עֹל פְּשָׁעַי בְּיָדוֹ יִשְׂתָּרְגוּ עָלוּ עַל־צַוָּארִי הִכְשִׁיל כֹּחִי נְתָנַנִי אֲדֹנָי בִּידֵי לֹא־אוּכַל קוּם:

15 *Hashem* in my midst has rejected All my heroes; He has proclaimed a set time against me To crush my young men. As in a press *Hashem* has trodden Fair Maiden *Yehuda*.

טו סִלָּה כָל־אַבִּירַי אֲדֹנָי בְּקִרְבִּי קָרָא עָלַי מוֹעֵד לִשְׁבֹּר בַּחוּרָי גַּת דָּרַךְ אֲדֹנָי לִבְתוּלַת בַּת־יְהוּדָה:

16 For these things do I weep, My eyes flow with tears: Far from me is any comforter Who might revive my spirit; My children are forlorn, For the foe has prevailed.

טז עַל־אֵלֶּה אֲנִי בוֹכִיָּה עֵינִי עֵינִי יֹרְדָה מַּיִם כִּי־רָחַק מִמֶּנִּי מְנַחֵם מֵשִׁיב נַפְשִׁי הָיוּ בָנַי שׁוֹמֵמִים כִּי גָבַר אוֹיֵב:

> *al ay-LEH a-NEE vo-khi-YAH ay-NEE ay-NEE YO-r'-dah MA-yim*
> *kee ra-KHAK mi-ME-nee m'-na-KHAYM may-SHEEV naf-SHEE*
> *ha-YU va-NAI sho-may-MEEM KEE ga-VAR o-YAYV*

Mourning the destruction of the Temple at the Western Wall on the ninth of *Av*

1:16 For these things do I weep, my eyes flow with tears The Sages explain that *Hashem* intentionally selected the ninth of the month of *Av* as the day on which both the first and second Temples would be destroyed. According to Jewish tradition, the reason for this is that it was on the ninth of *Av* that the twelve spies returned from their mission to scout out the land of Israel. As reported in *Sefer Bamidbar* (13–14), following the spies' pessimistic and libelous report, the people fearfully cried out to God: "How will we ever conquer the land? Why did you take us out of Egypt to die at the hands

¹⁷ *Tzion* spreads out her hands, She has no one to comfort her; *Hashem* has summoned against *Yaakov* His enemies all about him; *Yerushalayim* has become among them A thing unclean.

יז פֵּרְשָׂה צִיּוֹן בְּיָדֶיהָ אֵין מְנַחֵם לָהּ צִוָּה יְהֹוָה לְיַעֲקֹב סְבִיבָיו צָרָיו הָיְתָה יְרוּשָׁלַ͏ִם לְנִדָּה בֵּינֵיהֶם:

¹⁸ *Hashem* is in the right, For I have disobeyed Him. Hear, all you peoples, And behold my agony: My maidens and my youths Have gone into captivity!

יח צַדִּיק הוּא יְהֹוָה כִּי פִיהוּ מָרִיתִי שִׁמְעוּ־נָא כָל־עמים [הָעַמִּים] וּרְאוּ מַכְאֹבִי בְּתוּלֹתַי וּבַחוּרַי הָלְכוּ בַשֶּׁבִי:

¹⁹ I cried out to my friends, But they played me false. My *Kohanim* and my elders Have perished in the city As they searched for food To keep themselves alive.

יט קָרָאתִי לַמְאַהֲבַי הֵמָּה רִמּוּנִי כֹּהֲנַי וּזְקֵנַי בָּעִיר גָּוָעוּ כִּי־בִקְשׁוּ אֹכֶל לָמוֹ וְיָשִׁיבוּ אֶת־נַפְשָׁם:

²⁰ See, *Hashem*, the distress I am in! My heart is in anguish, I know how wrong I was To disobey. Outside the sword deals death; Indoors, the plague.

כ רְאֵה יְהֹוָה כִּי־צַר־לִי מֵעַי חֳמַרְמָרוּ נֶהְפַּךְ לִבִּי בְּקִרְבִּי כִּי מָרוֹ מָרִיתִי מִחוּץ שִׁכְּלָה־חֶרֶב בַּבַּיִת כַּמָּוֶת:

²¹ When they heard how I was sighing, There was none to comfort me; All my foes heard of my plight and exulted. For it is Your doing: You have brought on the day that You threatened. Oh, let them become like me!

כא שָׁמְעוּ כִּי נֶאֱנָחָה אָנִי אֵין מְנַחֵם לִי כָּל־אֹיְבַי שָׁמְעוּ רָעָתִי שָׂשׂוּ כִּי אַתָּה עָשִׂיתָ הֵבֵאתָ יוֹם־קָרָאתָ וְיִהְיוּ כָמוֹנִי:

sha-m'-U KEE ne-e-na-KHAH A-nee AYN m'-na-KHAYM LEE
kol o-y'-VAI sha-m'-U ra-a-TEE SA-su KEE a-TAH a-SEE-ta
hay-VAY-ta yom ka-RA-ta v'-yih-YU kha-MO-nee

---

of the Canaanites?" The Sages (*Taanit* 29a) record God's reprimand of the people for their lack of faith: "You cried on the ninth of *Av* for no reason, and so this day will become a day of crying for all generations." The events surrounding the destruction of the *Beit Hamikdash* are linked back to the biblical account of the twelve spies, to illustrate that all of Jewish history is inexorably interwoven; it all represents the unfolding of *Hashem's* master plan. Furthermore, we must never forget that one of the keys to the rebuilding of the *Beit Hamikdash* and the commencement of the Messianic Era is our unquestioning trust in God and appreciation for *Eretz Yisrael*. This is the very trait that the spies and nation failed to exhibit when they rejected His land, and it is one which we must constantly seek to achieve.

1:21 When they heard how I was sighing, there was none to comfort me The prophet *Yirmiyahu* captures the sense of utter loneliness that prevailed after the destruction of *Yerushalayim* and the exile of the people. He describes their feeling that there was no one to stand by their side or to provide any sort of comfort in their time of need. Over many centuries of exile, Jews repeatedly experienced this same sense of

abandonment. For example, over two and a half millennia following the destruction of *Yerushalayim* in *Yirmiyahu's* time, as Hitler's persecution mounted in the late 1930's, many Jews desired to flee from Europe. Unfortunately, though, not a single country was willing to absorb Jewish refugees. In July of 1938, delegates from over thirty countries met in Évian-les-Bains, France, to discuss the refugee crisis. Despite many sympathetic speeches for the tragic plight of the Jews, no country was willing to significantly change their immigration quota to admit additional Jewish refugees. As this verse bemoans, the entire world had closed their doors to the Jewish people, abandoning them in their time of need. With the establishment of the State of Israel, however, the Jewish people now have a home. Never again will they be left alone with no one to protect and comfort them. As Rabbi Joseph B. Soloveitchik writes in his essay *Kol Dodi Dofek*, 'The Voice of my Beloved Knocks,' "A Jew who flees from a hostile country now knows that he can find a secure refuge in the land of his ancestors...Jews who have been uprooted from their homes can find lodging in the Holy Land."

Rabbi Joseph
B. Soloveitchik
(1903–1993)

²² Let all their wrongdoing come before You, And deal with them As You have dealt with me For all my transgressions. For my sighs are many, And my heart is sick.

כב תָּבֹא כָל־רָעָתָם לְפָנֶיךָ וְעוֹלֵל לָמוֹ כַּאֲשֶׁר עוֹלַלְתָּ לִי עַל כָּל־פְּשָׁעָי כִּי־ רַבּוֹת אַנְחֹתַי וְלִבִּי דַוָּי:

2 ¹ Alas! *Hashem* in His wrath Has shamed Fair *Tzion*, Has cast down from heaven to earth The majesty of *Yisrael*. He did not remember His Footstool On His day of wrath.

ב א אֵיכָה יָעִיב בְּאַפּוֹ אֲדֹנָי אֶת־בַּת־צִיּוֹן הִשְׁלִיךְ מִשָּׁמַיִם אֶרֶץ תִּפְאֶרֶת יִשְׂרָאֵל וְלֹא־זָכַר הֲדֹם־רַגְלָיו בְּיוֹם אַפּוֹ:

ay-KHAH ya-EEV b'-a-PO a-do-NAI et bat tzi-YON hish-LEEKH mi-sha-MA-yim E-retz tif-E-ret yis-ra-AYL v'-LO za-KHAR ha-DOM rag-LAV b'-YOM a-PO

² *Hashem* has laid waste without pity All the habitations of *Yaakov*; He has razed in His anger Fair *Yehuda*'s strongholds. He has brought low in dishonor The kingdom and its leaders.

ב בִּלַּע אֲדֹנָי לֹא [וְלֹא] חָמַל אֵת כָּל־נְאוֹת יַעֲקֹב הָרַס בְּעֶבְרָתוֹ מִבְצְרֵי בַת־יְהוּדָה הִגִּיעַ לָאָרֶץ חִלֵּל מַמְלָכָה וְשָׂרֶיהָ:

³ In blazing anger He has cut down All the might of *Yisrael*; He has withdrawn His right hand In the presence of the foe; He has ravaged *Yaakov* like flaming fire, Consuming on all sides.

ג גָּדַע בָּחֳרִי אַף כֹּל קֶרֶן יִשְׂרָאֵל הֵשִׁיב אָחוֹר יְמִינוֹ מִפְּנֵי אוֹיֵב וַיִּבְעַר בְּיַעֲקֹב כְּאֵשׁ לֶהָבָה אָכְלָה סָבִיב:

⁴ He bent His bow like an enemy, Poised His right hand like a foe; He slew all who delighted the eye. He poured out His wrath like fire In the Tent of Fair *Tzion*.

ד דָּרַךְ קַשְׁתּוֹ כְּאוֹיֵב נִצָּב יְמִינוֹ כְּצָר וַיַּהֲרֹג כֹּל מַחֲמַדֵּי־עָיִן בְּאֹהֶל בַּת־צִיּוֹן שָׁפַךְ כָּאֵשׁ חֲמָתוֹ:

⁵ *Hashem* has acted like a foe, He has laid waste *Yisrael*, Laid waste all her citadels, Destroyed her strongholds. He has increased within Fair *Yehuda* Mourning and moaning.

ה הָיָה אֲדֹנָי כְּאוֹיֵב בִּלַּע יִשְׂרָאֵל בִּלַּע כָּל־ אַרְמְנוֹתֶיהָ שִׁחֵת מִבְצָרָיו וַיֶּרֶב בְּבַת־ יְהוּדָה תַּאֲנִיָּה וַאֲנִיָּה:

⁶ He has stripped His Booth like a garden, He has destroyed His *Mishkan*; *Hashem* has ended in *Tzion* Festival and *Shabbat*; In His raging anger He has spurned King and *Kohen*.

ו וַיַּחְמֹס כַּגַּן שֻׂכּוֹ שִׁחֵת מוֹעֲדוֹ שִׁכַּח יְהֹוָה בְּצִיּוֹן מוֹעֵד וְשַׁבָּת וַיִּנְאַץ בְּזַעַם־ אַפּוֹ מֶלֶךְ וְכֹהֵן:

va-yakh-MOS ka-GAN su-KO shi-KHAYT mo-a-DO shi-KACH a-do-NAI b'-tzi-YON mo-AYD v'-sha-BAT va-yin-ATZ b'-ZA-am a-PO ME-lekh v'-kho-HAYN

2:1 He did not remember His Footstool on His day of wrath To explain the metaphor of the "footstool" referred to in this verse, many commentaries point to other places in the Bible where the *Beit Hamikdash* is referred to as God's footstool (see, e.g., Psalms 132:7). This image expresses the notion that while *Hashem*'s essence is incomprehensible to man, as He resides, as it were, in another realm, His presence can be felt in the *Beit Hamikdash*. There, we catch a glimpse of God's metaphorical "feet." Even in the absence of the *Beit Hamikdash*, the Bible tells us that God's presence can be felt most closely in the Land of Israel, "a land which *Hashem* your God looks after, on which *Hashem* your God always keeps His eyes, from year's beginning to year's end." (Deuteronomy 11:12).

Sun shining over *Yerushalayim*

2:6 *Hashem* has ended in *Tzion* festival and *Shabbat* The destruction of the *Beit Hamikdash* led to a drastic reduction of holiness in the world. This verse emphasizes the tragedy inherent in the elimination of the observance of *Shabbat* in the *Beit Hamikdash*

Lamentations

7 *Hashem* has rejected His *Mizbayach*, Disdained His Sanctuary. He has handed over to the foe The walls of its citadels; They raised a shout in the House of *Hashem* As on a festival day.

ז זָנַח אֲדֹנָי מִזְבְּחוֹ נִאֵר מִקְדָּשׁוֹ הִסְגִּיר בְּיַד־אוֹיֵב חוֹמֹת אַרְמְנוֹתֶיהָ קוֹל נָתְנוּ בְּבֵית־יְהֹוָה כְּיוֹם מוֹעֵד:

8 *Hashem* resolved to destroy The wall of Fair *Tzion*; He measured with a line, refrained not From bringing destruction. He has made wall and rampart to mourn, Together they languish.

ח חָשַׁב יְהֹוָה לְהַשְׁחִית חוֹמַת בַּת־צִיּוֹן נָטָה קָו לֹא־הֵשִׁיב יָדוֹ מִבַּלֵּעַ וַיַּאֲבֶל־חֵל וְחוֹמָה יַחְדָּו אֻמְלָלוּ:

9 Her gates have sunk into the ground, He has smashed her bars to bits; Her king and her leaders are in exile, Instruction is no more; Her *neviim*, too, receive No vision from *Hashem*.

ט טָבְעוּ בָאָרֶץ שְׁעָרֶיהָ אִבַּד וְשִׁבַּר בְּרִיחֶיהָ מַלְכָּהּ וְשָׂרֶיהָ בַגּוֹיִם אֵין תּוֹרָה גַּם־נְבִיאֶיהָ לֹא־מָצְאוּ חָזוֹן מֵיְהֹוָה:

10 Silent sit on the ground The elders of Fair *Tzion*; They have strewn dust on their heads And girded themselves with sackcloth; The maidens of *Yerushalayim* have bowed Their heads to the ground.

י יֵשְׁבוּ לָאָרֶץ יִדְּמוּ זִקְנֵי בַת־צִיּוֹן הֶעֱלוּ עָפָר עַל־רֹאשָׁם חָגְרוּ שַׂקִּים הוֹרִידוּ לָאָרֶץ רֹאשָׁן בְּתוּלֹת יְרוּשָׁלָם:

11 My eyes are spent with tears, My heart is in tumult, My being melts away Over the ruin of my poor people, As babes and sucklings languish In the squares of the city.

יא כָּלוּ בַדְּמָעוֹת עֵינַי חֳמַרְמְרוּ מֵעַי נִשְׁפַּךְ לָאָרֶץ כְּבֵדִי עַל־שֶׁבֶר בַּת־עַמִּי בֵּעָטֵף עוֹלֵל וְיוֹנֵק בִּרְחֹבוֹת קִרְיָה:

12 They keep asking their mothers, "Where is bread and wine?" As they languish like battle-wounded In the squares of the town, As their life runs out In their mothers' bosoms.

יב לְאִמֹּתָם יֹאמְרוּ אַיֵּה דָּגָן וָיָיִן בְּהִתְעַטְּפָם כֶּחָלָל בִּרְחֹבוֹת עִיר בְּהִשְׁתַּפֵּךְ נַפְשָׁם אֶל־חֵיק אִמֹּתָם:

13 What can I take as witness or liken To you, O Fair *Yerushalayim*? What can I match with you to console you, O Fair Maiden *Tzion*? For your ruin is vast as the sea: Who can heal you?

יג מָה־אֲעִידֵךְ מָה אֲדַמֶּה־לָּךְ הַבַּת יְרוּשָׁלַם מָה אַשְׁוֶה־לָּךְ וַאֲנַחֲמֵךְ בְּתוּלַת בַּת־צִיּוֹן כִּי־גָדוֹל כַּיָּם שִׁבְרֵךְ מִי יִרְפָּא־לָךְ:

14 Your seers prophesied to you Delusion and folly. They did not expose your iniquity So as to restore your fortunes, But prophesied to you oracles Of delusion and deception.

יד נְבִיאַיִךְ חָזוּ לָךְ שָׁוְא וְתָפֵל וְלֹא־גִלּוּ עַל־עֲוֹנֵךְ לְהָשִׁיב שְׁבִיתֵךְ [שְׁבוּתֵךְ] וַיֶּחֱזוּ לָךְ מַשְׂאוֹת שָׁוְא וּמַדּוּחִים:

Achad Ha'am
(1856–1927)

due to the destruction. The famous Jewish author Achad Ha'am once remarked: "More than the Jews have kept the Sabbath, the Sabbath has kept the Jews." Indeed, in many ways, the tranquility and spiritual rejuvenation which *Shabbat* offers have proven invaluable to the Jew's ability to persevere in the face of so much oppression. Many of the Jewish people's worst enemies were aware of the power of the *Shabbat*, and thus sought to eradicate it from Jewish life. For example, Antiochus Epiphanes, the villain of the Hanukkah story, prohibited *Shabbat* observance, as did many subsequent oppressors. Despite the myriad attempts to erase the Sabbath from Jewish consciousness, it has remained a central and defining feature of Jewish life until this very day.

15 All who pass your way Clap their hands at you;
They hiss and wag their head At Fair *Yerushalayim*:
"Is this the city that was called Perfect in Beauty,
Joy of All the Earth?"

טו סָפְקוּ עָלַיִךְ כַּפַּיִם כָּל־עֹבְרֵי דֶרֶךְ שָׁרְקוּ
וַיָּנִעוּ רֹאשָׁם עַל־בַּת יְרוּשָׁלַ͏ִם הֲזֹאת הָעִיר
שֶׁיֹּאמְרוּ כְּלִילַת יֹפִי מָשׂוֹשׂ
לְכָל־הָאָרֶץ:

*sa-f'-KU a-LA-yikh ka-PA-yim kol O-v'-ray DE-rekh sha-r'-KU
va-ya-NI-u ro-SHAM al BAT y'-ru-sha-LA-im ha-ZOT ha-EER
she-yo-m'-RU k'-lee-LAT YO-fee ma-SOS l-khol ha-A-retz*

16 All your enemies Jeer at you; They hiss and gnash
their teeth, And cry: "We've ruined her! Ah, this is
the day we hoped for; We have lived to see it!"

טז פָּצוּ עָלַיִךְ פִּיהֶם כָּל־אוֹיְבַיִךְ שָׁרְקוּ
וַיַּחַרְקוּ־שֵׁן אָמְרוּ בִּלָּעְנוּ אַךְ זֶה הַיּוֹם
שֶׁקִּוִּינֻהוּ מָצָאנוּ רָאִינוּ:

17 *Hashem* has done what He purposed, Has carried
out the decree That He ordained long ago; He has
torn down without pity. He has let the foe rejoice
over you, Has exalted the might of your enemies.

יז עָשָׂה יְהֹוָה אֲשֶׁר זָמָם בִּצַּע אֶמְרָתוֹ
אֲשֶׁר צִוָּה מִימֵי־קֶדֶם הָרַס וְלֹא חָמָל
וַיְשַׂמַּח עָלַיִךְ אוֹיֵב הֵרִים קֶרֶן צָרָיִךְ:

18 Their heart cried out to *Hashem*. O wall of Fair
Tzion, Shed tears like a torrent Day and night! Give
yourself no respite, Your eyes no rest.

יח צָעַק לִבָּם אֶל־אֲדֹנָי חוֹמַת בַּת־צִיּוֹן
הוֹרִידִי כַנַּחַל דִּמְעָה יוֹמָם וָלַיְלָה אַל־
תִּתְּנִי פוּגַת לָךְ אַל־תִּדֹּם בַּת־עֵינֵךְ:

19 Arise, cry out in the night At the beginning of
the watches, Pour out your heart like water In the
presence of *Hashem*! Lift up your hands to Him
For the life of your infants, Who faint for hunger At
every street corner.

יט קוּמִי רֹנִּי בליל [בַלַּיְלָה] לְרֹאשׁ
אַשְׁמֻרוֹת שִׁפְכִי כַמַּיִם לִבֵּךְ נֹכַח פְּנֵי
אֲדֹנָי שְׂאִי אֵלָיו כַּפַּיִךְ עַל־נֶפֶשׁ עוֹלָלַיִךְ
הָעֲטוּפִים בְּרָעָב בְּרֹאשׁ כָּל־חוּצוֹת:

20 See, *Hashem*, and behold, To whom You have
done this! Alas, women eat their own fruit, Their
new-born babes! Alas, *Kohen* and *Navi* are slain In
the Sanctuary of *Hashem*!

כ רְאֵה יְהֹוָה וְהַבִּיטָה לְמִי עוֹלַלְתָּ כֹּה
אִם־תֹּאכַלְנָה נָשִׁים פִּרְיָם עֹלְלֵי טִפֻּחִים
אִם־יֵהָרֵג בְּמִקְדַּשׁ אֲדֹנָי כֹּהֵן וְנָבִיא:

21 Prostrate in the streets lie Both young and old. My
maidens and youths Are fallen by the sword; You
slew them on Your day of wrath, You slaughtered
without pity.

כא שָׁכְבוּ לָאָרֶץ חוּצוֹת נַעַר וְזָקֵן בְּתוּלֹתַי
וּבַחוּרַי נָפְלוּ בֶחָרֶב הָרַגְתָּ בְּיוֹם אַפֶּךָ
טָבַחְתָּ לֹא חָמָלְתָּ:

Beautiful Jerusalem

2:15 Is this the city that was called Perfect in Beauty, Joy of All the Earth? This verse demonstrates the grandeur that once was Jerusalem. However, it is peculiar that in the hands of Babylon and of numerous subsequent conquerors, the city of *Yerushalayim* and the entire Land of Israel lay almost completely in ruins. In his notes on *Sefer Vayikra* (26:32), the *Ramban* explains that *Eretz Yisrael* has a supernatural quality to it. While under foreign occupation, the land is little more than a barren desert. However, when it is under the sovereignty of the People of Israel, the land comes to life, flourishes, and yields great produce. Indeed, for nearly two millennia, as the land switched hands numerous times between various foreign occupiers, including Romans, Arabs, Turks and others, the land lay desolate. Amazingly, the modern rebirth of the Jewish homeland has brought with it an astounding development of the land, to the point where once again the Jewish people can claim a flourishing country. In agriculture, technology, and culture, contemporary Israel ranks among the most advanced countries of the world. Indeed, Jerusalem itself has returned to a point where visitors once again remark that the city is "Perfect in Beauty, Joy of All the Earth."

²² You summoned, as on a festival, My neighbors from roundabout. On the day of the wrath of *Hashem*, None survived or escaped; Those whom I bore and reared My foe has consumed.

כב תִּקְרָא כְיוֹם מוֹעֵד מְגוּרַי מִסָּבִיב וְלֹא הָיָה בְּיוֹם אַף־יְהֹוָה פָּלִיט וְשָׂרִיד אֲשֶׁר־טִפַּחְתִּי וְרִבִּיתִי אֹיְבִי כִלָּם:

3 ¹ I am the man who has known affliction Under the rod of His wrath;

ג א אֲנִי הַגֶּבֶר רָאָה עֳנִי בְּשֵׁבֶט עֶבְרָתוֹ:

² Me He drove on and on In unrelieved darkness;

ב אוֹתִי נָהַג וַיֹּלַךְ חֹשֶׁךְ וְלֹא־אוֹר:

³ On none but me He brings down His hand Again and again, without cease.

ג אַךְ בִּי יָשֻׁב יַהֲפֹךְ יָדוֹ כָּל־הַיּוֹם:

⁴ He has worn away my flesh and skin; He has shattered my bones.

ד בִּלָּה בְשָׂרִי וְעוֹרִי שִׁבַּר עַצְמוֹתָי:

⁵ All around me He has built Misery and hardship;

ה בָּנָה עָלַי וַיַּקַּף רֹאשׁ וּתְלָאָה:

⁶ He has made me dwell in darkness, Like those long dead.

ו בְּמַחֲשַׁכִּים הוֹשִׁיבַנִי כְּמֵתֵי עוֹלָם:

⁷ He has walled me in and I cannot break out; He has weighed me down with chains.

ז גָּדַר בַּעֲדִי וְלֹא אֵצֵא הִכְבִּיד נְחָשְׁתִּי:

⁸ And when I cry and plead, He shuts out my prayer;

ח גַּם כִּי אֶזְעַק וַאֲשַׁוֵּעַ שָׂתַם תְּפִלָּתִי:

GAM KEE ez-AK va-a-sha-VAY-a sa-TAM t'-fi-la-TEE

⁹ He has walled in my ways with hewn blocks, He has made my paths a maze.

ט גָּדַר דְּרָכַי בְּגָזִית נְתִיבֹתַי עִוָּה:

¹⁰ He is a lurking bear to me, A lion in hiding;

י דֹּב אֹרֵב הוּא לִי אריה [אֲרִי] בְּמִסְתָּרִים:

¹¹ He has forced me off my way and mangled me, He has left me numb.

יא דְּרָכַי סוֹרֵר וַיְפַשְּׁחֵנִי שָׂמַנִי שֹׁמֵם:

¹² He has bent His bow and made me The target of His arrows:

יב דָּרַךְ קַשְׁתּוֹ וַיַּצִּיבֵנִי כַּמַּטָּרָא לַחֵץ:

¹³ He has shot into my vitals The shafts of His quiver.

יג הֵבִיא בְּכִלְיוֹתָי בְּנֵי אַשְׁפָּתוֹ:

¹⁴ I have become a laughingstock to all people, The butt of their gibes all day long.

יד הָיִיתִי שְּׂחֹק לְכָל־עַמִּי נְגִינָתָם כָּל־הַיּוֹם:

¹⁵ He has filled me with bitterness, Sated me with wormwood.

טו הִשְׂבִּיעַנִי בַמְּרוֹרִים הִרְוַנִי לַעֲנָה:

3:8 And when I cry and plead, He shuts out my prayer While God always hears our prayers, He doesn't always grant our requests. Even in difficult times, *Hashem* does not always respond to our prayers in the affirmative, but instead "He shuts out my prayer." It is noteworthy that in the central Jewish prayer, known as the *Amida* and recited three times a day, *Hashem* is referred to as, "He who listens to our prayers" and not, "He who answers our prayers." God's will is inscrutable. Like any parent, at times He says "no." But especially at those times, He is always there to listen with love and to hear our cries.

Soldier praying at the Western Wall

¹⁶ He has broken my teeth on gravel, Has ground me into the dust.

טז וַיַּגְרֵס בֶּחָצָץ שִׁנָּי הִכְפִּישַׁנִי בָּאֵפֶר:

¹⁷ My life was bereft of peace, I forgot what happiness was.

יז וַתִּזְנַח מִשָּׁלוֹם נַפְשִׁי נָשִׁיתִי טוֹבָה:

¹⁸ I thought my strength and hope Had perished before *Hashem*.

יח וָאֹמַר אָבַד נִצְחִי וְתוֹחַלְתִּי מֵיהֹוָה:

¹⁹ To recall my distress and my misery Was wormwood and poison;

יט זְכָר־עָנְיִי וּמְרוּדִי לַעֲנָה וָרֹאשׁ:

²⁰ Whenever I thought of them, I was bowed low.

כ זָכוֹר תִּזְכּוֹר וְתָשִׁיחַ [וְתָשׁוֹחַ] עָלַי נַפְשִׁי:

²¹ But this do I call to mind, Therefore I have hope:

כא זֹאת אָשִׁיב אֶל־לִבִּי עַל־כֵּן אוֹחִיל:

²² The kindness of *Hashem* has not ended, His mercies are not spent.

כב חַסְדֵי יְהֹוָה כִּי לֹא־תָמְנוּ כִּי לֹא־כָלוּ רַחֲמָיו:

²³ They are renewed every morning – Ample is Your grace!

כג חֲדָשִׁים לַבְּקָרִים רַבָּה אֱמוּנָתֶךָ:

²⁴ "*Hashem* is my portion," I say with full heart; Therefore will I hope in Him.

כד חֶלְקִי יְהֹוָה אָמְרָה נַפְשִׁי עַל־כֵּן אוֹחִיל לוֹ:

²⁵ *Hashem* is good to those who trust in Him, To the one who seeks Him;

כה טוֹב יְהֹוָה לְקֹוָו לְנֶפֶשׁ תִּדְרְשֶׁנּוּ:

²⁶ It is good to wait patiently Till rescue comes from *Hashem*.

כו טוֹב וְיָחִיל וְדוּמָם לִתְשׁוּעַת יְהֹוָה:

²⁷ It is good for a man, when young, To bear a yoke;

כז טוֹב לַגֶּבֶר כִּי־יִשָּׂא עֹל בִּנְעוּרָיו:

²⁸ Let him sit alone and be patient, When He has laid it upon him.

כח יֵשֵׁב בָּדָד וְיִדֹּם כִּי נָטַל עָלָיו:

²⁹ Let him put his mouth to the dust – There may yet be hope.

כט יִתֵּן בֶּעָפָר פִּיהוּ אוּלַי יֵשׁ תִּקְוָה:

³⁰ Let him offer his cheek to the smiter; Let him be surfeited with mockery.

ל יִתֵּן לְמַכֵּהוּ לֶחִי יִשְׂבַּע בְּחֶרְפָּה:

³¹ For *Hashem* does not Reject forever,

לא כִּי לֹא יִזְנַח לְעוֹלָם אֲדֹנָי:

KEE LO yiz-NAKH l'-o-LAM a-do-NAI

Appreciating the flourishing Land of Israel

3:31 For the Lord does not reject forever Throughout the many episodes of persecution, Jews have remembered the critical message of this verse: The suffering of the Jewish people will not be eternal. Already in the days of *Moshe*, *Hashem* assured His people that though they may face His wrath and anger, though He may send nations to oppress them, they will always remain His chosen nation. Their suffering will eventually come to an end, and *Hashem* will redeem His people, as it says: "Yet, even then, when they are in the land of their enemies, I will not reject them or spurn them so as to destroy them, annulling My covenant with them: for I *Hashem* am their God" (Leviticus 26:44). To the contrary, "I will remember My covenant with *Yaakov*; I will remember also My covenant with *Yitzchak*, and also My covenant with *Avraham* I will remember; and I will remember the land" (Leviticus 26:42). Indeed, after years of persecution and suffering, the Jewish people are thriving and the Land of Israel is flourishing, thus demonstrating the eternal truth of this verse.

Lamentations

32 But first afflicts, then pardons In His abundant kindness.

לב כִּי אִם־הוֹגָה וְרִחַם כְּרֹב חסדו [חֲסָדָיו:]

33 For He does not willfully bring grief Or affliction to man,

לג כִּי לֹא עִנָּה מִלִּבּוֹ וַיַּגֶּה בְּנֵי־אִישׁ:

34 Crushing under His feet All the prisoners of the earth.

לד לְדַכֵּא תַּחַת רַגְלָיו כֹּל אֲסִירֵי אָרֶץ:

35 To deny a man his rights In the presence of the Most High,

לה לְהַטּוֹת מִשְׁפַּט־גָּבֶר נֶגֶד פְּנֵי עֶלְיוֹן:

36 To wrong a man in his cause – This *Hashem* does not choose.

לו לְעַוֵּת אָדָם בְּרִיבוֹ אֲדֹנָי לֹא רָאָה:

37 Whose decree was ever fulfilled, Unless *Hashem* willed it?

לז מִי זֶה אָמַר וַתֶּהִי אֲדֹנָי לֹא צִוָּה:

38 Is it not at the word of the Most High, That weal and woe befall?

לח מִפִּי עֶלְיוֹן לֹא תֵצֵא הָרָעוֹת וְהַטּוֹב:

39 Of what shall a living man complain? Each one of his own sins!

לט מַה־יִּתְאוֹנֵן אָדָם חָי גֶּבֶר עַל־חטאו [חֲטָאָיו:]

40 Let us search and examine our ways, And turn back to *Hashem*;

מ נַחְפְּשָׂה דְרָכֵינוּ וְנַחְקֹרָה וְנָשׁוּבָה עַד־יְהֹוָה:

41 Let us lift up our hearts with our hands To *Hashem* in heaven:

מא נִשָּׂא לְבָבֵנוּ אֶל־כַּפָּיִם אֶל־אֵל בַּשָּׁמָיִם:

42 We have transgressed and rebelled, And You have not forgiven.

מב נַחְנוּ פָשַׁעְנוּ וּמָרִינוּ אַתָּה לֹא סָלָחְתָּ:

43 You have clothed Yourself in anger and pursued us, You have slain without pity.

מג סַכֹּתָה בָאַף וַתִּרְדְּפֵנוּ הָרַגְתָּ לֹא חָמָלְתָּ:

44 You have screened Yourself off with a cloud, That no prayer may pass through.

מד סַכּוֹתָה בֶעָנָן לָךְ מֵעֲבוֹר תְּפִלָּה:

45 You have made us filth and refuse In the midst of the peoples.

מה סְחִי וּמָאוֹס תְּשִׂימֵנוּ בְּקֶרֶב הָעַמִּים:

46 All our enemies loudly Rail against us.

מו פָּצוּ עָלֵינוּ פִּיהֶם כָּל־אֹיְבֵינוּ:

pa-TZU a-LAY-nu pee-HEM kol o-y'-VAY-nu

Abba Eban
(1915–2002)

3:46 All our enemies loudly rail against us Many times, the enemies of the Jewish people eagerly awaited the day when the Jews would finally meet their demise. But these plans and expectations have always been divinely foiled. This verse reflects the hatred that Israel's enemies, both historical and contemporary, have always felt towards her. In the spring of 1967, for example, Israel's fate seemed truly doomed. Nearly all of her neighbors sought to wipe her off the map, including Egypt, Jordan, Syria, Iraq, and Saudi Arabia. Here is how Abba Eban, serving at that time as Israel's Foreign Minister, described the mood in the days leading up to the Six Day War: "There was no doubt that the howling mobs in Cairo, Damascus and Baghdad were seeing savage visions of murder and booty. Israel, for its part, had learned from Jewish history that no outrage against its men, women and children was inconceivable. Many things in Jewish history are too terrible to be believed, but nothing in that history is too terrible to have happened. Memories of the European slaughter were taking form and substance in countless Israeli hearts. They flowed into our room like turgid air and sat heavy on all our minds. As has always been the case, God had different plans, and the young State of Israel mightily and miraculously defeated its enemies."

⁴⁷ Panic and pitfall are our lot, Death and destruction.

מז פַּחַד וָפַחַת הָיָה לָנוּ הַשֵּׁאת וְהַשָּׁבֶר:

⁴⁸ My eyes shed streams of water Over the ruin of my poor people.

מח פַּלְגֵי־מַיִם תֵּרַד עֵינִי עַל־שֶׁבֶר בַּת־עַמִּי:

⁴⁹ My eyes shall flow without cease, Without respite,

מט עֵינִי נִגְּרָה וְלֹא תִדְמֶה מֵאֵין הֲפֻגוֹת:

⁵⁰ Until *Hashem* looks down And beholds from heaven.

נ עַד־יַשְׁקִיף וְיֵרֶא יְהֹוָה מִשָּׁמָיִם:

⁵¹ My eyes have brought me grief Over all the maidens of my city.

נא עֵינִי עוֹלְלָה לְנַפְשִׁי מִכֹּל בְּנוֹת עִירִי:

⁵² My foes have snared me like a bird, Without any cause.

נב צוֹד צָדוּנִי כַּצִּפּוֹר אֹיְבַי חִנָּם:

⁵³ They have ended my life in a pit And cast stones at me.

נג צָמְתוּ בַבּוֹר חַיָּי וַיַּדּוּ־אֶבֶן בִּי:

⁵⁴ Waters flowed over my head; I said: I am lost!

נד צָפוּ־מַיִם עַל־רֹאשִׁי אָמַרְתִּי נִגְזָרְתִּי:

⁵⁵ I have called on Your name, *Hashem*, From the depths of the Pit.

נה קָרָאתִי שִׁמְךָ יְהֹוָה מִבּוֹר תַּחְתִּיּוֹת:

⁵⁶ Hear my plea; Do not shut Your ear To my groan, to my cry!

נו קוֹלִי שָׁמָעְתָּ אַל־תַּעְלֵם אָזְנְךָ לְרַוְחָתִי לְשַׁוְעָתִי:

⁵⁷ You have ever drawn nigh when I called You; You have said, "Do not fear!"

נז קָרַבְתָּ בְּיוֹם אֶקְרָאֶךָּ אָמַרְתָּ אַל־תִּירָא:

⁵⁸ You championed my cause, O *Hashem*, You have redeemed my life.

נח רַבְתָּ אֲדֹנָי רִיבֵי נַפְשִׁי גָּאַלְתָּ חַיָּי:

RAV-ta a-do-NAI ree-VAY naf-SHEE ga-AL-ta kha-YAI

⁵⁹ You have seen, *Hashem*, the wrong done me; Oh, vindicate my right!

נט רָאִיתָה יְהֹוָה עַוָּתָתִי שָׁפְטָה מִשְׁפָּטִי:

⁶⁰ You have seen all their malice, All their designs against me;

ס רָאִיתָה כָּל־נִקְמָתָם כָּל־מַחְשְׁבֹתָם לִי:

⁶¹ You have heard, *Hashem*, their taunts, All their designs against me,

סא שָׁמַעְתָּ חֶרְפָּתָם יְהֹוָה כָּל־מַחְשְׁבֹתָם עָלָי:

⁶² The mouthings and pratings of my adversaries Against me all day long.

סב שִׂפְתֵי קָמַי וְהֶגְיוֹנָם עָלַי כָּל־הַיּוֹם:

⁶³ See how, at their ease or at work, I am the butt of their gibes.

סג שִׁבְתָּם וְקִימָתָם הַבִּיטָה אֲנִי מַנְגִּינָתָם:

3:58 You have redeemed my life Indeed, God is the ultimate redeemer. Time and again, *Hashem* lifts the Jewish people up from the brink of destruction and depths of despair and helps them to stand upright once again. A shining example of this is the founding of the State of Israel. Merely three years following the end of the darkest period in Jewish history, when a third of world Jewry was brutally murdered and the future of the Jewish people seemed most bleak, God restored His nation to a position of dignity and strength. The significance of the founding of the State of Israel in 1948 was not just the return of the Jewish people to their homeland; it was the reestablishment of Jewish sovereignty, and the affirmation that *Hashem* did not break His word. He was, and remains, the redeemer of His people.

David Ben Gurion declaring the State of Israel, 1948

64 Give them, *Hashem*, their deserts According to their deeds.

סד תָּשִׁיב לָהֶם גְּמוּל יְהֹוָה כְּמַעֲשֵׂה יְדֵיהֶם:

65 Give them anguish of heart; Your curse be upon them!

סה תִּתֵּן לָהֶם מְגִנַּת־לֵב תַּאֲלָתְךָ לָהֶם:

66 Oh, pursue them in wrath and destroy them From under the heavens of *Hashem*!

סו תִּרְדֹּף בְּאַף וְתַשְׁמִידֵם מִתַּחַת שְׁמֵי יְהֹוָה:

4 1 Alas! The gold is dulled, Debased the finest gold! The sacred gems are spilled At every street corner.

ד א אֵיכָה יוּעַם זָהָב יִשְׁנֶא הַכֶּתֶם הַטּוֹב תִּשְׁתַּפֵּכְנָה אַבְנֵי־קֹדֶשׁ בְּרֹאשׁ כָּל־חוּצוֹת:

2 The precious children of *Tzion*; Once valued as gold – Alas, they are accounted as earthen pots, Work of a potter's hands!

ב בְּנֵי צִיּוֹן הַיְקָרִים הַמְסֻלָּאִים בַּפָּז אֵיכָה נֶחְשְׁבוּ לְנִבְלֵי־חֶרֶשׂ מַעֲשֵׂה יְדֵי יוֹצֵר:

3 Even jackals offer the breast And suckle their young; But my poor people has turned cruel, Like ostriches of the desert.

ג גַּם־תַּנִּין [תַּנִּים] חָלְצוּ שַׁד הֵינִיקוּ גּוּרֵיהֶן בַּת־עַמִּי לְאַכְזָר כִּי עֵנִים [כַּיְעֵנִים] בַּמִּדְבָּר:

4 The tongue of the suckling cleaves To its palate for thirst. Little children beg for bread; None gives them a morsel.

ד דָּבַק לְשׁוֹן יוֹנֵק אֶל־חִכּוֹ בַּצָּמָא עוֹלָלִים שָׁאֲלוּ לֶחֶם פֹּרֵשׂ אֵין לָהֶם:

5 Those who feasted on dainties Lie famished in the streets; Those who were reared in purple Have embraced refuse heaps.

ה הָאֹכְלִים לְמַעֲדַנִּים נָשַׁמּוּ בַּחוּצוֹת הָאֱמֻנִים עֲלֵי תוֹלָע חִבְּקוּ אַשְׁפַּתּוֹת:

6 The guilt of my poor people Exceeded the iniquity of Sodom, Which was overthrown in a moment, Without a hand striking it.

ו וַיִּגְדַּל עֲוֹן בַּת־עַמִּי מֵחַטַּאת סְדֹם הַהֲפוּכָה כְמוֹ־רָגַע וְלֹא־חָלוּ בָהּ יָדָיִם:

7 Her elect were purer than snow, Whiter than milk; Their limbs were ruddier than coral, Their bodies were like sapphire.

ז זַכּוּ נְזִירֶיהָ מִשֶּׁלֶג צַחוּ מֵחָלָב אָדְמוּ עֶצֶם מִפְּנִינִים סַפִּיר גִּזְרָתָם:

8 Now their faces are blacker than soot, They are not recognized in the streets; Their skin has shriveled on their bones, It has become dry as wood.

ח חָשַׁךְ מִשְּׁחוֹר תָּאֳרָם לֹא נִכְּרוּ בַּחוּצוֹת צָפַד עוֹרָם עַל־עַצְמָם יָבֵשׁ הָיָה כָעֵץ:

9 Better off were the slain of the sword Than those slain by famine, Who pined away, [as though] wounded, For lack of the fruits of the field.

ט טוֹבִים הָיוּ חַלְלֵי־חֶרֶב מֵחַלְלֵי רָעָב שֶׁהֵם יָזוּבוּ מְדֻקָּרִים מִתְּנוּבֹת שָׂדָי:

10 With their own hands, tenderhearted women Have cooked their children; Such became their fare, In the disaster of my poor people.

י יְדֵי נָשִׁים רַחֲמָנִיּוֹת בִּשְּׁלוּ יַלְדֵיהֶן הָיוּ לְבָרוֹת לָמוֹ בְּשֶׁבֶר בַּת־עַמִּי:

11 *Hashem* vented all His fury, Poured out His blazing wrath; He kindled a fire in *Tzion* Which consumed its foundations.

יא כִּלָּה יְהֹוָה אֶת־חֲמָתוֹ שָׁפַךְ חֲרוֹן אַפּוֹ וַיַּצֶּת־אֵשׁ בְּצִיּוֹן וַתֹּאכַל יְסוֹדֹתֶיהָ:

12 The kings of the earth did not believe, Nor any of the inhabitants of the world, That foe or adversary could enter The gates of *Yerushalayim*.

יב לֹא הֶאֱמִינוּ מַלְכֵי־אֶרֶץ וְכֹל [כֹּל] יֹשְׁבֵי תֵבֵל כִּי יָבֹא צַר וְאוֹיֵב בְּשַׁעֲרֵי יְרוּשָׁלָ͏ִם:

¹³ It was for the sins of her *Neviim*, The iniquities of her *Kohanim*, Who had shed in her midst the blood of the just.

יג מֵחַטֹּאת נְבִיאֶיהָ עֲוֹנוֹת כֹּהֲנֶיהָ
הַשֹּׁפְכִים בְּקִרְבָּהּ דַּם צַדִּיקִים:

¹⁴ They wandered blindly through the streets, Defiled with blood, So that no one was able To touch their garments.

יד נָעוּ עִוְרִים בַּחוּצוֹת נְגֹאֲלוּ בַּדָּם בְּלֹא
יוּכְלוּ יִגְּעוּ בִּלְבֻשֵׁיהֶם:

¹⁵ "Away! Unclean!" people shouted at them, "Away! Away! Touch not!" So they wandered and wandered again; For the nations had resolved: "They shall stay here no longer."

טו סוּרוּ טָמֵא קָרְאוּ לָמוֹ סוּרוּ סוּרוּ אַל־
תִּגָּעוּ כִּי נָצוּ גַּם־נָעוּ אָמְרוּ בַּגּוֹיִם לֹא
יוֹסִיפוּ לָגוּר:

*SU-ru ta-MAY KA-r'-u LA-mo SU-ru SU-ru al ti-GA-u KEE
na-TZU gam na-U a-m'-RU ba-go-YIM LO yo-SI-fu la-GUR*

¹⁶ *Hashem*'s countenance has turned away from them, He will look on them no more. They showed no regard for *Kohanim*, No favor to elders.

טז פְּנֵי יְהֹוָה חִלְּקָם לֹא יוֹסִיף לְהַבִּיטָם
פְּנֵי כֹהֲנִים לֹא נָשָׂאוּ זְקֵנִים [וּזְקֵנִים]
לֹא חָנָנוּ:

¹⁷ Even now our eyes pine away In vain for deliverance. As we waited, still we wait For a nation that cannot help.

יז עוֹדֵינָה [עוֹדֵינוּ] תִּכְלֶינָה עֵינֵינוּ אֶל־
עֶזְרָתֵנוּ הָבֶל בְּצִפִּיָּתֵנוּ צִפִּינוּ אֶל־גּוֹי
לֹא יוֹשִׁעַ:

¹⁸ Our steps were checked, We could not walk in our squares. Our doom is near, our days are done – Alas, our doom has come!

יח צָדוּ צְעָדֵינוּ מִלֶּכֶת בִּרְחֹבֹתֵינוּ קָרַב
קִצֵּינוּ מָלְאוּ יָמֵינוּ כִּי־בָא קִצֵּינוּ:

¹⁹ Our pursuers were swifter Than the eagles in the sky; They chased us in the mountains, Lay in wait for us in the wilderness.

יט קַלִּים הָיוּ רֹדְפֵינוּ מִנִּשְׁרֵי שָׁמָיִם עַל־
הֶהָרִים דְּלָקֻנוּ בַּמִּדְבָּר אָרְבוּ לָנוּ:

*ka-LEEM ha-YU ro-d'-FAY-nu mi-nish-RAY sha-MA-yim al
he-ha-REEM d-la-KU-nu ba-mid-BAR a-r'-VU LA-nu*

4:15 For the nations had resolved: "They shall stay here no longer." The insulting jeers described in this verse were repeated not too long ago. Following the liberation of the Nazi concentration camps, Jews were not only denied entry into many foreign countries, but even the borders of their homeland were closed. After the conclusion of World War II, Palestine (as the Land of Israel was then called) was under British sovereignty and the British government put a strict quota on the number of Jewish refugees allowed to enter. Furthermore, many of those who defied the quota and managed to cross the border into the Promised Land without British permission were rounded up and placed in detention camps, such as the one in the northern coastal city of Atlit. However, the will of *Hashem* could not be thwarted. After the founding of the State of Israel in 1948, the declaration "They shall stay here no longer" quickly became obsolete. With the Knesset's passing of the Law of Return, every Jew in the world became entitled to move to Israel and obtain citizenship in the new country. Since then, millions of Jews have moved from all corners of the globe to the Holy Land. For the first time in almost two thousand years, almost half of the Jews in the world now live in Israel and indeed, "they stay here" once again.

Atlit detention camp museum

4:19 They chased us in the mountains This verse conveys a sense that the enemy lurks on all terrains and in all locations, and is impossible to escape. Unfortunately, even after arriving on the shores of *Eretz Yisrael* following the Holocaust, Jewish refugees

20 The breath of our life, *Hashem*'s anointed, Was captured in their traps – He in whose shade we had thought To live among the nations.

כ רוּחַ אַפֵּינוּ מְשִׁיחַ יְהוָֹה נִלְכַּד בִּשְׁחִיתוֹתָם אֲשֶׁר אָמַרְנוּ בְּצִלּוֹ נִחְיֶה בַגּוֹיִם:

21 Rejoice and exult, Fair *Edom*, Who dwell in the land of Uz! To you, too, the cup shall pass, You shall get drunk and expose your nakedness.

כא שִׂישִׂי וְשִׂמְחִי בַּת־אֱדוֹם יוֹשַׁבְתִּי [יוֹשֶׁבֶת] בְּאֶרֶץ עוּץ גַּם־עָלַיִךְ תַּעֲבָר־כּוֹס תִּשְׁכְּרִי וְתִתְעָרִי:

22 Your iniquity, Fair *Tzion*, is expiated; He will exile you no longer. Your iniquity, Fair *Edom*, He will note; He will uncover your sins.

כב תַּם־עֲוֹנֵךְ בַּת־צִיּוֹן לֹא יוֹסִיף לְהַגְלוֹתֵךְ פָּקַד עֲוֹנֵךְ בַּת־אֱדוֹם גִּלָּה עַל־חַטֹּאתָיִךְ:

5 1 Remember, *Hashem*, what has befallen us; Behold, and see our disgrace!

ה א זְכֹר יְהוָֹה מֶה־הָיָה לָנוּ הַבִּיט [הַבִּיטָה] וּרְאֵה אֶת־חֶרְפָּתֵנוּ:

2 Our heritage has passed to aliens, Our homes to strangers.

ב נַחֲלָתֵנוּ נֶהֶפְכָה לְזָרִים בָּתֵּינוּ לְנָכְרִים:

na-kha-la-TAY-nu ne-hef-KHAH l'-za-REEM ba-TAY-nu l'-nokh-REEM

3 We have become orphans, fatherless; Our mothers are like widows.

ג יְתוֹמִים הָיִינוּ אֵין [וְאֵין] אָב אִמֹּתֵינוּ כְּאַלְמָנוֹת:

4 We must pay to drink our own water, Obtain our own kindling at a price.

ד מֵימֵינוּ בְּכֶסֶף שָׁתִינוּ עֵצֵינוּ בִּמְחִיר יָבֹאוּ:

5 We are hotly pursued; Exhausted, we are given no rest.

ה עַל צַוָּארֵנוּ נִרְדָּפְנוּ יָגַעְנוּ לֹא [וְלֹא] הוּנַח לָנוּ:

6 We hold out a hand to Egypt; To Assyria, for our fill of bread.

ו מִצְרַיִם נָתַנּוּ יָד אַשּׁוּר לִשְׂבֹּעַ לָחֶם:

7 Our fathers sinned and are no more; And we must bear their guilt.

ז אֲבֹתֵינוּ חָטְאוּ אֵינָם [וְאֵינָם] אֲנַחְנוּ [וַאֲנַחְנוּ] עֲוֹנֹתֵיהֶם סָבָלְנוּ:

8 Slaves are ruling over us, With none to rescue us from them.

ח עֲבָדִים מָשְׁלוּ בָנוּ פֹּרֵק אֵין מִיָּדָם:

Battle hill of the 35 fallen soldiers in Gush Etzion

from Europe encountered a situation similar to that described in this verse. Having survived the Nazis, these Jews were met by a new enemy: The local Arab population, which fought violently to keep them away from their ancient homeland. This enemy also waged war on a number of fronts, including the mountains and the wilderness, as described in this verse. In January of 1948, a terrible tragedy took place in the Judean hills. A group of thirty-five soldiers was dispatched to bring provisions and food to the beleaguered communities of *Gush Etzion*, the Etzion bloc. They set out on foot at night to avoid detection, but the sun rose before they managed to reach their destination. Still in the vicinity of hostile villages, they were detected by some Arab women who had gone down to the valley to gather branches. Arab mobs were quickly deployed and after a lengthy battle, all thirty-five of the soldiers were killed in a bloody massacre. "They chased us in the mountains, lay in wait for us in the wilderness."

5:2 Our heritage has passed to aliens In the past century, we have merited to witness a reversal of this prophetic statement with our own eyes. Whereas *Yirmiyahu* bemoans the fact that Jewish land has been seized by foreigners, today, Jews have returned to their ancient homeland and reclaimed lands that have belonged to them from the time that they were promised by *Hashem* to *Avraham* and his descendants for eternity.

⁹ We get our bread at the peril of our lives, Because of the sword of the wilderness.

ט בְּנַפְשֵׁנוּ נָבִיא לַחְמֵנוּ מִפְּנֵי חֶרֶב הַמִּדְבָּר:

¹⁰ Our skin glows like an oven, With the fever of famine.

י עוֹרֵנוּ כְּתַנּוּר נִכְמָרוּ מִפְּנֵי זַלְעֲפוֹת רָעָב:

¹¹ They have ravished women in *Tzion*, Maidens in the towns of *Yehuda*.

יא נָשִׁים בְּצִיּוֹן עִנּוּ בְּתֻלֹת בְּעָרֵי יְהוּדָה:

¹² Princes have been hanged by them; No respect has been shown to elders.

יב שָׂרִים בְּיָדָם נִתְלוּ פְּנֵי זְקֵנִים לֹא נֶהְדָּרוּ:

¹³ Young men must carry millstones, And youths stagger under loads of wood.

יג בַּחוּרִים טְחוֹן נָשָׂאוּ וּנְעָרִים בָּעֵץ כָּשָׁלוּ:

¹⁴ The old men are gone from the gate, The young men from their music.

יד זְקֵנִים מִשַּׁעַר שָׁבָתוּ בַּחוּרִים מִנְּגִינָתָם:

¹⁵ Gone is the joy of our hearts; Our dancing is turned into mourning.

טו שָׁבַת מְשׂוֹשׂ לִבֵּנוּ נֶהְפַּךְ לְאֵבֶל מְחֹלֵנוּ:

¹⁶ The crown has fallen from our head; Woe to us that we have sinned!

טז נָפְלָה עֲטֶרֶת רֹאשֵׁנוּ אוֹי־נָא לָנוּ כִּי חָטָאנוּ:

¹⁷ Because of this our hearts are sick, Because of these our eyes are dimmed:

יז עַל־זֶה הָיָה דָוֶה לִבֵּנוּ עַל־אֵלֶּה חָשְׁכוּ עֵינֵינוּ:

¹⁸ Because of Mount *Tzion*, which lies desolate; Jackals prowl over it.

יח עַל הַר־צִיּוֹן שֶׁשָּׁמֵם שׁוּעָלִים הִלְּכוּ־בוֹ:

AL har tzi-YON she-sha-MAYM shu-a-LEEM hi-l'-khu VO

¹⁹ But You, *Hashem*, are enthroned forever, Your throne endures through the ages.

יט אַתָּה יְהֹוָה לְעוֹלָם תֵּשֵׁב כִּסְאֲךָ לְדֹר וָדוֹר:

²⁰ Why have You forgotten us utterly, Forsaken us for all time?

כ לָמָּה לָנֶצַח תִּשְׁכָּחֵנוּ תַּעַזְבֵנוּ לְאֹרֶךְ יָמִים:

Jews pray at the Western Wall, remnant of the western retaining wall of *Har HaBayit*

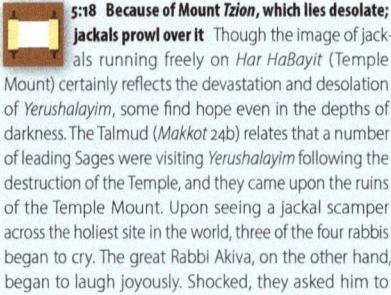

5:18 Because of Mount *Tzion*, which lies desolate; jackals prowl over it Though the image of jackals running freely on *Har HaBayit* (Temple Mount) certainly reflects the devastation and desolation of *Yerushalayim*, some find hope even in the depths of darkness. The Talmud (*Makkot* 24b) relates that a number of leading Sages were visiting *Yerushalayim* following the destruction of the Temple, and they came upon the ruins of the Temple Mount. Upon seeing a jackal scamper across the holiest site in the world, three of the four rabbis began to cry. The great Rabbi Akiva, on the other hand, began to laugh joyously. Shocked, they asked him to explain his behavior. Rabbi Akiva explained that if the prophecies of destruction had indeed been fulfilled, we can be certain that the promises of redemption will also be fulfilled. The Jews have always maintained immutable optimism and unwavering faith that the Almighty will preserve His covenant with them, and in modern times He has begun to fulfill His promises of redemption.

46

²¹ Take us back, *Hashem*, to Yourself, And let us come back; Renew our days as of old!

כא הֲשִׁיבֵנוּ יְהֹוָה אֵלֶיךָ ונשוב [וְנָשׁוּבָה] חַדֵּשׁ יָמֵינוּ כְּקֶדֶם:

ha-shee-VAY-nu a-do-NAI ay-LE-kha v'-na-SHU-vah kha-DAYSH ya-MAY-nu k'-KE-dem

²² For truly, You have rejected us, Bitterly raged against us. Take us back, *Hashem*, to Yourself, And let us come back; Renew our days as of old!

כב כִּי אִם־מָאֹס מְאַסְתָּנוּ קָצַפְתָּ עָלֵינוּ עַד־מְאֹד: [השיבנו יהוה אליך ונשובה חדש ימינו כקדם]

Young North American immigrants return to the Promised Land

5:21 Take us back, *Hashem* This verse is one of the most significant verses in the entire book. Traditionally, when *Megillat Eicha* is read in synagogues on the ninth of *Av*, this verse is repeated at the conclusion of the reading, to highlight its significance and to end on a positive note. The verse emphasizes that *Hashem* will one day return the Jewish people to the Land of Israel, and renew the intimate relationship with Him centered around a rebuilt Temple in *Yerushalayim*. Moreover, it reminds us that a relationship with our Maker is a two-way street; we return to God, and God returns to us. Our generation has been blessed with the beginning of the fulfillment of this promise. The Jewish people have started their return to the land of their fathers, and the realization of the dream of redemption has begun. We sincerely pray for the fulfillment of the final redemption, a complete return to *Hashem* and the coming of the *Mashiach*.

Megillat Kohelet
The Scroll of Ecclesiastes

Introduction and commentary by Batya Markowitz

Megillat Kohelet (Ecclesiastes) gets its Hebrew name from its author King *Shlomo*, who calls himself "*Kohelet*." The name is related to the word *hak-hel* (הקהל), 'gathering', since *Shlomo* often shared his wisdom in public gatherings. *Megillat Kohelet* is a book of observations on life, made by the wisest man to ever live. According to the Sages, it was written towards the end of *Shlomo's* life, after he had gathered much wisdom and life experience. Fitting for a book of insight, this book was written in *Yerushalayim*, a city known for its wisdom.

Throughout *Megillat Kohelet*, King *Shlomo* comments on the futility of life in this world. He warns not to be drawn to excessive celebration, and instructs that it is better to pursue knowledge than pleasure. He observes that *Hashem* created a perfect world in which "A season is set for everything" (3:1). Solomon ponders the age-old question of why righteous people suffer while the wicked prosper. He illustrates how meaningless the pursuit of wealth and luxuries is, and points out the things that really matter in life, such as a good reputation, charity and good deeds. He decries bad personality traits such as jealousy, stinginess, and anger.

At first glance, certain verses in *Megillat Kohelet* seem inherently contradictory or antithetical to Judaism, and for this reason the Sages considered not including it in the Bible. Ultimately, though, they arrived at the conclusion that *Kohelet* should be included, since its overall message is that life is infused with meaning when following the word of God and His *Torah*. *Megillat Kohelet* begins by saying that the physical world on its own is meaningless, and ends by stating: "The sum of the matter, when all is said and done: Revere *Hashem* and observe His commandments! For this applies to all mankind" (12:13).

Megillat Kohelet was originally read at the biblical *hak-hel* ceremony described in *Sefer Devarim* 31. Once every seven years, at the conclusion of the Sabbatical year, the king would address the people who had made the pilgrimage to *Yerushalayim* for the holiday of *Sukkot*. Traditionally, the king would read portions of the *Torah* at this ceremony. King *Shlomo* added the words of caution that are included in his book, *Megillat Kohelet,* and later kings read from this scroll as well.

To this day, *Megillat Kohelet* is read on *Sukkot* each year. In the Land of Israel, the holiday of *Sukkot* falls right before the rainy season. Crops that have been harvested and dried in the fields throughout the summer are stored before the first rains come. This time of year provides a great sense of accomplishment for the farmer who has toiled all year to finally reap the fruits of his labor. To avoid getting caught up in the self-satisfaction and the materialism, *Megillat Kohelet* is read specifically at this time, to warn a person that the goal of life is not material success, but rather the means to achieve the higher purpose of closeness with the Almighty.

Map of Ancient *Yerushalayim*

Kohelet (1:1) states that the book contains the words of *Kohelet* son of *David* who lived in *Yerushalayim*. The Sages identify *Kohelet* as *Shlomo*, who ruled in *Yerushalayim* following the death of his father *David*. The following is a map of *Yerushalayim* as it looked in the time of King *Shlomo*. For comparison, the map also contains the city limits at the end of the monarchy as well as the present day walls of the Old City of *Yerushalayim*.

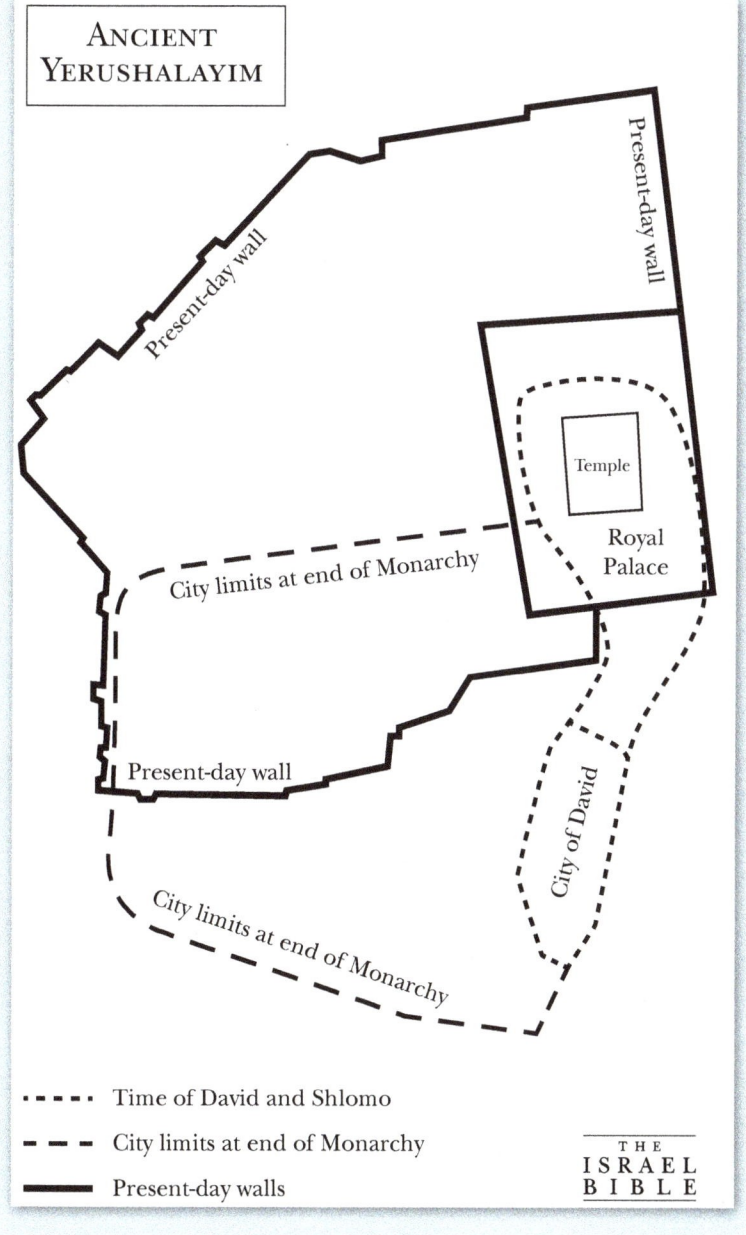

ANCIENT YERUSHALAYIM

Present-day wall

Present-day wall

Temple

Royal Palace

City limits at end of Monarchy

Present-day wall

City of David

City limits at end of Monarchy

- - - - - Time of David and Shlomo
- - - City limits at end of Monarchy
——— Present-day walls

THE ISRAEL BIBLE

1

1 The words of *Kohelet* son of *David*, king in *Yerushalayim*.

א דִּבְרֵי קֹהֶלֶת בֶּן־דָּוִד מֶלֶךְ בִּירוּשָׁלָםִ:

div-RAY ko-HE-let ben da-VID ME-lekh bee-ru-sha-LA-im

2 Utter futility! – said *Kohelet* – Utter futility! All is futile!

ב הֲבֵל הֲבָלִים אָמַר קֹהֶלֶת הֲבֵל הֲבָלִים הַכֹּל הָבֶל:

3 What real value is there for a man In all the gains he makes beneath the sun?

ג מַה־יִּתְרוֹן לָאָדָם בְּכָל־עֲמָלוֹ שֶׁיַּעֲמֹל תַּחַת הַשָּׁמֶשׁ:

4 One generation goes, another comes, But the earth remains the same forever.

ד דּוֹר הֹלֵךְ וְדוֹר בָּא וְהָאָרֶץ לְעוֹלָם עֹמָדֶת:

5 The sun rises, and the sun sets – And glides back to where it rises.

ה וְזָרַח הַשֶּׁמֶשׁ וּבָא הַשָּׁמֶשׁ וְאֶל־מְקוֹמוֹ שׁוֹאֵף זוֹרֵחַ הוּא שָׁם:

6 Southward blowing, Turning northward, Ever turning blows the wind; On its rounds the wind returns.

ו הוֹלֵךְ אֶל־דָּרוֹם וְסוֹבֵב אֶל־צָפוֹן סוֹבֵב סֹבֵב הוֹלֵךְ הָרוּחַ וְעַל־סְבִיבֹתָיו שָׁב הָרוּחַ:

7 All streams flow into the sea, Yet the sea is never full; To the place [from] which they flow The streams flow back again.

ז כָּל־הַנְּחָלִים הֹלְכִים אֶל־הַיָּם וְהַיָּם אֵינֶנּוּ מָלֵא אֶל־מְקוֹם שֶׁהַנְּחָלִים הֹלְכִים שָׁם הֵם שָׁבִים לָלָכֶת:

8 All such things are wearisome: No man can ever state them; The eye never has enough of seeing, Nor the ear enough of hearing.

ח כָּל־הַדְּבָרִים יְגֵעִים לֹא־יוּכַל אִישׁ לְדַבֵּר לֹא־תִשְׂבַּע עַיִן לִרְאוֹת וְלֹא־תִמָּלֵא אֹזֶן מִשְּׁמֹעַ:

9 Only that shall happen Which has happened, Only that occur Which has occurred; There is nothing new Beneath the sun!

ט מַה־שֶּׁהָיָה הוּא שֶׁיִּהְיֶה וּמַה־שֶּׁנַּעֲשָׂה הוּא שֶׁיֵּעָשֶׂה וְאֵין כָּל־חָדָשׁ תַּחַת הַשָּׁמֶשׁ:

10 Sometimes there is a phenomenon of which they say, "Look, this one is new!" – it occurred long since, in ages that went by before us.

י יֵשׁ דָּבָר שֶׁיֹּאמַר רְאֵה־זֶה חָדָשׁ הוּא כְּבָר הָיָה לְעֹלָמִים אֲשֶׁר הָיָה מִלְּפָנֵנוּ:

11 The earlier ones are not remembered; so too those that will occur later will no more be remembered than those that will occur at the very end.

יא אֵין זִכְרוֹן לָרִאשֹׁנִים וְגַם לָאַחֲרֹנִים שֶׁיִּהְיוּ לֹא־יִהְיֶה לָהֶם זִכָּרוֹן עִם שֶׁיִּהְיוּ לָאַחֲרֹנָה:

12 I, *Kohelet*, was king in *Yerushalayim* over *Yisrael*.

יב אֲנִי קֹהֶלֶת הָיִיתִי מֶלֶךְ עַל־יִשְׂרָאֵל בִּירוּשָׁלָםִ:

Silhouette of two Jerusalem residents at sunset

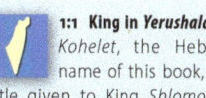

1:1 King in *Yerushalayim*
Kohelet, the Hebrew name of this book, is a title given to King *Shlomo*. Although he was king of all of Israel, the wisest of all men is called the "king in *Yerushalayim*" since *Yerushalayim* is known as a city of wisdom and a place that lends itself to deeper understanding. Furthermore, many sages resided in *Yerushalayim*, the political and spiritual capital of the united Kingdom of Israel. King *Shlomo* wants to add validity to his work by emphasizing that the observations recorded here were analyzed and approved by the wise residents of Jerusalem.

¹³ I set my mind to study and to probe with wisdom all that happens under the sun. – An unhappy business, that, which *Hashem* gave men to be concerned with!

יג וְנָתַתִּי אֶת־לִבִּי לִדְרוֹשׁ וְלָתוּר בַּחָכְמָה עַל כָּל־אֲשֶׁר נַעֲשָׂה תַּחַת הַשָּׁמָיִם הוּא עִנְיַן רָע נָתַן אֱלֹהִים לִבְנֵי הָאָדָם לַעֲנוֹת בּוֹ:

¹⁴ I observed all the happenings beneath the sun, and I found that all is futile and pursuit of wind:

יד רָאִיתִי אֶת־כָּל־הַמַּעֲשִׂים שֶׁנַּעֲשׂוּ תַּחַת הַשָּׁמֶשׁ וְהִנֵּה הַכֹּל הֶבֶל וּרְעוּת רוּחַ:

¹⁵ A twisted thing that cannot be made straight, A lack that cannot be made good.

טו מְעֻוָּת לֹא־יוּכַל לִתְקֹן וְחֶסְרוֹן לֹא־יוּכַל לְהִמָּנוֹת:

¹⁶ I said to myself: "Here I have grown richer and wiser than any that ruled before me over *Yerushalayim*, and my mind has zealously absorbed wisdom and learning."

טז דִּבַּרְתִּי אֲנִי עִם־לִבִּי לֵאמֹר אֲנִי הִנֵּה הִגְדַּלְתִּי וְהוֹסַפְתִּי חָכְמָה עַל כָּל־אֲשֶׁר־הָיָה לְפָנַי עַל־יְרוּשָׁלָ͏ִם וְלִבִּי רָאָה הַרְבֵּה חָכְמָה וָדָעַת:

¹⁷ And so I set my mind to appraise wisdom and to appraise madness and folly. And I learned – that this too was pursuit of wind:

יז וָאֶתְּנָה לִבִּי לָדַעַת חָכְמָה וָדַעַת הוֹלֵלוֹת וְשִׂכְלוּת יָדַעְתִּי שֶׁגַּם־זֶה הוּא רַעְיוֹן רוּחַ:

¹⁸ For as wisdom grows, vexation grows; To increase learning is to increase heartache.

יח כִּי בְּרֹב חָכְמָה רָב־כָּעַס וְיוֹסִיף דַּעַת יוֹסִיף מַכְאוֹב:

2 ¹ I said to myself, "Come, I will treat you to merriment. Taste mirth!" That too, I found, was futile.

ב א אָמַרְתִּי אֲנִי בְּלִבִּי לְכָה־נָּא אֲנַסְּכָה בְשִׂמְחָה וּרְאֵה בְטוֹב וְהִנֵּה גַם־הוּא הָבֶל:

² Of revelry I said, "It's mad!" Of merriment, "What good is that?"

ב לִשְׂחוֹק אָמַרְתִּי מְהוֹלָל וּלְשִׂמְחָה מַה־זֶּה עֹשָׂה:

³ I ventured to tempt my flesh with wine, and to grasp folly, while letting my mind direct with wisdom, to the end that I might learn which of the two was better for men to practice in their few days of life under heaven.

ג תַּרְתִּי בְלִבִּי לִמְשׁוֹךְ בַּיַּיִן אֶת־בְּשָׂרִי וְלִבִּי נֹהֵג בַּחָכְמָה וְלֶאֱחֹז בְּסִכְלוּת עַד אֲשֶׁר־אֶרְאֶה אֵי־זֶה טוֹב לִבְנֵי הָאָדָם אֲשֶׁר יַעֲשׂוּ תַּחַת הַשָּׁמַיִם מִסְפַּר יְמֵי חַיֵּיהֶם:

⁴ I multiplied my possessions. I built myself houses and I planted vineyards.

ד הִגְדַּלְתִּי מַעֲשָׂי בָּנִיתִי לִי בָּתִּים נָטַעְתִּי לִי כְּרָמִים:

⁵ I laid out gardens and groves, in which I planted every kind of fruit tree.

ה עָשִׂיתִי לִי גַּנּוֹת וּפַרְדֵּסִים וְנָטַעְתִּי בָהֶם עֵץ כָּל־פֶּרִי:

a-SEE-tee LEE ga-NOT u-far-day-SEEM v'-na-TA-tee va-HEM AYTZ kol PE-ree

Ecclesiastes

A lemon tree in *Yerushalayim*

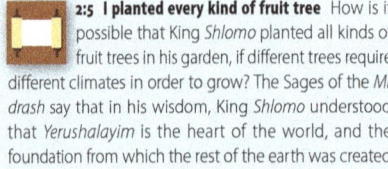

2:5 I planted every kind of fruit tree How is it possible that King *Shlomo* planted all kinds of fruit trees in his garden, if different trees require different climates in order to grow? The Sages of the *Midrash* say that in his wisdom, King *Shlomo* understood that *Yerushalayim* is the heart of the world, and the foundation from which the rest of the earth was created. Since it contains spiritual channels that lead to all other places, *Shlomo* was able to plant every kind of fruit tree in *Yerushalayim*. According to tradition, he knew which part of *Yerushalayim* gives its strength to Africa and which location is connected to India, and was able to plant the trees of these climates in those areas.

⁶ I constructed pools of water, enough to irrigate a forest shooting up with trees.

ו עָשִׂיתִי לִי בְּרֵכוֹת מָיִם לְהַשְׁקוֹת מֵהֶם יַעַר צוֹמֵחַ עֵצִים:

⁷ I bought male and female slaves, and I acquired stewards. I also acquired more cattle, both herds and flocks, than all who were before me in *Yerushalayim.*

ז קָנִיתִי עֲבָדִים וּשְׁפָחוֹת וּבְנֵי־בַיִת הָיָה לִי גַּם מִקְנֶה בָקָר וָצֹאן הַרְבֵּה הָיָה לִי מִכֹּל שֶׁהָיוּ לְפָנַי בִּירוּשָׁלָֽם:

⁸ I further amassed silver and gold and treasures of kings and provinces; and I got myself male and female singers, as well as the luxuries of commoners – coffers and coffers of them.

ח כָּנַסְתִּי לִי גַּם־כֶּסֶף וְזָהָב וּסְגֻלַּת מְלָכִים וְהַמְּדִינוֹת עָשִׂיתִי לִי שָׁרִים וְשָׁרוֹת וְתַעֲנֻגוֹת בְּנֵי הָאָדָם שִׁדָּה וְשִׁדּוֹת:

⁹ Thus, I gained more wealth than anyone before me in *Yerushalayim.* In addition, my wisdom remained with me:

ט וְגָדַלְתִּי וְהוֹסַפְתִּי מִכֹּל שֶׁהָיָה לְפָנַי בִּירוּשָׁלָ͏ִם אַף חָכְמָתִי עָמְדָה לִּי:

¹⁰ I withheld from my eyes nothing they asked for, and denied myself no enjoyment; rather, I got enjoyment out of all my wealth. And that was all I got out of my wealth.

י וְכֹל אֲשֶׁר שָׁאֲלוּ עֵינַי לֹא אָצַלְתִּי מֵהֶם לֹא־מָנַעְתִּי אֶת־לִבִּי מִכָּל־שִׂמְחָה כִּי־לִבִּי שָׂמֵחַ מִכָּל־עֲמָלִי וְזֶה־הָיָה חֶלְקִי מִכָּל־עֲמָלִי:

¹¹ Then my thoughts turned to all the fortune my hands had built up, to the wealth I had acquired and won – and oh, it was all futile and pursuit of wind; there was no real value under the sun!

יא וּפָנִיתִי אֲנִי בְּכָל־מַעֲשַׂי שֶׁעָשׂוּ יָדַי וּבֶעָמָל שֶׁעָמַלְתִּי לַעֲשׂוֹת וְהִנֵּה הַכֹּל הֶבֶל וּרְעוּת רוּחַ וְאֵין יִתְרוֹן תַּחַת הַשָּׁמֶשׁ:

¹² For what will the man be like who will succeed the one who is ruling over what was built up long ago? My thoughts also turned to appraising wisdom and madness and folly.*

יב וּפָנִיתִי אֲנִי לִרְאוֹת חָכְמָה וְהוֹלֵלוֹת וְסִכְלוּת כִּי מֶה הָאָדָם שֶׁיָּבוֹא אַחֲרֵי הַמֶּלֶךְ אֵת אֲשֶׁר־כְּבָר עָשׂוּהוּ:

¹³ I found that Wisdom is superior to folly As light is superior to darkness;

יג וְרָאִיתִי אָנִי שֶׁיֵּשׁ יִתְרוֹן לַחָכְמָה מִן־הַסִּכְלוּת כִּיתְרוֹן הָאוֹר מִן־הַחֹשֶׁךְ:

¹⁴ A wise man has his eyes in his head, Whereas a fool walks in darkness. But I also realized that the same fate awaits them both.

יד הֶחָכָם עֵינָיו בְּרֹאשׁוֹ וְהַכְּסִיל בַּחֹשֶׁךְ הוֹלֵךְ וְיָדַעְתִּי גַם־אָנִי שֶׁמִּקְרֶה אֶחָד יִקְרֶה אֶת־כֻּלָּם:

¹⁵ So I reflected: "The fate of the fool is also destined for me; to what advantage, then, have I been wise?" And I came to the conclusion that that too was futile,

טו וְאָמַרְתִּי אֲנִי בְּלִבִּי כְּמִקְרֵה הַכְּסִיל גַּם־אֲנִי יִקְרֵנִי וְלָמָּה חָכַמְתִּי אֲנִי אָז יוֹתֵר וְדִבַּרְתִּי בְלִבִּי שֶׁגַּם־זֶה הָבֶל:

¹⁶ because the wise man, just like the fool, is not remembered forever; for, as the succeeding days roll by, both are forgotten. Alas, the wise man dies, just like the fool!

טז כִּי אֵין זִכְרוֹן לֶחָכָם עִם־הַכְּסִיל לְעוֹלָם בְּשֶׁכְּבָר הַיָּמִים הַבָּאִים הַכֹּל נִשְׁכָּח וְאֵיךְ יָמוּת הֶחָכָם עִם־הַכְּסִיל:

¹⁷ And so I loathed life. For I was distressed by all that goes on under the sun, because everything is futile and pursuit of wind.

יז וְשָׂנֵאתִי אֶת־הַחַיִּים כִּי רַע עָלַי הַמַּעֲשֶׂה שֶׁנַּעֲשָׂה תַּחַת הַשָּׁמֶשׁ כִּי־הַכֹּל הֶבֶל וּרְעוּת רוּחַ:

---

* order of the two sentences reversed for clarity

¹⁸ So, too, I loathed all the wealth that I was gaining under the sun. For I shall leave it to the man who will succeed me –

יח וְשָׂנֵאתִי אֲנִי אֶת־כָּל־עֲמָלִי שֶׁאֲנִי עָמֵל תַּחַת הַשָּׁמֶשׁ שֶׁאַנִּיחֶנּוּ לָאָדָם שֶׁיִּהְיֶה אַחֲרָי:

¹⁹ and who knows whether he will be wise or foolish? – and he will control all the wealth that I gained by toil and wisdom under the sun. That too is futile.

יט וּמִי יוֹדֵעַ הֶחָכָם יִהְיֶה אוֹ סָכָל וְיִשְׁלַט בְּכָל־עֲמָלִי שֶׁעָמַלְתִּי וְשֶׁחָכַמְתִּי תַּחַת הַשָּׁמֶשׁ גַּם־זֶה הָבֶל:

²⁰ And so I came to view with despair all the gains I had made under the sun.

כ וְסַבּוֹתִי אֲנִי לְיַאֵשׁ אֶת־לִבִּי עַל כָּל־הֶעָמָל שֶׁעָמַלְתִּי תַּחַת הַשָּׁמֶשׁ:

²¹ For sometimes a person whose fortune was made with wisdom, knowledge, and skill must hand it on to be the portion of somebody who did not toil for it. That too is futile, and a grave evil.

כא כִּי־יֵשׁ אָדָם שֶׁעֲמָלוֹ בְּחָכְמָה וּבְדַעַת וּבְכִשְׁרוֹן וּלְאָדָם שֶׁלֹּא עָמַל־בּוֹ יִתְּנֶנּוּ חֶלְקוֹ גַּם־זֶה הֶבֶל וְרָעָה רַבָּה:

²² For what does a man get for all the toiling and worrying he does under the sun?

כב כִּי מֶה־הֹוֶה לָאָדָם בְּכָל־עֲמָלוֹ וּבְרַעְיוֹן לִבּוֹ שֶׁהוּא עָמֵל תַּחַת הַשָּׁמֶשׁ:

²³ All his days his thoughts are grief and heartache, and even at night his mind has no respite. That too is futile!

כג כִּי כָל־יָמָיו מַכְאֹבִים וָכַעַס עִנְיָנוֹ גַּם־בַּלַּיְלָה לֹא־שָׁכַב לִבּוֹ גַּם־זֶה הֶבֶל הוּא:

²⁴ There is nothing worthwhile for a man but to eat and drink and afford himself enjoyment with his means. And even that, I noted, comes from *Hashem*.

כד אֵין־טוֹב בָּאָדָם שֶׁיֹּאכַל וְשָׁתָה וְהֶרְאָה אֶת־נַפְשׁוֹ טוֹב בַּעֲמָלוֹ גַּם־זֹה רָאִיתִי אָנִי כִּי מִיַּד הָאֱלֹהִים הִיא:

²⁵ For who eats and who enjoys but myself?

כה כִּי מִי יֹאכַל וּמִי יָחוּשׁ חוּץ מִמֶּנִּי:

²⁶ To the man, namely, who pleases Him He has given the wisdom and shrewdness to enjoy himself; and to him who displeases, He has given the urge to gather and amass – only for handing on to one who is pleasing to *Hashem*. That too is futile and pursuit of wind.

כו כִּי לְאָדָם שֶׁטּוֹב לְפָנָיו נָתַן חָכְמָה וְדַעַת וְשִׂמְחָה וְלַחוֹטֶא נָתַן עִנְיָן לֶאֱסוֹף וְלִכְנוֹס לָתֵת לְטוֹב לִפְנֵי הָאֱלֹהִים גַּם־זֶה הֶבֶל וּרְעוּת רוּחַ:

3 ¹ A season is set for everything, a time for every experience under heaven:

ג א לַכֹּל זְמָן וְעֵת לְכָל־חֵפֶץ תַּחַת הַשָּׁמָיִם:

² A time for being born and a time for dying, A time for planting and a time for uprooting the planted;

ב עֵת לָלֶדֶת וְעֵת לָמוּת עֵת לָטַעַת וְעֵת לַעֲקוֹר נָטוּעַ:

³ A time for slaying and a time for healing, A time for tearing down and a time for building up;

ג עֵת לַהֲרוֹג וְעֵת לִרְפּוֹא עֵת לִפְרוֹץ וְעֵת לִבְנוֹת:

⁴ A time for weeping and a time for laughing, A time for wailing and a time for dancing;

ד עֵת לִבְכּוֹת וְעֵת לִשְׂחוֹק עֵת סְפוֹד וְעֵת רְקוֹד:

5 A time for throwing stones and a time for gathering stones, A time for embracing and a time for shunning embraces;

ה עֵת לְהַשְׁלִיךְ אֲבָנִים וְעֵת כְּנוֹס אֲבָנִים עֵת לַחֲבוֹק וְעֵת לִרְחֹק מֵחַבֵּק:

AYT l'-hash-LEEKH a-va-NEEM v'-AYT k'-NOS a-va-NEEM
AYT la-kha-VOK v'-AYT lir-KHOK may-kha-BAYK

6 A time for seeking and a time for losing, A time for keeping and a time for discarding;

ו עֵת לְבַקֵּשׁ וְעֵת לְאַבֵּד עֵת לִשְׁמוֹר וְעֵת לְהַשְׁלִיךְ:

7 A time for ripping and a time for sewing, A time for silence and a time for speaking;

ז עֵת לִקְרוֹעַ וְעֵת לִתְפּוֹר עֵת לַחֲשׁוֹת וְעֵת לְדַבֵּר:

8 A time for loving and a time for hating; A time for war and a time for peace.

ח עֵת לֶאֱהֹב וְעֵת לִשְׂנֹא עֵת מִלְחָמָה וְעֵת שָׁלוֹם:

9 What value, then, can the man of affairs get from what he earns?

ט מַה־יִּתְרוֹן הָעוֹשֶׂה בַּאֲשֶׁר הוּא עָמֵל:

10 I have observed the business that *Hashem* gave man to be concerned with:

י רָאִיתִי אֶת־הָעִנְיָן אֲשֶׁר נָתַן אֱלֹהִים לִבְנֵי הָאָדָם לַעֲנוֹת בּוֹ:

11 He brings everything to pass precisely at its time; He also puts eternity in their mind, but without man ever guessing, from first to last, all the things that *Hashem* brings to pass.

יא אֶת־הַכֹּל עָשָׂה יָפֶה בְעִתּוֹ גַּם אֶת־הָעֹלָם נָתַן בְּלִבָּם מִבְּלִי אֲשֶׁר לֹא־יִמְצָא הָאָדָם אֶת־הַמַּעֲשֶׂה אֲשֶׁר־עָשָׂה הָאֱלֹהִים מֵרֹאשׁ וְעַד־סוֹף:

12 Thus I realized that the only worthwhile thing there is for them is to enjoy themselves and do what is good in their lifetime;

יב יָדַעְתִּי כִּי אֵין טוֹב בָּם כִּי אִם־לִשְׂמוֹחַ וְלַעֲשׂוֹת טוֹב בְּחַיָּיו:

13 also, that whenever a man does eat and drink and get enjoyment out of all his wealth, it is a gift of *Hashem*.

יג וְגַם כָּל־הָאָדָם שֶׁיֹּאכַל וְשָׁתָה וְרָאָה טוֹב בְּכָל־עֲמָלוֹ מַתַּת אֱלֹהִים הִיא:

14 I realized, too, that whatever *Hashem* has brought to pass will recur evermore: Nothing can be added to it And nothing taken from it – and *Hashem* has brought to pass that men revere Him.

יד יָדַעְתִּי כִּי כָּל־אֲשֶׁר יַעֲשֶׂה הָאֱלֹהִים הוּא יִהְיֶה לְעוֹלָם עָלָיו אֵין לְהוֹסִיף וּמִמֶּנּוּ אֵין לִגְרֹעַ וְהָאֱלֹהִים עָשָׂה שֶׁיִּרְאוּ מִלְּפָנָיו:

15 What is occurring occurred long since, And what is to occur occurred long since: and *Hashem* seeks the pursued.

טו מַה־שֶּׁהָיָה כְּבָר הוּא וַאֲשֶׁר לִהְיוֹת כְּבָר הָיָה וְהָאֱלֹהִים יְבַקֵּשׁ אֶת־נִרְדָּף:

16 And, indeed, I have observed under the sun: Alongside justice there is wickedness, Alongside righteousness there is wickedness.

טז וְעוֹד רָאִיתִי תַּחַת הַשָּׁמֶשׁ מְקוֹם הַמִּשְׁפָּט שָׁמָּה הָרֶשַׁע וּמְקוֹם הַצֶּדֶק שָׁמָּה הָרָשַׁע:

3:5 A time for throwing stones According to the Sages, the phrase, "a time for throwing stones" is a reference to the destruction of *Yerushalayim*, when its grand walls were reduced to a heap of rocks. The phrase, "and a time to gather stones" refers to the second stage of exile, when King *Yechonya*, and those exiled with him, carried the stones and earth of *Yerushalayim* to Babylonia, in order to build synagogues and study halls from the precious and sacred earth of the Holy Land. Additionally, just as God allowed *Yerushalayim* to be destroyed and reduced to stones, He also allowed the stones to be gathered for *Yerushalayim* to be built once again.

Stone buildings in the Old City of *Yerushalayim*

17 I mused: "*Hashem* will doom both righteous and wicked, for there is a time for every experience and for every happening."

יז אָמַרְתִּי אֲנִי בְּלִבִּי אֶת־הַצַּדִּיק וְאֶת־הָרָשָׁע יִשְׁפֹּט הָאֱלֹהִים כִּי־עֵת לְכָל־חֵפֶץ וְעַל כָּל־הַמַּעֲשֶׂה שָׁם:

18 So I decided, as regards men, to dissociate them [from] the divine beings and to face the fact that they are beasts.

יח אָמַרְתִּי אֲנִי בְּלִבִּי עַל־דִּבְרַת בְּנֵי הָאָדָם לְבָרָם הָאֱלֹהִים וְלִרְאוֹת שְׁהֶם־בְּהֵמָה הֵמָּה לָהֶם:

19 For in respect of the fate of man and the fate of beast, they have one and the same fate: as the one dies so dies the other, and both have the same lifebreath; man has no superiority over beast, since both amount to nothing.

יט כִּי מִקְרֶה בְנֵי־הָאָדָם וּמִקְרֶה הַבְּהֵמָה וּמִקְרֶה אֶחָד לָהֶם כְּמוֹת זֶה כֵּן מוֹת זֶה וְרוּחַ אֶחָד לַכֹּל וּמוֹתַר הָאָדָם מִן־הַבְּהֵמָה אָיִן כִּי הַכֹּל הָבֶל:

20 Both go to the same place; both came from dust and both return to dust.

כ הַכֹּל הוֹלֵךְ אֶל־מָקוֹם אֶחָד הַכֹּל הָיָה מִן־הֶעָפָר וְהַכֹּל שָׁב אֶל־הֶעָפָר:

21 Who knows if a man's lifebreath does rise upward and if a beast's breath does sink down into the earth?

כא מִי יוֹדֵעַ רוּחַ בְּנֵי הָאָדָם הָעֹלָה הִיא לְמָעְלָה וְרוּחַ הַבְּהֵמָה הַיֹּרֶדֶת הִיא לְמַטָּה לָאָרֶץ:

22 I saw that there is nothing better for man than to enjoy his possessions, since that is his portion. For who can enable him to see what will happen afterward?

כב וְרָאִיתִי כִּי אֵין טוֹב מֵאֲשֶׁר יִשְׂמַח הָאָדָם בְּמַעֲשָׂיו כִּי־הוּא חֶלְקוֹ כִּי מִי יְבִיאֶנּוּ לִרְאוֹת בְּמֶה שֶׁיִּהְיֶה אַחֲרָיו:

4 1 I further observed all the oppression that goes on under the sun: the tears of the oppressed, with none to comfort them; and the power of their oppressors – with none to comfort them.

ד א וְשַׁבְתִּי אֲנִי וָאֶרְאֶה אֶת־כָּל־הָעֲשֻׁקִים אֲשֶׁר נַעֲשִׂים תַּחַת הַשָּׁמֶשׁ וְהִנֵּה דִּמְעַת הָעֲשֻׁקִים וְאֵין לָהֶם מְנַחֵם וּמִיַּד עֹשְׁקֵיהֶם כֹּחַ וְאֵין לָהֶם מְנַחֵם:

v'-shav-TEE a-NEE va-er-EH et kol HA-a-shu-KEEM a-SHER na-a-SEEM TA-khat ha-SHA-mesh v'-hi-NAY dim-AT ha-a-shu-KEEM v'-AYN la-HEM m'-na-KHAYM u-mi-YAD o-sh'-kay-HEM KO-akh v'-AYN la-HEM m'-na-KHAYM

2 Then I accounted those who died long since more fortunate than those who are still living;

ב וְשַׁבֵּחַ אֲנִי אֶת־הַמֵּתִים שֶׁכְּבָר מֵתוּ מִן־הַחַיִּים אֲשֶׁר הֵמָּה חַיִּים עֲדֶנָה:

3 and happier than either are those who have not yet come into being and have never witnessed the miseries that go on under the sun.

ג וְטוֹב מִשְּׁנֵיהֶם אֵת אֲשֶׁר־עֲדֶן לֹא הָיָה אֲשֶׁר לֹא־רָאָה אֶת־הַמַּעֲשֶׂה הָרָע אֲשֶׁר נַעֲשָׂה תַּחַת הַשָּׁמֶשׁ:

4 I have also noted that all labor and skillful enterprise come from men's envy of each other – another futility and pursuit of wind!

ד וְרָאִיתִי אֲנִי אֶת־כָּל־עָמָל וְאֵת כָּל־כִּשְׁרוֹן הַמַּעֲשֶׂה כִּי הִיא קִנְאַת־אִישׁ מֵרֵעֵהוּ גַּם־זֶה הֶבֶל וּרְעוּת רוּחַ:

4:1 With none to comfort them When the verse mentions "all the oppression that goes on," it refers to the suffering of the Jewish people in exile. *Kohelet* observes, however, that not only do the people suffer in exile, but that they lack the leadership to comfort them. *Sforno* notes that the phrase "with none to comfort them" is repeated twice in this verse, hinting that they were lacking the leadership to teach them the two keys for redemption: repentance and prayer. First, the People of Israel need a leader who will guide them towards repentance, for sincere repentance leads to redemption. Second, they need a leader who will show them how to pray effectively so that their prayers will be answered, and they will be returned to the Land of Israel.

Jewish men praying at sunset

5 [True,] The fool folds his hands together And has to eat his own flesh.

ה הַכְּסִיל חֹבֵק אֶת־יָדָיו וְאֹכֵל אֶת־בְּשָׂרוֹ׃

6 [But no less truly,] Better is a handful of gratification Than two fistfuls of labor which is pursuit of wind.

ו טוֹב מְלֹא כַף נָחַת מִמְּלֹא חָפְנַיִם עָמָל וּרְעוּת רוּחַ׃

7 And I have noted this further futility under the sun:

ז וְשַׁבְתִּי אֲנִי וָאֶרְאֶה הֶבֶל תַּחַת הַשָּׁמֶשׁ׃

8 the case of the man who is alone, with no companion, who has neither son nor brother; yet he amasses wealth without limit, and his eye is never sated with riches. For whom, now, is he amassing it while denying himself enjoyment? That too is a futility and an unhappy business.

ח יֵשׁ אֶחָד וְאֵין שֵׁנִי גַּם בֵּן וָאָח אֵין־לוֹ וְאֵין קֵץ לְכָל־עֲמָלוֹ גַּם־עֵינָיו [עֵינוֹ] לֹא־תִשְׂבַּע עֹשֶׁר וּלְמִי אֲנִי עָמֵל וּמְחַסֵּר אֶת־נַפְשִׁי מִטּוֹבָה גַּם־זֶה הֶבֶל וְעִנְיַן רָע הוּא׃

9 Two are better off than one, in that they have greater benefit from their earnings.

ט טוֹבִים הַשְּׁנַיִם מִן־הָאֶחָד אֲשֶׁר יֵשׁ־לָהֶם שָׂכָר טוֹב בַּעֲמָלָם׃

10 For should they fall, one can raise the other; but woe betide him who is alone and falls with no companion to raise him!

י כִּי אִם־יִפֹּלוּ הָאֶחָד יָקִים אֶת־חֲבֵרוֹ וְאִילוֹ הָאֶחָד שֶׁיִּפּוֹל וְאֵין שֵׁנִי לַהֲקִימוֹ׃

11 Further, when two lie together they are warm; but how can he who is alone get warm?

יא גַּם אִם־יִשְׁכְּבוּ שְׁנַיִם וְחַם לָהֶם וּלְאֶחָד אֵיךְ יֵחָם׃

12 Also, if one attacks, two can stand up to him. A threefold cord is not readily broken!

יב וְאִם־יִתְקְפוֹ הָאֶחָד הַשְּׁנַיִם יַעַמְדוּ נֶגְדּוֹ וְהַחוּט הַמְשֻׁלָּשׁ לֹא בִמְהֵרָה יִנָּתֵק׃

13 Better a poor but wise youth than an old but foolish king who no longer has the sense to heed warnings.

יג טוֹב יֶלֶד מִסְכֵּן וְחָכָם מִמֶּלֶךְ זָקֵן וּכְסִיל אֲשֶׁר לֹא־יָדַע לְהִזָּהֵר עוֹד׃

14 For the former can emerge from a dungeon to become king; while the latter, even if born to kingship, can become a pauper.

יד כִּי־מִבֵּית הָסוּרִים יָצָא לִמְלֹךְ כִּי גַּם בְּמַלְכוּתוֹ נוֹלַד רָשׁ׃

15 [However,] I reflected about all the living who walk under the sun with that youthful successor who steps into his place.

טו רָאִיתִי אֶת־כָּל־הַחַיִּים הַמְהַלְּכִים תַּחַת הַשָּׁמֶשׁ עִם הַיֶּלֶד הַשֵּׁנִי אֲשֶׁר יַעֲמֹד תַּחְתָּיו׃

16 Unnumbered are the multitudes of all those who preceded them; and later generations will not acclaim him either. For that too is futile and pursuit of wind.

טז אֵין־קֵץ לְכָל־הָעָם לְכֹל אֲשֶׁר־הָיָה לִפְנֵיהֶם גַּם הָאַחֲרוֹנִים לֹא יִשְׂמְחוּ־בוֹ כִּי־גַם־זֶה הֶבֶל וְרַעְיוֹן רוּחַ׃

17 Be not overeager to go to the House of *Hashem*: more acceptable is obedience than the offering of fools, for they know nothing [but] to do wrong.

יז שְׁמֹר רַגְלֶיךָ [רַגְלְךָ] כַּאֲשֶׁר תֵּלֵךְ אֶל־בֵּית הָאֱלֹהִים וְקָרוֹב לִשְׁמֹעַ מִתֵּת הַכְּסִילִים זָבַח כִּי־אֵינָם יוֹדְעִים לַעֲשׂוֹת רָע׃

5 1 Keep your mouth from being rash, and let not your throat be quick to bring forth speech before *Hashem*. For *Hashem* is in heaven and you are on earth; that is why your words should be few.

ה א אַל־תְּבַהֵל עַל־פִּיךָ וְלִבְּךָ אַל־יְמַהֵר לְהוֹצִיא דָבָר לִפְנֵי הָאֱלֹהִים כִּי הָאֱלֹהִים בַּשָּׁמַיִם וְאַתָּה עַל־הָאָרֶץ עַל־כֵּן יִהְיוּ דְבָרֶיךָ מְעַטִּים׃

2 Just as dreams come with much brooding, so does foolish utterance come with much speech.

ב כִּי בָּא הַחֲלוֹם בְּרֹב עִנְיָן וְקוֹל כְּסִיל בְּרֹב דְּבָרִים:

3 When you make a vow to *Hashem*, do not delay to fulfill it. For He has no pleasure in fools; what you vow, fulfill.

ג כַּאֲשֶׁר תִּדֹּר נֶדֶר לֵאלֹהִים אַל־תְּאַחֵר לְשַׁלְּמוֹ כִּי אֵין חֵפֶץ בַּכְּסִילִים אֵת אֲשֶׁר־תִּדֹּר שַׁלֵּם:

4 It is better not to vow at all than to vow and not fulfill.

ד טוֹב אֲשֶׁר לֹא־תִדֹּר מִשֶּׁתִּדּוֹר וְלֹא תְשַׁלֵּם:

5 Don't let your mouth bring you into disfavor, and don't plead before the messenger that it was an error, but fear *Hashem*;* else *Hashem* may be angered by your talk and destroy your possessions.

ה אַל־תִּתֵּן אֶת־פִּיךָ לַחֲטִיא אֶת־בְּשָׂרֶךָ וְאַל־תֹּאמַר לִפְנֵי הַמַּלְאָךְ כִּי שְׁגָגָה הִיא לָמָּה יִקְצֹף הָאֱלֹהִים עַל־קוֹלֶךָ וְחִבֵּל אֶת־מַעֲשֵׂה יָדֶיךָ:

6 For much dreaming leads to futility and to superfluous talk.

ו כִּי בְרֹב חֲלֹמוֹת וַהֲבָלִים וּדְבָרִים הַרְבֵּה כִּי אֶת־הָאֱלֹהִים יְרָא:

7 If you see in a province oppression of the poor and suppression of right and justice, don't wonder at the fact; for one high official is protected by a higher one, and both of them by still higher ones.

ז אִם־עֹשֶׁק רָשׁ וְגֵזֶל מִשְׁפָּט וָצֶדֶק תִּרְאֶה בַמְּדִינָה אַל־תִּתְמַהּ עַל־הַחֵפֶץ כִּי גָבֹהַּ מֵעַל גָּבֹהַּ שֹׁמֵר וּגְבֹהִים עֲלֵיהֶם:

8 Thus the greatest advantage in all the land is his: he controls a field that is cultivated.

ח וְיִתְרוֹן אֶרֶץ בַּכֹּל הִיא [הוּא] מֶלֶךְ לְשָׂדֶה נֶעֱבָד:

9 A lover of money never has his fill of money, nor a lover of wealth his fill of income. That too is futile.

ט אֹהֵב כֶּסֶף לֹא־יִשְׂבַּע כֶּסֶף וּמִי־אֹהֵב בֶּהָמוֹן לֹא תְבוּאָה גַּם־זֶה הָבֶל:

o-HAYV KE-sef lo yis-BA KE-sef u-MEE o-HAYV be-ha-MON LO t'-vu-AH gam ZEH HA-vel

10 As his substance increases, so do those who consume it; what, then, does the success of its owner amount to but feasting his eyes?

י בִּרְבוֹת הַטּוֹבָה רַבּוּ אוֹכְלֶיהָ וּמַה־כִּשְׁרוֹן לִבְעָלֶיהָ כִּי אִם־רְאִית [רְאוּת] עֵינָיו:

11 A worker's sleep is sweet, whether he has much or little to eat; but the rich man's abundance doesn't let him sleep.

יא מְתוּקָה שְׁנַת הָעֹבֵד אִם־מְעַט וְאִם־הַרְבֵּה יֹאכֵל וְהַשָּׂבָע לֶעָשִׁיר אֵינֶנּוּ מַנִּיחַ לוֹ לִישׁוֹן:

12 Here is a grave evil I have observed under the sun: riches hoarded by their owner to his misfortune,

יב יֵשׁ רָעָה חוֹלָה רָאִיתִי תַּחַת הַשָּׁמֶשׁ עֹשֶׁר שָׁמוּר לִבְעָלָיו לְרָעָתוֹ:

13 in that those riches are lost in some unlucky venture; and if he begets a son, he has nothing in hand.

יג וְאָבַד הָעֹשֶׁר הַהוּא בְּעִנְיָן רָע וְהוֹלִיד בֵּן וְאֵין בְּיָדוֹ מְאוּמָה:

---

* "but fear Hashem" moved up from verse 6 for clarity

א **5:9 That too is futile** The word *hevel* (הבל), 'futile,' appears many times throughout *Megillat Kohelet* as a description of the pursuit of various physical pleasures. Although the word is translated as 'futile,' it literally means 'vapor.' Vapor has the power to distort what a person sees. For example, the hot air rising from desert sands creates the mirage of an oasis. In this verse, *Kohelet* observes that amassing wealth is "*hevel*."

More than just futile, the pursuit of wealth is similar to vapor, since it has the power to distort a person's reality and values. *Kohelet* warns not to pursue wealth, because one who does so will never be satisfied.

הבל

Oasis in the desert at *Ein Gedi*

Ecclesiastes

14 Another grave evil is this: He must depart just as he came* As he came out of his mother's womb, so must he depart at last, naked as he came. He can take nothing of his wealth to carry with him.

יד כַּאֲשֶׁר יָצָא מִבֶּטֶן אִמּוֹ עָרוֹם יָשׁוּב לָלֶכֶת כְּשֶׁבָּא וּמְאוּמָה לֹא־יִשָּׂא בַעֲמָלוֹ שֶׁיֹּלֵךְ בְּיָדוֹ:

15 So what is the good of his toiling for the wind?

טו וְגַם־זֹה רָעָה חוֹלָה כָּל־עֻמַּת שֶׁבָּא כֵּן יֵלֵךְ וּמַה־יִּתְרוֹן לוֹ שֶׁיַּעֲמֹל לָרוּחַ:

16 Besides, all his days he eats in darkness, with much vexation and grief and anger.

טז גַּם כָּל־יָמָיו בַּחֹשֶׁךְ יֹאכֵל וְכָעַס הַרְבֵּה וְחָלְיוֹ וָקָצֶף:

17 Only this, I have found, is a real good: that one should eat and drink and get pleasure with all the gains he makes under the sun, during the numbered days of life that *Hashem* has given him; for that is his portion.

יז הִנֵּה אֲשֶׁר־רָאִיתִי אָנִי טוֹב אֲשֶׁר־יָפֶה לֶאֱכוֹל־וְלִשְׁתּוֹת וְלִרְאוֹת טוֹבָה בְּכָל־עֲמָלוֹ שֶׁיַּעֲמֹל תַּחַת־הַשֶּׁמֶשׁ מִסְפַּר יְמֵי־חַיָּו [חַיָּיו] אֲשֶׁר־נָתַן־לוֹ הָאֱלֹהִים כִּי־הוּא חֶלְקוֹ:

18 Also, whenever a man is given riches and property by *Hashem*, and is also permitted by Him to enjoy them and to take his portion and get pleasure for his gains – that is a gift of *Hashem*.

יח גַּם כָּל־הָאָדָם אֲשֶׁר נָתַן־לוֹ הָאֱלֹהִים עֹשֶׁר וּנְכָסִים וְהִשְׁלִיטוֹ לֶאֱכֹל מִמֶּנּוּ וְלָשֵׂאת אֶת־חֶלְקוֹ וְלִשְׂמֹחַ בַּעֲמָלוֹ זֹה מַתַּת אֱלֹהִים הִיא:

19 For [such a man] will not brood much over the days of his life, because *Hashem* keeps him busy enjoying himself.

יט כִּי לֹא הַרְבֵּה יִזְכֹּר אֶת־יְמֵי חַיָּיו כִּי הָאֱלֹהִים מַעֲנֶה בְּשִׂמְחַת לִבּוֹ:

6 1 There is an evil I have observed under the sun, and a grave one it is for man:

ו א יֵשׁ רָעָה אֲשֶׁר רָאִיתִי תַּחַת הַשָּׁמֶשׁ וְרַבָּה הִיא עַל־הָאָדָם:

2 that *Hashem* sometimes grants a man riches, property, and wealth, so that he does not want for anything his appetite may crave, but *Hashem* does not permit him to enjoy it; instead, a stranger will enjoy it. That is futility and a grievous ill.

ב אִישׁ אֲשֶׁר יִתֶּן־לוֹ הָאֱלֹהִים עֹשֶׁר וּנְכָסִים וְכָבוֹד וְאֵינֶנּוּ חָסֵר לְנַפְשׁוֹ מִכֹּל אֲשֶׁר־יִתְאַוֶּה וְלֹא־יַשְׁלִיטֶנּוּ הָאֱלֹהִים לֶאֱכֹל מִמֶּנּוּ כִּי אִישׁ נָכְרִי יֹאכֲלֶנּוּ זֶה הֶבֶל וָחֳלִי רָע הוּא:

EESH a-SHER yi-ten LO ha-e-lo-HEEM O-sher un-kha-SEEM
v'-kha-VOD v'-ay-NE-nu kha-SAYR l'-naf-SHO mi-KOL a-sher yit-a-VEH
v'-LO yash-lee-TE-nu ha-e-lo-HEEM le-KHOL mi-ME-nu KEE
EESH nokh-REE yo-kh'-LE-nu ZEH HE-vel va-kho-LEE RA HU

3 Even if a man should beget a hundred children and live many years – no matter how many the days of his years may come to, if his gullet is not sated through his wealth, I say: The stillbirth, though it was not even accorded a burial, is more fortunate than he.

ג אִם־יוֹלִיד אִישׁ מֵאָה וְשָׁנִים רַבּוֹת יִחְיֶה וְרַב שֶׁיִּהְיוּ יְמֵי־שָׁנָיו וְנַפְשׁוֹ לֹא־תִשְׂבַּע מִן־הַטּוֹבָה וְגַם־קְבוּרָה לֹא־הָיְתָה לּוֹ אָמַרְתִּי טוֹב מִמֶּנּוּ הַנָּפֶל:

---

* "Another grave evil is this: He must depart just as he came" moved up from verse 15 for clarity

---

אוֹשֶׁר
עוֹשֶׁר

6:2 *Hashem* sometimes grants a man riches The Hebrew word for 'riches' is *osher*, spelled with the letter *ayin* (עושר). The Hebrew word for 'happiness' is also *osher*, but spelled with the letter *alef* (אושר). While the two words are homophones, they are not synonymous. Some people mistakenly believe that wealth leads to happiness. The Sages ("Ethics of the Fathers" 4:1), however, teach the exact opposite. "Who is wealthy? One who is happy with his lot." Only when a person is happy and satisfied with the material possessions that he has, no matter their value, can he be considered truly wealthy.

4 Though it comes into futility and departs into darkness, and its very name is covered with darkness,

ד כִּֽי־בַהֶ֥בֶל בָּ֖א וּבַחֹ֣שֶׁךְ יֵלֵ֑ךְ וּבַחֹ֖שֶׁךְ שְׁמ֥וֹ יְכֻסֶּֽה׃

5 though it has never seen or experienced the sun, it is better off than he –

ה גַּם־שֶׁ֥מֶשׁ לֹא־רָאָ֖ה וְלֹ֣א יָדָ֑ע נַ֥חַת לָזֶ֖ה מִזֶּֽה׃

6 yes, even if the other lived a thousand years twice over but never had his fill of enjoyment! For are not both of them bound for the same place?

ו וְאִלּ֣וּ חָיָ֗ה אֶ֤לֶף שָׁנִים֙ פַּעֲמַ֔יִם וְטוֹבָ֖ה לֹ֣א רָאָ֑ה הֲלֹ֛א אֶל־מָק֥וֹם אֶחָ֖ד הַכֹּ֥ל הוֹלֵֽךְ׃

7 All of man's earning is for the sake of his mouth, yet his gullet is not sated.

ז כָּל־עֲמַ֥ל הָאָדָ֖ם לְפִ֑יהוּ וְגַם־הַנֶּ֖פֶשׁ לֹ֥א תִמָּלֵֽא׃

8 What advantage then has the wise man over the fool, what advantage has the pauper who knows how to get on in life?

ח כִּ֣י מַה־יּוֹתֵ֤ר לֶחָכָם֙ מִֽן־הַכְּסִ֔יל מַה־לֶּעָנִ֣י יוֹדֵ֔עַ לַהֲלֹ֖ךְ נֶ֥גֶד הַֽחַיִּֽים׃

9 Is the feasting of the eyes more important than the pursuit of desire? That, too, is futility and pursuit of wind.

ט ט֛וֹב מַרְאֵ֥ה עֵינַ֖יִם מֵֽהֲלָךְ־נָ֑פֶשׁ גַּם־זֶ֥ה הֶ֖בֶל וּרְע֥וּת רֽוּחַ׃

10 Whatever happens, it was designated long ago and it was known that it would happen; as for man, he cannot contend with what is stronger than he.

י מַה־שֶּֽׁהָיָ֗ה כְּבָר֙ נִקְרָ֣א שְׁמ֔וֹ וְנוֹדָ֖ע אֲשֶׁר־ה֣וּא אָדָ֑ם וְלֹֽא־יוּכַ֣ל לָדִ֔ין עִ֥ם שהתקיף [שֶׁתַּקִּ֖יף] מִמֶּֽנּוּ׃

11 Often, much talk means much futility. How does it benefit a man?

יא כִּ֛י יֵשׁ־דְּבָרִ֥ים הַרְבֵּ֖ה מַרְבִּ֣ים הָ֑בֶל מַה־יֹּתֵ֖ר לָאָדָֽם׃

12 Who can possibly know what is best for a man to do in life – the few days of his fleeting life? For who can tell him what the future holds for him under the sun?

יב כִּ֣י מִֽי־יוֹדֵעַ֩ מַה־טּ֨וֹב לָֽאָדָ֜ם בַּֽחַיִּ֗ים מִסְפַּ֛ר יְמֵֽי־חַיֵּ֥י הֶבְל֖וֹ וְיַעֲשֵׂ֣ם כַּצֵּ֑ל אֲשֶׁ֣ר מִֽי־יַגִּ֣יד לָֽאָדָ֗ם מַה־יִּהְיֶ֧ה אַחֲרָ֛יו תַּ֥חַת הַשָּֽׁמֶשׁ׃

7 1 A good name is better than fragrant oil, and the day of death than the day of birth.

ז א ט֥וֹב שֵׁ֖ם מִשֶּׁ֣מֶן ט֑וֹב וְי֣וֹם הַמָּ֔וֶת מִיּ֖וֹם הִוָּלְדֽוֹ׃

2 It is better to go to a house of mourning than to a house of feasting; for that is the end of every man, and a living one should take it to heart.

ב ט֞וֹב לָלֶ֣כֶת אֶל־בֵּֽית־אֵ֗בֶל מִלֶּ֙כֶת֙ אֶל־בֵּ֣ית מִשְׁתֶּ֔ה בַּאֲשֶׁ֕ר ה֖וּא ס֣וֹף כָּל־הָאָדָ֑ם וְהַחַ֖י יִתֵּ֥ן אֶל־לִבּֽוֹ׃

3 Vexation is better than revelry; for though the face be sad, the heart may be glad.

ג ט֥וֹב כַּ֖עַס מִשְּׂחֹ֑ק כִּֽי־בְרֹ֥עַ פָּנִ֖ים יִ֥יטַב לֵֽב׃

4 Wise men are drawn to a house of mourning, and fools to a house of merrymaking.

ד לֵ֤ב חֲכָמִים֙ בְּבֵ֣ית אֵ֔בֶל וְלֵ֥ב כְּסִילִ֖ים בְּבֵ֥ית שִׂמְחָֽה׃

5 It is better to listen to a wise man's reproof than to listen to the praise of fools.

ה ט֕וֹב לִשְׁמֹ֖עַ גַּעֲרַ֣ת חָכָ֑ם מֵאִ֕ישׁ שֹׁמֵ֖עַ שִׁ֥יר כְּסִילִֽים׃

6 For the levity of the fool is like the crackling of nettles under a kettle. But that too is illusory;

ו כִּ֣י כְק֤וֹל הַסִּירִים֙ תַּ֣חַת הַסִּ֔יר כֵּ֖ן שְׂחֹ֣ק הַכְּסִ֑יל וְגַם־זֶ֖ה הָֽבֶל׃

7 for cheating may rob the wise man of reason and destroy the prudence of the cautious.

ז כִּ֣י הָעֹ֔שֶׁק יְהוֹלֵ֖ל חָכָ֑ם וִֽיאַבֵּ֥ד אֶת־לֵ֖ב מַתָּנָֽה׃

8 The end of a matter is better than the beginning of it. Better a patient spirit than a haughty spirit.

ח ט֣וֹב אַחֲרִ֣ית דָּבָ֔ר מֵֽרֵאשִׁית֑וֹ ט֥וֹב אֶֽרֶךְ־ר֖וּחַ מִגְּבַהּ־רֽוּחַ׃

⁹ Don't let your spirit be quickly vexed, for vexation abides in the breasts of fools.

ט אַל־תְּבַהֵל בְּרוּחֲךָ לִכְעוֹס כִּי כַעַס בְּחֵיק כְּסִילִים יָנוּחַ:

¹⁰ Don't say, "How has it happened that former times were better than these?" For it is not wise of you to ask that question.

י אַל־תֹּאמַר מֶה הָיָה שֶׁהַיָּמִים הָרִאשֹׁנִים הָיוּ טוֹבִים מֵאֵלֶּה כִּי לֹא מֵחָכְמָה שָׁאַלְתָּ עַל־זֶה:

¹¹ Wisdom is as good as a patrimony, and even better, for those who behold the sun.

יא טוֹבָה חָכְמָה עִם־נַחֲלָה וְיֹתֵר לְרֹאֵי הַשָּׁמֶשׁ:

to-VAH khokh-MAH im na-kha-LAH v'-yo-TAYR l'-ro-AY ha-SHA-mesh

¹² For to be in the shelter of wisdom is to be also in the shelter of money, and the advantage of intelligence is that wisdom preserves the life of him who possesses it.

יב כִּי בְּצֵל הַחָכְמָה בְּצֵל הַכָּסֶף וְיִתְרוֹן דַּעַת הַחָכְמָה תְּחַיֶּה בְעָלֶיהָ:

¹³ Consider *Hashem*'s doing! Who can straighten what He has twisted?

יג רְאֵה אֶת־מַעֲשֵׂה הָאֱלֹהִים כִּי מִי יוּכַל לְתַקֵּן אֵת אֲשֶׁר עִוְּתוֹ:

¹⁴ So in a time of good fortune enjoy the good fortune; and in a time of misfortune, reflect: The one no less than the other was *Hashem*'s doing; consequently, man may find no fault with Him.

יד בְּיוֹם טוֹבָה הֱיֵה בְטוֹב וּבְיוֹם רָעָה רְאֵה גַּם אֶת־זֶה לְעֻמַּת־זֶה עָשָׂה הָאֱלֹהִים עַל־דִּבְרַת שֶׁלֹּא יִמְצָא הָאָדָם אַחֲרָיו מְאוּמָה:

¹⁵ In my own brief span of life, I have seen both these things: sometimes a good man perishes in spite of his goodness, and sometimes a wicked one endures in spite of his wickedness.

טו אֶת־הַכֹּל רָאִיתִי בִּימֵי הֶבְלִי יֵשׁ צַדִּיק אֹבֵד בְּצִדְקוֹ וְיֵשׁ רָשָׁע מַאֲרִיךְ בְּרָעָתוֹ:

¹⁶ So don't overdo goodness and don't act the wise man to excess, or you may be dumfounded.

טז אַל־תְּהִי צַדִּיק הַרְבֵּה וְאַל־תִּתְחַכַּם יוֹתֵר לָמָּה תִּשּׁוֹמֵם:

¹⁷ Don't overdo wickedness and don't be a fool, or you may die before your time.

יז אַל־תִּרְשַׁע הַרְבֵּה וְאַל־תְּהִי סָכָל לָמָּה תָמוּת בְּלֹא עִתֶּךָ:

¹⁸ It is best that you grasp the one without letting go of the other, for one who fears *Hashem* will do his duty by both.

יח טוֹב אֲשֶׁר תֶּאֱחֹז בָּזֶה וְגַם־מִזֶּה אַל־תַּנַּח אֶת־יָדֶךָ כִּי־יְרֵא אֱלֹהִים יֵצֵא אֶת־כֻּלָּם:

7:11 Wisdom is as good as a patrimony The Sages teach that the wisdom in this verse is the knowledge of the *Torah*, and the patrimony refers to the Land of Israel, which is the eternal inheritance of the Jewish people. *Tova chochma im nachala* (טובה חכמה עם נחלה), translated here as 'Wisdom is as good as a patrimony,' literally means "Wisdom is good with an inheritance." This means that the wisdom of the *Torah* is enhanced by the "inheritance" that is *Eretz Yisrael*. The Sages further teach that "there is no *Torah* like the *Torah* of the Land of Israel," since the very air of Israel makes a person wise. Israel is the Jews' "natural habitat," and it is therefore the place in which they can flourish and reach their spiritual potential. Mizrachi, the religious-Zionist movement founded in nineteenth century Vilna, reflected this sentiment in their motto: "The Land of Israel for the People of Israel, according to the *Torah* of Israel." Among other things, Mizrachi's mission, from its inception until today, has been working towards the economic and spiritual development of *Eretz Yisrael*.

Students studying Talmud in Tiberias

¹⁹ Wisdom is more of a stronghold to a wise man than ten magnates that a city may contain.

²⁰ For there is not one good man on earth who does what is best and doesn't err.

²¹ Finally, don't pay attention to everything that is said, so that you may not hear your slave reviling you;

²² for well you remember the many times that you yourself have reviled others.

²³ All this I tested with wisdom. I thought I could fathom it, but it eludes me.

²⁴ [The secret of] what happens is elusive and deep, deep down; who can discover it?

²⁵ I put my mind to studying, exploring, and seeking wisdom and the reason of things, and to studying wickedness, stupidity, madness, and folly.

²⁶ Now, I find woman more bitter than death; she is all traps, her hands are fetters and her heart is snares. He who is pleasing to *Hashem* escapes her, and he who is displeasing is caught by her.

²⁷ See, this is what I found, said *Kohelet*, item by item in my search for the reason of things.

²⁸ As for what I sought further but did not find, I found only one human being in a thousand, and the one I found among so many was never a woman.

²⁹ But, see, this I did find: *Hashem* made men plain, but they have engaged in too much reasoning.

8 ¹ Who is like the wise man, and who knows the meaning of the adage: "A man's wisdom lights up his face, So that his deep discontent is dissembled"?

² I do! "Obey the king's orders – and don't rush into uttering an oath by *Hashem*."

³ Leave his presence; do not tarry in a dangerous situation, for he can do anything he pleases;

⁴ inasmuch as a king's command is authoritative, and none can say to him, "What are you doing?"

⁵ One who obeys orders will not suffer from the dangerous situation. A wise man, however, will bear in mind that there is a time of doom.

יט הַחׇכְמָה תָּעֹז לֶחָכָם מֵעֲשָׂרָה שַׁלִּיטִים אֲשֶׁר הָיוּ בָּעִיר:

כ כִּי אָדָם אֵין צַדִּיק בָּאָרֶץ אֲשֶׁר יַעֲשֶׂה־טּוֹב וְלֹא יֶחֱטָא:

כא גַּם לְכׇל־הַדְּבָרִים אֲשֶׁר יְדַבֵּרוּ אַל־תִּתֵּן לִבֶּךָ אֲשֶׁר לֹא־תִשְׁמַע אֶת־עַבְדְּךָ מְקַלְלֶךָ:

כב כִּי גַּם־פְּעָמִים רַבּוֹת יָדַע לִבֶּךָ אֲשֶׁר גַּם־[אַתָּה] קִלַּלְתָּ אֲחֵרִים:

כג כׇּל־זֹה נִסִּיתִי בַחׇכְמָה אָמַרְתִּי אֶחְכָּמָה וְהִיא רְחוֹקָה מִמֶּנִּי:

כד רָחוֹק מַה־שֶּׁהָיָה וְעָמֹק עָמֹק מִי יִמְצָאֶנּוּ:

כה סַבּוֹתִי אֲנִי וְלִבִּי לָדַעַת וְלָתוּר וּבַקֵּשׁ חׇכְמָה וְחֶשְׁבּוֹן וְלָדַעַת רֶשַׁע כֶּסֶל וְהַסִּכְלוּת הוֹלֵלוֹת:

כו וּמוֹצֶא אֲנִי מַר מִמָּוֶת אֶת־הָאִשָּׁה אֲשֶׁר־הִיא מְצוֹדִים וַחֲרָמִים לִבָּהּ אֲסוּרִים יָדֶיהָ טוֹב לִפְנֵי הָאֱלֹהִים יִמָּלֵט מִמֶּנָּה וְחוֹטֵא יִלָּכֶד בָּהּ:

כז רְאֵה זֶה מָצָאתִי אָמְרָה קֹהֶלֶת אַחַת לְאַחַת לִמְצֹא חֶשְׁבּוֹן:

כח אֲשֶׁר עוֹד־בִּקְשָׁה נַפְשִׁי וְלֹא מָצָאתִי אָדָם אֶחָד מֵאֶלֶף מָצָאתִי וְאִשָּׁה בְכׇל־אֵלֶּה לֹא מָצָאתִי:

כט לְבַד רְאֵה־זֶה מָצָאתִי אֲשֶׁר עָשָׂה הָאֱלֹהִים אֶת־הָאָדָם יָשָׁר וְהֵמָּה בִקְשׁוּ חִשְּׁבֹנוֹת רַבִּים:

ח א מִי כְּהֶחָכָם וּמִי יוֹדֵעַ פֵּשֶׁר דָּבָר חׇכְמַת אָדָם תָּאִיר פָּנָיו וְעֹז פָּנָיו יְשֻׁנֶּא:

ב אֲנִי פִּי־מֶלֶךְ שְׁמוֹר וְעַל דִּבְרַת שְׁבוּעַת אֱלֹהִים:

ג אַל־תִּבָּהֵל מִפָּנָיו תֵּלֵךְ אַל־תַּעֲמֹד בְּדָבָר רָע כִּי כׇּל־אֲשֶׁר יַחְפֹּץ יַעֲשֶׂה:

ד בַּאֲשֶׁר דְּבַר־מֶלֶךְ שִׁלְטוֹן וּמִי יֹאמַר־לוֹ מַה־תַּעֲשֶׂה:

ה שׁוֹמֵר מִצְוָה לֹא יֵדַע דָּבָר רָע וְעֵת וּמִשְׁפָּט יֵדַע לֵב חָכָם:

⁶ For there is a time for every experience, including the doom; for a man's calamity overwhelms him.

כִּי לְכָל־חֵפֶץ יֵשׁ עֵת וּמִשְׁפָּט כִּי־רָעַת הָאָדָם רַבָּה עָלָיו:

> *KEE l'-khol KHAY-fetz YAYSH AYT u-mish-PAT*
> *kee ra-AT ha-a-DAM ra-BAH a-LAV*

⁷ Indeed, he does not know what is to happen; even when it is on the point of happening, who can tell him?

כִּי־אֵינֶנּוּ יֹדֵעַ מַה־שֶּׁיִּהְיֶה כִּי כַּאֲשֶׁר יִהְיֶה מִי יַגִּיד לוֹ:

⁸ No man has authority over the lifebreath – to hold back the lifebreath; there is no authority over the day of death. There is no mustering out from that war; wickedness is powerless to save its owner.

אֵין אָדָם שַׁלִּיט בָּרוּחַ לִכְלוֹא אֶת־הָרוּחַ וְאֵין שִׁלְטוֹן בְּיוֹם הַמָּוֶת וְאֵין מִשְׁלַחַת בַּמִּלְחָמָה וְלֹא־יְמַלֵּט רֶשַׁע אֶת־בְּעָלָיו:

⁹ All these things I observed; I noted all that went on under the sun, while men still had authority over men to treat them unjustly.

אֶת־כָּל־זֶה רָאִיתִי וְנָתוֹן אֶת־לִבִּי לְכָל־מַעֲשֶׂה אֲשֶׁר נַעֲשָׂה תַּחַת הַשָּׁמֶשׁ עֵת אֲשֶׁר שָׁלַט הָאָדָם בְּאָדָם לְרַע לוֹ:

¹⁰ And then I saw scoundrels coming from the Holy Site and being brought to burial, while such as had acted righteously were forgotten in the city. And here is another frustration:

וּבְכֵן רָאִיתִי רְשָׁעִים קְבֻרִים וָבָאוּ וּמִמְּקוֹם קָדוֹשׁ יְהַלֵּכוּ וְיִשְׁתַּכְּחוּ בָעִיר אֲשֶׁר כֵּן־עָשׂוּ גַּם־זֶה הָבֶל:

¹¹ the fact that the sentence imposed for evil deeds is not executed swiftly, which is why men are emboldened to do evil –

אֲשֶׁר אֵין־נַעֲשָׂה פִתְגָם מַעֲשֵׂה הָרָעָה מְהֵרָה עַל־כֵּן מָלֵא לֵב בְּנֵי־הָאָדָם בָּהֶם לַעֲשׂוֹת רָע:

¹² the fact that a sinner may do evil a hundred times and his [punishment] still be delayed. For although I am aware that "It will be well with those who revere *Hashem* since they revere Him,

אֲשֶׁר חֹטֶא עֹשֶׂה רָע מְאַת וּמַאֲרִיךְ לוֹ כִּי גַּם־יוֹדֵעַ אָנִי אֲשֶׁר יִהְיֶה־טּוֹב לְיִרְאֵי הָאֱלֹהִים אֲשֶׁר יִירְאוּ מִלְּפָנָיו:

¹³ and it will not be well with the scoundrel, and he will not live long, because he does not revere *Hashem*" –

וְטוֹב לֹא־יִהְיֶה לָרָשָׁע וְלֹא־יַאֲרִיךְ יָמִים כַּצֵּל אֲשֶׁר אֵינֶנּוּ יָרֵא מִלִּפְנֵי אֱלֹהִים:

¹⁴ here is a frustration that occurs in the world: sometimes an upright man is requited according to the conduct of the scoundrel; and sometimes the scoundrel is requited according to the conduct of the upright. I say all that is frustration.

יֵשׁ־הֶבֶל אֲשֶׁר נַעֲשָׂה עַל־הָאָרֶץ אֲשֶׁר יֵשׁ צַדִּיקִים אֲשֶׁר מַגִּיעַ אֲלֵהֶם כְּמַעֲשֵׂה הָרְשָׁעִים וְיֵשׁ רְשָׁעִים שֶׁמַּגִּיעַ אֲלֵהֶם כְּמַעֲשֵׂה הַצַּדִּיקִים אָמַרְתִּי שֶׁגַּם־זֶה הָבֶל:

8:6 For there is a time for every experience The word *chaifetz* (חפץ), translated here as 'experience,' also means 'desire.' *Sforno* explains that this verse means that God desires that various biblical commandments be observed at specific times of the year. Each season contains unique powers. The month of *Elul*, for example, which precedes the High Holidays, is conducive to repentance. *Adar*, the month in which the joyous holiday of *Purim* is celebrated, is a month of happiness, while *Av*, the month in which the two Temples in *Yerushalayim* were destroyed, is a month of mourning.

Each year, a person can tap into the different powers corresponding to the different times of year. The Sages tell us that the exodus from Egypt took place in the month of *Nisan*, the month in which the holiday of *Pesach* is celebrated, and that the ultimate redemption will take place then as well. Therefore, a prayer for redemption is included in the *Pesach* seder, which ends with the words "next year in *Yerushalayim*."

Purim celebrations in the streets of Yerushalayim

¹⁵ I therefore praised enjoyment. For the only good a man can have under the sun is to eat and drink and enjoy himself. That much can accompany him, in exchange for his wealth, through the days of life that *Hashem* has granted him under the sun.

טו וְשִׁבַּחְתִּי אֲנִי אֶת־הַשִּׂמְחָה אֲשֶׁר אֵין־טוֹב לָאָדָם תַּחַת הַשֶּׁמֶשׁ כִּי אִם־לֶאֱכוֹל וְלִשְׁתּוֹת וְלִשְׂמוֹחַ וְהוּא יִלְוֶנּוּ בַעֲמָלוֹ יְמֵי חַיָּיו אֲשֶׁר־נָתַן־לוֹ הָאֱלֹהִים תַּחַת הַשָּׁמֶשׁ:

¹⁶ For I have set my mind to learn wisdom and to observe the business that goes on in the world – even to the extent of going without sleep day and night –

טז כַּאֲשֶׁר נָתַתִּי אֶת־לִבִּי לָדַעַת חָכְמָה וְלִרְאוֹת אֶת־הָעִנְיָן אֲשֶׁר נַעֲשָׂה עַל־הָאָרֶץ כִּי גַם בַּיּוֹם וּבַלַּיְלָה שֵׁנָה בְּעֵינָיו אֵינֶנּוּ רֹאֶה:

¹⁷ and I have observed all that *Hashem* brings to pass. Indeed, man cannot guess the events that occur under the sun. For man tries strenuously, but fails to guess them; and even if a sage should think to discover them he would not be able to guess them.

יז וְרָאִיתִי אֶת־כָּל־מַעֲשֵׂה הָאֱלֹהִים כִּי לֹא יוּכַל הָאָדָם לִמְצוֹא אֶת־הַמַּעֲשֶׂה אֲשֶׁר נַעֲשָׂה תַחַת־הַשֶּׁמֶשׁ בְּשֶׁל אֲשֶׁר יַעֲמֹל הָאָדָם לְבַקֵּשׁ וְלֹא יִמְצָא וְגַם אִם־יֹאמַר הֶחָכָם לָדַעַת לֹא יוּכַל לִמְצֹא:

9 ¹ For all this I noted, and I ascertained all this: that the actions of even the righteous and the wise are determined by *Hashem*. Even love! Even hate! Man knows none of these in advance –

ט א כִּי אֶת־כָּל־זֶה נָתַתִּי אֶל־לִבִּי וְלָבוּר אֶת־כָּל־זֶה אֲשֶׁר הַצַּדִּיקִים וְהַחֲכָמִים וַעֲבָדֵיהֶם בְּיַד הָאֱלֹהִים גַּם־אַהֲבָה גַם־שִׂנְאָה אֵין יוֹדֵעַ הָאָדָם הַכֹּל לִפְנֵיהֶם:

² none! For the same fate is in store for all: for the righteous, and for the wicked; for the good and pure, and for the impure; for him who sacrifices, and for him who does not; for him who is pleasing, and for him who is displeasing; and for him who swears, and for him who shuns oaths.

ב הַכֹּל כַּאֲשֶׁר לַכֹּל מִקְרֶה אֶחָד לַצַּדִּיק וְלָרָשָׁע לַטּוֹב וְלַטָּהוֹר וְלַטָּמֵא וְלַזֹּבֵחַ וְלַאֲשֶׁר אֵינֶנּוּ זֹבֵחַ כַּטּוֹב כַּחֹטֶא הַנִּשְׁבָּע כַּאֲשֶׁר שְׁבוּעָה יָרֵא:

³ That is the sad thing about all that goes on under the sun: that the same fate is in store for all. (Not only that, but men's hearts are full of sadness, and their minds of madness, while they live; and then – to the dead!)

ג זֶה רָע בְּכֹל אֲשֶׁר־נַעֲשָׂה תַּחַת הַשֶּׁמֶשׁ כִּי־מִקְרֶה אֶחָד לַכֹּל וְגַם לֵב בְּנֵי־הָאָדָם מָלֵא־רָע וְהוֹלֵלוֹת בִּלְבָבָם בְּחַיֵּיהֶם וְאַחֲרָיו אֶל־הַמֵּתִים:

⁴ For he who is reckoned among the living has something to look forward to – even a live dog is better than a dead lion –

ד כִּי־מִי אֲשֶׁר יבחר [יְחֻבַּר] אֶל כָּל־הַחַיִּים יֵשׁ בִּטָּחוֹן כִּי־לְכֶלֶב חַי הוּא טוֹב מִן־הָאַרְיֵה הַמֵּת:

⁵ since the living know they will die. But the dead know nothing; they have no more recompense, for even the memory of them has died.

ה כִּי הַחַיִּים יוֹדְעִים שֶׁיָּמֻתוּ וְהַמֵּתִים אֵינָם יוֹדְעִים מְאוּמָה וְאֵין־עוֹד לָהֶם שָׂכָר כִּי נִשְׁכַּח זִכְרָם:

⁶ Their loves, their hates, their jealousies have long since perished; and they have no more share till the end of time in all that goes on under the sun.

ו גַּם אַהֲבָתָם גַּם־שִׂנְאָתָם גַּם־קִנְאָתָם כְּבָר אָבָדָה וְחֵלֶק אֵין־לָהֶם עוֹד לְעוֹלָם בְּכֹל אֲשֶׁר־נַעֲשָׂה תַּחַת הַשָּׁמֶשׁ:

⁷ Go, eat your bread in gladness, and drink your wine in joy; for your action was long ago approved by *Hashem*.

ז לֵךְ אֱכֹל בְּשִׂמְחָה לַחְמֶךָ וּשְׁתֵה בְלֶב־טוֹב יֵינֶךָ כִּי כְבָר רָצָה הָאֱלֹהִים אֶת־מַעֲשֶׂיךָ:

8   Let your clothes always be freshly washed, and your head never lack ointment.

בְּכָל־עֵת יִהְיוּ בְגָדֶיךָ לְבָנִים וְשֶׁמֶן עַל־רֹאשְׁךָ אַל־יֶחְסָר׃

b'-khol AYT yih-YU v'-ga-DE-kha l'-va-NEEM
v'-SHE-men al ro-sh'-KHA al yekh-SAR

9   Enjoy happiness with a woman you love all the fleeting days of life that have been granted to you under the sun – all your fleeting days. For that alone is what you can get out of life and out of the means you acquire under the sun.

רְאֵה חַיִּים עִם־אִשָּׁה אֲשֶׁר־אָהַבְתָּ כָּל־יְמֵי חַיֵּי הֶבְלֶךָ אֲשֶׁר נָתַן־לְךָ תַּחַת הַשֶּׁמֶשׁ כֹּל יְמֵי הֶבְלֶךָ כִּי הוּא חֶלְקְךָ בַּחַיִּים וּבַעֲמָלְךָ אֲשֶׁר־אַתָּה עָמֵל תַּחַת הַשָּׁמֶשׁ׃

10 Whatever it is in your power to do, do with all your might. For there is no action, no reasoning, no learning, no wisdom in Sheol, where you are going.

כֹּל אֲשֶׁר תִּמְצָא יָדְךָ לַעֲשׂוֹת בְּכֹחֲךָ עֲשֵׂה כִּי אֵין מַעֲשֶׂה וְחֶשְׁבּוֹן וְדַעַת וְחָכְמָה בִּשְׁאוֹל אֲשֶׁר אַתָּה הֹלֵךְ שָׁמָּה׃

11 I have further observed under the sun that The race is not won by the swift, Nor the battle by the valiant; Nor is bread won by the wise, Nor wealth by the intelligent, Nor favor by the learned. For the time of mischance comes to all.

שַׁבְתִּי וְרָאֹה תַחַת־הַשֶּׁמֶשׁ כִּי לֹא לַקַּלִּים הַמֵּרוֹץ וְלֹא לַגִּבּוֹרִים הַמִּלְחָמָה וְגַם לֹא לַחֲכָמִים לֶחֶם וְגַם לֹא לַנְּבֹנִים עֹשֶׁר וְגַם לֹא לַיֹּדְעִים חֵן כִּי־עֵת וָפֶגַע יִקְרֶה אֶת־כֻּלָּם׃

12 And a man cannot even know his time. As fishes are enmeshed in a fatal net, and as birds are trapped in a snare, so men are caught at the time of calamity, when it comes upon them without warning.

כִּי גַם לֹא־יֵדַע הָאָדָם אֶת־עִתּוֹ כַּדָּגִים שֶׁנֶּאֱחָזִים בִּמְצוֹדָה רָעָה וְכַצִּפֳּרִים הָאֲחֻזוֹת בַּפָּח כָּהֵם יוּקָשִׁים בְּנֵי הָאָדָם לְעֵת רָעָה כְּשֶׁתִּפּוֹל עֲלֵיהֶם פִּתְאֹם׃

13 This thing too I observed under the sun about wisdom, and it affected me profoundly.

גַּם־זֹה רָאִיתִי חָכְמָה תַּחַת הַשָּׁמֶשׁ וּגְדוֹלָה הִיא אֵלָי׃

14 There was a little city, with few men in it; and to it came a great king, who invested it and built mighty siege works against it.

עִיר קְטַנָּה וַאֲנָשִׁים בָּהּ מְעָט וּבָא־אֵלֶיהָ מֶלֶךְ גָּדוֹל וְסָבַב אֹתָהּ וּבָנָה עָלֶיהָ מְצוֹדִים גְּדֹלִים׃

15 Present in the city was a poor wise man who might have saved it with his wisdom, but nobody thought of that poor man.

וּמָצָא בָהּ אִישׁ מִסְכֵּן חָכָם וּמִלַּט־הוּא אֶת־הָעִיר בְּחָכְמָתוֹ וְאָדָם לֹא זָכַר אֶת־הָאִישׁ הַמִּסְכֵּן הַהוּא׃

16 So I observed: Wisdom is better than valor; but A poor man's wisdom is scorned, And his words are not heeded.

וְאָמַרְתִּי אָנִי טוֹבָה חָכְמָה מִגְּבוּרָה וְחָכְמַת הַמִּסְכֵּן בְּזוּיָה וּדְבָרָיו אֵינָם נִשְׁמָעִים׃

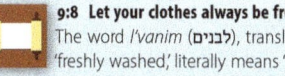 **9:8 Let your clothes always be freshly washed** The word *l'vanim* (לבנים), translated here as 'freshly washed,' literally means 'white.' Some explain that this verse refers to the High Priest's service in the Temple on *Yom Kippur*, the Day of Atonement. When he entered the Holy of Holies on that holiest day of the year, the *Kohen Gadol* wore special clothing that were entirely white, instead of his regular colorful attire. The goal of his service was to bring atonement to the entire Jewish people. The High Priest conducted the service wearing white, which is synonymous with purity, as *Ye-*shayahu states regarding the purification of sin: "Be your sins like crimson, they can turn snow-white" (Isaiah 1:18). This verse instructs every person that their garments should always be white and freshly washed, meaning that one should strive to be in a constant state of purity and innocence.

Clean white laundry drying in the sun, Akko

¹⁷ Words spoken softly by wise men are heeded sooner than those shouted by a lord in folly.

דִּבְרֵי חֲכָמִים בְּנַחַת נִשְׁמָעִים מִזַּעֲקַת מוֹשֵׁל בַּכְּסִילִים: יז

¹⁸ Wisdom is more valuable than weapons of war, but a single error destroys much of value.

טוֹבָה חָכְמָה מִכְּלֵי קְרָב וְחוֹטֶא אֶחָד יְאַבֵּד טוֹבָה הַרְבֵּה: יח

10 ¹ Dead flies turn the perfumer's ointment fetid and putrid; so a little folly outweighs massive wisdom.

זְבוּבֵי מָוֶת יַבְאִישׁ יַבִּיעַ שֶׁמֶן רוֹקֵחַ יָקָר מֵחָכְמָה מִכָּבוֹד סִכְלוּת מְעָט: י א

² A wise man's mind tends toward the right hand, a fool's toward the left.

לֵב חָכָם לִימִינוֹ וְלֵב כְּסִיל לִשְׂמֹאלוֹ: ב

³ A fool's mind is also wanting when he travels, and he lets everybody know he is a fool.

וְגַם־בַּדֶּרֶךְ כשהסכל [כְּשֶׁסָּכָל] הֹלֵךְ לִבּוֹ חָסֵר וְאָמַר לַכֹּל סָכָל הוּא: ג

⁴ If the wrath of a lord flares up against you, don't give up your post; for when wrath abates, grave offenses are pardoned.

אִם־רוּחַ הַמּוֹשֵׁל תַּעֲלֶה עָלֶיךָ מְקוֹמְךָ אַל־תַּנַּח כִּי מַרְפֵּא יַנִּיחַ חֲטָאִים גְּדוֹלִים: ד

⁵ Here is an evil I have seen under the sun as great as an error committed by a ruler:

יֵשׁ רָעָה רָאִיתִי תַּחַת הַשָּׁמֶשׁ כִּשְׁגָגָה שֶׁיֹּצָא מִלִּפְנֵי הַשַּׁלִּיט: ה

⁶ Folly was placed on lofty heights, while rich men sat in low estate.

נִתַּן הַסֶּכֶל בַּמְּרוֹמִים רַבִּים וַעֲשִׁירִים בַּשֵּׁפֶל יֵשֵׁבוּ: ו

⁷ I have seen slaves on horseback, and nobles walking on the ground like slaves.

רָאִיתִי עֲבָדִים עַל־סוּסִים וְשָׂרִים הֹלְכִים כַּעֲבָדִים עַל־הָאָרֶץ: ז

⁸ He who digs a pit will fall into it; he who breaches a stone fence will be bitten by a snake.

חֹפֵר גּוּמָץ בּוֹ יִפּוֹל וּפֹרֵץ גָּדֵר יִשְּׁכֶנּוּ נָחָשׁ: ח

⁹ He who quarries stones will be hurt by them; he who splits wood will be harmed by it.

מַסִּיעַ אֲבָנִים יֵעָצֵב בָּהֶם בּוֹקֵעַ עֵצִים יִסָּכֶן בָּם: ט

¹⁰ If the ax has become dull and he has not whetted the edge, he must exert more strength. Thus the advantage of a skill [depends on the exercise of] prudence.

אִם־קֵהָה הַבַּרְזֶל וְהוּא לֹא־פָנִים קִלְקַל וַחֲיָלִים יְגַבֵּר וְיִתְרוֹן הכשיר [הַכְשֵׁר] חָכְמָה: י

¹¹ If the snake bites because no spell was uttered, no advantage is gained by the trained charmer.

אִם־יִשֹּׁךְ הַנָּחָשׁ בְּלוֹא־לָחַשׁ וְאֵין יִתְרוֹן לְבַעַל הַלָּשׁוֹן: יא

¹² A wise man's talk brings him favor, but a fool's lips are his undoing.

דִּבְרֵי פִי־חָכָם חֵן וְשִׂפְתוֹת כְּסִיל תְּבַלְּעֶנּוּ: יב

¹³ His talk begins as silliness and ends as disastrous madness.

תְּחִלַּת דִּבְרֵי־פִיהוּ סִכְלוּת וְאַחֲרִית פִּיהוּ הוֹלֵלוּת רָעָה: יג

¹⁴ Yet the fool talks and talks! A man cannot know what will happen; who can tell him what the future holds?

וְהַסָּכָל יַרְבֶּה דְבָרִים לֹא־יֵדַע הָאָדָם מַה־שֶׁיִּהְיֶה וַאֲשֶׁר יִהְיֶה מֵאַחֲרָיו מִי יַגִּיד לוֹ: יד

¹⁵ A fool's exertions tire him out, for he doesn't know how to get to a town.

עֲמַל הַכְּסִילִים תְּיַגְּעֶנּוּ אֲשֶׁר לֹא־יָדַע לָלֶכֶת אֶל־עִיר: טו

¹⁶ Alas for you, O land whose king is a lackey and whose ministers dine in the morning!

טז אִי־לָ֣ךְ אֶ֔רֶץ שֶׁמַּלְכֵּ֖ךְ נָ֑עַר וְשָׂרַ֖יִךְ בַּבֹּ֥קֶר יֹאכֵֽלוּ׃

¹⁷ Happy are you, O land whose king is a master and whose ministers dine at the proper time – with restraint, not with guzzling!

יז אַשְׁרֵ֣יךְ אֶ֔רֶץ שֶׁמַּלְכֵּ֖ךְ בֶּן־חוֹרִ֑ים וְשָׂרַ֤יִךְ בָּעֵ֣ת יֹאכֵ֔לוּ בִּגְבוּרָ֖ה וְלֹ֥א בַשְּׁתִֽי׃

¹⁸ Through slothfulness the ceiling sags, Through lazy hands the house caves in.

יח בַּעֲצַלְתַּ֖יִם יִמַּ֣ךְ הַמְּקָרֶ֑ה וּבְשִׁפְל֥וּת יָדַ֖יִם יִדְלֹ֥ף הַבָּֽיִת׃

¹⁹ They make a banquet for revelry; wine makes life merry, and money answers every need.

יט לִשְׂחוֹק֙ עֹשִׂ֣ים לֶ֔חֶם וְיַ֖יִן יְשַׂמַּ֣ח חַיִּ֑ים וְהַכֶּ֖סֶף יַעֲנֶ֥ה אֶת־הַכֹּֽל׃

lis-KHOK o-SEEM LE-khem v'-YA-yin y'-sa-MAKH kha-YEEM v'-ha-KE-sef ya-a-NEH et ha-KOL

²⁰ Don't revile a king even among your intimates. Don't revile a rich man even in your bedchamber; For a bird of the air may carry the utterance, And a winged creature may report the word.

כ גַּ֣ם בְּמַדָּֽעֲךָ֗ מֶ֚לֶךְ אַל־תְּקַלֵּ֔ל וּבְחַדְרֵי֙ מִשְׁכָּ֣בְךָ֔ אַל־תְּקַלֵּ֖ל עָשִׁ֑יר כִּ֣י ע֤וֹף הַשָּׁמַ֙יִם֙ יוֹלִ֣יךְ אֶת־הַקּ֔וֹל וּבַ֥עַל הכנפים [כְּנָפַ֖יִם] יַגֵּ֥יד דָּבָֽר׃

11 ¹ Send your bread forth upon the waters; for after many days you will find it.

א שַׁלַּ֥ח לַחְמְךָ֖ עַל־פְּנֵ֣י הַמָּ֑יִם כִּֽי־בְרֹ֥ב הַיָּמִ֖ים תִּמְצָאֶֽנּוּ׃

² Distribute portions to seven or even to eight, for you cannot know what misfortune may occur on earth.

ב תֶּן־חֵ֥לֶק לְשִׁבְעָ֖ה וְגַ֣ם לִשְׁמוֹנָ֑ה כִּ֚י לֹ֣א תֵדַ֔ע מַה־יִּהְיֶ֥ה רָעָ֖ה עַל־הָאָֽרֶץ׃

³ If the clouds are filled, they will pour down rain on the earth; and if a tree falls to the south or to the north, the tree will stay where it falls.

ג אִם־יִמָּלְא֨וּ הֶעָבִ֥ים גֶּ֙שֶׁם֙ עַל־הָאָ֣רֶץ יָרִ֔יקוּ וְאִם־יִפּ֥וֹל עֵ֛ץ בַּדָּר֖וֹם וְאִ֣ם בַּצָּפ֑וֹן מְק֛וֹם שֶׁיִּפּ֥וֹל הָעֵ֖ץ שָׁ֥ם יְהֽוּא׃

⁴ If one watches the wind, he will never sow; and if one observes the clouds, he will never reap.

ד שֹׁמֵ֥ר ר֖וּחַ לֹ֣א יִזְרָ֑ע וְרֹאֶ֥ה בֶעָבִ֖ים לֹ֥א יִקְצֽוֹר׃

⁵ Just as you do not know how the lifebreath passes into the limbs within the womb of the pregnant woman, so you cannot foresee the actions of *Hashem*, who causes all things to happen.

ה כַּאֲשֶׁ֨ר אֵֽינְךָ֤ יוֹדֵ֙עַ֙ מַה־דֶּ֣רֶךְ הָר֔וּחַ כַּעֲצָמִ֖ים בְּבֶ֣טֶן הַמְּלֵאָ֑ה כָּ֗כָה לֹ֤א תֵדַע֙ אֶת־מַעֲשֵׂ֣ה הָאֱלֹהִ֔ים אֲשֶׁ֥ר יַעֲשֶׂ֖ה אֶת־הַכֹּֽל׃

⁶ Sow your seed in the morning, and don't hold back your hand in the evening, since you don't know which is going to succeed, the one or the other, or if both are equally good.

ו בַּבֹּ֙קֶר֙ זְרַ֣ע אֶת־זַרְעֶ֔ךָ וְלָעֶ֖רֶב אַל־תַּנַּ֣ח יָדֶ֑ךָ כִּ֣י אֵֽינְךָ֤ יוֹדֵ֙עַ֙ אֵ֣י זֶ֤ה יִכְשָׁר֙ הֲזֶ֣ה אוֹ־זֶ֔ה וְאִם־שְׁנֵיהֶ֥ם כְּאֶחָ֖ד טוֹבִֽים׃

כֶּסֶף **10:19 Money answers every need** Following the previous verse which opposes laziness, this verse encourages man to be industrious and to earn money. *Metzudat David* comments that unlike other pleasures, money is helpful in all situations. Whether a person is sick or healthy, happy or depressed, everybody benefits from financial stability. The Hebrew word for 'money' is *kesef* (כסף), related to the verb *kasaf* (כ-ס-ף) which means to 'yearn.' Money is something for which all people yearn, and that is what gives it its value. However, as King *Shlomo* warns in other verses (see 5:9), the pursuit of wealth for its own sake is futile; it must only be used in the service of *Hashem*.

Tel Aviv/Ramat Gan financial district at sunset

7 How sweet is the light, what a delight for the eyes to behold the sun!

ז וּמָתוֹק הָאוֹר וְטוֹב לַעֵינַיִם לִרְאוֹת אֶת־הַשָּׁמֶשׁ:

8 Even if a man lives many years, let him enjoy himself in all of them, remembering how many the days of darkness are going to be. The only future is nothingness!

ח כִּי אִם־שָׁנִים הַרְבֵּה יִחְיֶה הָאָדָם בְּכֻלָּם יִשְׂמָח וְיִזְכֹּר אֶת־יְמֵי הַחֹשֶׁךְ כִּי־הַרְבֵּה יִהְיוּ כָּל־שֶׁבָּא הָבֶל:

9 O youth, enjoy yourself while you are young! Let your heart lead you to enjoyment in the days of your youth. Follow the desires of your heart and the glances of your eyes – but know well that *Hashem* will call you to account for all such things –

ט שְׂמַח בָּחוּר בְּיַלְדוּתֶיךָ וִיטִיבְךָ לִבְּךָ בִּימֵי בְחוּרוֹתֶךָ וְהַלֵּךְ בְּדַרְכֵי לִבְּךָ וּבְמַרְאֵי עֵינֶיךָ וְדַע כִּי עַל־כָּל־אֵלֶּה יְבִיאֲךָ הָאֱלֹהִים בַּמִּשְׁפָּט:

s'-MAKH ba-KHUR b'-yal-du-TE-kha vee-tee-v'-KHA li-b'-KHA bee-MAY v'-khu-ro-TE-kha v'-ha-LAYKH b'-dar-KHAY li-b'-KHA uv-mar-AY ay-NE-kha v'-DA KEE al kol AY-leh y'-vee-a-KHA ha-e-lo-HEEM ba-mish-PAT

10 and banish care from your mind, and pluck sorrow out of your flesh! For youth and black hair are fleeting.

י וְהָסֵר כַּעַס מִלִּבֶּךָ וְהַעֲבֵר רָעָה מִבְּשָׂרֶךָ כִּי־הַיַּלְדוּת וְהַשַּׁחֲרוּת הָבֶל:

12 1 So appreciate your vigor in the days of your youth, before those days of sorrow come and those years arrive of which you will say, "I have no pleasure in them";

יב א וּזְכֹר אֶת־בּוֹרְאֶיךָ בִּימֵי בְּחוּרֹתֶיךָ עַד אֲשֶׁר לֹא־יָבֹאוּ יְמֵי הָרָעָה וְהִגִּיעוּ שָׁנִים אֲשֶׁר תֹּאמַר אֵין־לִי בָהֶם חֵפֶץ:

2 before sun and light and moon and stars grow dark, and the clouds come back again after the rain:

ב עַד אֲשֶׁר לֹא־תֶחְשַׁךְ הַשֶּׁמֶשׁ וְהָאוֹר וְהַיָּרֵחַ וְהַכּוֹכָבִים וְשָׁבוּ הֶעָבִים אַחַר הַגָּשֶׁם:

3 When the guards of the house become shaky, And the men of valor are bent, And the maids that grind, grown few, are idle, And the ladies that peer through the windows grow dim,

ג בַּיּוֹם שֶׁיָּזֻעוּ שֹׁמְרֵי הַבַּיִת וְהִתְעַוְּתוּ אַנְשֵׁי הֶחָיִל וּבָטְלוּ הַטֹּחֲנוֹת כִּי מִעֵטוּ וְחָשְׁכוּ הָרֹאוֹת בָּאֲרֻבּוֹת:

4 And the doors to the street are shut – With the noise of the hand mill growing fainter, And the song of the bird growing feebler, And all the strains of music dying down;

ד וְסֻגְּרוּ דְלָתַיִם בַּשּׁוּק בִּשְׁפַל קוֹל הַטַּחֲנָה וְיָקוּם לְקוֹל הַצִּפּוֹר וְיִשַּׁחוּ כָּל־בְּנוֹת הַשִּׁיר:

An adolescent boy at the Mediterranean coast near Ashkelon

11:9 O youth, enjoy yourself while you are young! The Hebrew word for 'youth' is *bachur* (בחור), related to the word *bachar* (בחר) which means to 'chose'. The years of one's youth, from adolescence to early adulthood, are specifically a time of life-impacting choices. The young adult observes the world critically, and makes decisions that can impact the rest of his or her life regarding where to live, who to marry and what to do professionally. The young person mentioned here is encouraged to "follow the desires of your heart and the glances of your eyes," but is cautioned not to be led astray by desires, and is reminded that there will be accountability for these choices.

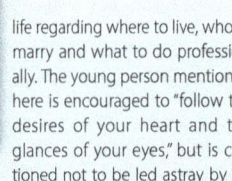

בחור
בחר

Ecclesiastes

5 When one is afraid of heights And there is terror on the road. – For the almond tree may blossom, The grasshopper be burdened, And the caper bush may bud again; But man sets out for his eternal abode, With mourners all around in the street. –

ה גַּם מִגָּבֹהַּ יִרָאוּ וְחַתְחַתִּים בַּדֶּרֶךְ וְיָנֵאץ הַשָּׁקֵד וְיִסְתַּבֵּל הֶחָגָב וְתָפֵר הָאֲבִיּוֹנָה כִּי־הֹלֵךְ הָאָדָם אֶל־בֵּית עוֹלָמוֹ וְסָבְבוּ בַשּׁוּק הַסֹּפְדִים:

6 Before the silver cord snaps And the golden bowl crashes, The jar is shattered at the spring, And the jug is smashed at the cistern.

ו עַד אֲשֶׁר לֹא־ירחק [יֵרָתֵק] חֶבֶל הַכֶּסֶף וְתָרֻץ גֻּלַּת הַזָּהָב וְתִשָּׁבֶר כַּד עַל־הַמַּבּוּעַ וְנָרֹץ הַגַּלְגַּל אֶל־הַבּוֹר:

7 And the dust returns to the ground As it was, And the lifebreath returns to *Hashem* Who bestowed it.

ז וְיָשֹׁב הֶעָפָר עַל־הָאָרֶץ כְּשֶׁהָיָה וְהָרוּחַ תָּשׁוּב אֶל־הָאֱלֹהִים אֲשֶׁר נְתָנָהּ:

8 Utter futility – said *Kohelet* – All is futile!

ח הֲבֵל הֲבָלִים אָמַר הַקּוֹהֶלֶת הַכֹּל הָבֶל:

9 A further word: Because *Kohelet* was a sage, he continued to instruct the people. He listened to and tested the soundness of many maxims.

ט וְיֹתֵר שֶׁהָיָה קֹהֶלֶת חָכָם עוֹד לִמַּד־דַּעַת אֶת־הָעָם וְאִזֵּן וְחִקֵּר תִּקֵּן מְשָׁלִים הַרְבֵּה:

v'-yo-TAYR she-ha-YAH ko-HE-let kha-KHAM OD li-mad DA-at et ha-AM v'-i-ZAYN v'-khi-KAYR ti-KAYN m'-sha-LEEM har-BAY

10 *Kohelet* sought to discover useful sayings and recorded genuinely truthful sayings.

י בִּקֵּשׁ קֹהֶלֶת לִמְצֹא דִּבְרֵי־חֵפֶץ וְכָתוּב יֹשֶׁר דִּבְרֵי אֱמֶת:

11 The sayings of the wise are like goads, like nails fixed in prodding sticks. They were given by one Shepherd.

יא דִּבְרֵי חֲכָמִים כַּדָּרְבֹנוֹת וּכְמַשְׂמְרוֹת נְטוּעִים בַּעֲלֵי אֲסֻפּוֹת נִתְּנוּ מֵרֹעֶה אֶחָד:

12 A further word: Against them, my son, be warned! The making of many books is without limit And much study is a wearying of the flesh.

יב וְיֹתֵר מֵהֵמָּה בְּנִי הִזָּהֵר עֲשׂוֹת סְפָרִים הַרְבֵּה אֵין קֵץ וְלַהַג הַרְבֵּה יְגִעַת בָּשָׂר:

13 The sum of the matter, when all is said and done: Revere *Hashem* and observe His commandments! For this applies to all mankind:

יג סוֹף דָּבָר הַכֹּל נִשְׁמָע אֶת־הָאֱלֹהִים יְרָא וְאֶת־מִצְוֹתָיו שְׁמוֹר כִּי־זֶה כָּל־הָאָדָם:

14 that *Hashem* will call every creature to account for everything unknown, be it good or bad. The sum of the matter, when all is said and done: Revere *Hashem* and observe His commandments! For this applies to all mankind.

יד כִּי אֶת־כָּל־מַעֲשֶׂה הָאֱלֹהִים יָבִא בְמִשְׁפָּט עַל כָּל־נֶעְלָם אִם־טוֹב וְאִם־רָע: [סוֹף דבר הכל נשמע את־האלהים ירא ואת־מצותיו שמור כי־זה כל־האדם]

A rocky hill with an impressive scale statue in *Yerushalayim*

איזן
אוזן
אזנים

12:9 He listened The Hebrew word *izayn* (איזן), translated here as 'listened,' is related to the words *ozen* (אוזן), 'ear,' and *moznayim* (מאזנים), 'scale.' Commentators note that King *Shlomo*'s greatness was not that he heard and internalized much wisdom, but that he was also able to present it clearly, so that others could hear and understand it as well. Additionally, King *Shlomo* calculated and weighed the ideas presented to him in order to arrive at the ultimate truth. The deeper connection between the Hebrew words *ozen* and *moznayim* reflect the biological fact that the ear not only receives sound, but also aids a person's balance and equilibrium.

Megillat Esther
The Scroll of Esther

Introduction and commentary by Batya Markowitz

Esther comes from the Hebrew word *hester* (הסתר), which means 'hidden.'
Megilla (מגילה), 'scroll,' is related to the word *ligalot* (לגלות), which means
'to reveal.' The challenge of reading *Megillat Esther* (Esther) is to reveal the
hidden messages veiled within the exciting plot. At first glance, the story
seems to be one of royal intrigue, power, wealth and politics. Superficially,
the events of the *Megilla* seem to be the result of the whims of an
intoxicated king. The name of God does not appear even once in the entire
story, making *Megillat Esther* the only book of the *Tanakh* that does not
mention His holy name. The reader's job, therefore, is to uncover *Hashem*'s
hidden hand guiding what appears to be a string of coincidences.

Megillat Esther contains an account of events that took place when the
Jewish people were living in Persia. Following the destruction of the first
Beit Hamikdash at the hands of the Babylonians, the Jews were exiled to
Babylon. Not long afterwards, the Babylonians were defeated by Cyrus,
king of Persia, and the Jewish residents of Babylon found themselves under
Persian rule. The story of *Esther* takes place against this backdrop of Persian
exile.

Cyrus the Great was the first Persian king to control Babylon. In the
first year of his reign he made a famous decree, granting permission for
the Jews to return to *Yerushalayim* and rebuild their Temple (Ezra 1:1–3).
Unfortunately, not many heeded the call. Though construction of the *Beit
Hamikdash* begins soon after this first, small, wave of exiles return, it is
quickly halted. It is not until the second year of King Darius's reign that
construction of the Temple resumes, and it is finally completed in Darius's
sixth year. Jewish tradition places King Ahasuerus between Cyrus and
Darius. The Sages even suggest that Darius was the son of Ahasuerus and
Esther. In their opinion, the story of *Esther* takes place after the Cyrus
declaration, but before the reconstruction of the *Beit Hamikdash*. According
to this opinion, the Jews of the story are the very ones who disregard
the decree of Cyrus, and choose to remain in exile rather than returning

to *Eretz Yisrael* to participate in the reconstruction of the Temple and *Yerushalayim*.

According to the Sages (*Megilla* 11a), Ahasuerus halted the reconstruction of the *Beit Hamikdash*, and he threw a feast when he believed that the Jews have been forsaken and would never return to *Yerushalayim*. He deliberately offered *Esther* only "half the kingdom," (Esther 5:3) refusing to restart the construction of the *Beit Hamikdash*. Meanwhile, *Mordechai*, a former citizen of *Yerushalayim* living in Shushan, the capital of the Persian empire, was teaching about the *Beit Hamikdash* and putting aside money for its construction. At the same time, however, the Jews of the Persian Empire have weakened their connection to *Eretz Yisrael*. They could have immigrated to Israel years before during Cyrus' rule, but instead opted to remain in exile. The opening of *Megillat Esther* even finds them at Ahasuerus's feast where the Temple vessels were on display. It has been suggested that the events of the story, and the evil decree of Haman, were Divine retribution for forsaking the Land of Israel and the *Beit Hamikdash*.

The miracle of the story of *Esther* carries an important message to the people of that time, and for all ages. Living in exile, the Jews felt physically distanced from their land, and spiritually distanced from their God. They no longer deserved the open miracles they had experienced in the past in their homeland. Nevertheless, the story of *Esther* teaches that *Hashem* has not, and will not, abandon His people. Although He is hidden in exile, He is very much present, pulling the strings from behind the scenes. The God who created the world and who split the sea is the same God who deposed Vashti, chose *Esther* and hanged Haman.

In a subtle way, *Megillat Esther* reminds exiled Jews throughout the ages of some very fundamental ideas. First, they must never forsake *Yerushalayim*, but must remember her no matter where they find themselves. Second, even outside of Israel, where *Hashem*'s presence is less obvious, they must discover and reveal the hidden God, and must see Him in all aspects of day-to-day life, not just in open miracles. And finally, they must always remember that *Hashem* will never forsake His promise to return the Children of Israel to the Land of Israel.

List of the *Neviim* (Prophets) and *Neviot* (Prophetesses)

Esther was not only a heroine of the Jewish people, but, according to the Sages, she was also a prophetess. The Talmud *(Megillah* 14a) states that there were 48 prophets and 7 prophetesses. The following is a list of prophets and prophetesses based on *Rashi*'s enumeration, as well as the main places in *Tanakh* that they are mentioned:

The 48 *Neviim*	Biblical Reference
Avraham	Genesis 11:26–25:11
Yitzchak	Genesis 21:1–28:9
Yaakov	Genesis 25:19–50:13
Moshe	Exodus 2–Deuteronomy 34
Aharon	Exodus 4:14–Numbers 20:29
Yehoshua son of **Nun**	The Book of Joshua
Pinchas son of **Elazar**	Numbers 25:1–15
Elkana	I Samuel 1
Eli	I Samuel 1–4:18
Shmuel son of **Elkana**	I Samuel 1–25:1
Gad	I Samuel 22:5, II Samuel 24:11,19
Natan	II Samuel 7, 12, II Kings 1
David son of **Yishai**	I Samuel 15–II Kings 2:13
Achiya the **Shilonite**	I Kings 11:29–39, 14:1–16
Shlomo son of **David**	I Kings 2–11
Ido	II Chronicles 12:15, 13:22
Shemaya	I Kings 12:22–24, II Chronicles 12:5–15
Eliyahu	I Kings 17:1-II Kings 2:12
Michaihu	I Kings 22
Ovadya	The Book of Obadiah
Chanani	II Chronicles 16:7–10
Yehu son of **Chanani**	I Kings 16:1–7
Azarya son of **Oded**	II Chronicles 15:1–8
Yachaziel son of **Zecharya**	II Chronicles 20:14–17
Eliezer son of **Dodavahu**	II Chronicles 20:37
Elisha son of **Shafat**	II Kings 2–9, 13:14–21
Yona son of **Amitai**	The Book of Jonah
Hoshea son of **B'eri**	The Book of Hosea
Amos	The Book of Amos
Amotz	Father of *Yeshayahu** – Isaiah 1:1
Oded	II Chronicles 28:9–11

The 48 *Neviim*	Biblical Reference
Yeshayahu son of **Amotz**	The Book of Isaiah
Micha of **Moreshet**	The Book of Micah
Yoel son of **Petuel**	The Book of Joel
Nachum	The Book of Nahum
Uriah son of **Shemaya**	Jeremiah 26:20–23
Chavakuk	The Book of Habakkuk
Tzefanya son of **Kushi**	The Book of Zephaniah
Yirmiyahu son of **Chilkiyahu**	The Book of Jeremiah
Yechezkel son of **Buzi**	The Book of Ezekiel
Neriya	Father of *Baruch* and *Seraya** – Jeremiah 32:12,16 36:4,8,14,32 43:3,6 45:1 51:59
Baruch son of **Neriya**	Jeremiah 32, 36, 43:2–7, 45
Seraya son of **Neriya**	Jeremiah 51:59–64
Machaseya	Father of *Neriya** – Jeremiah 32:12, 51:59
Chagai	The Book of Haggai
Zecharya	The Book of Zechariah
Malachi	The Book of Malachi
Mordechai	The Book of Esther

The 7 *Neviot*	
Sara	Genesis 11:29–23:20
Miriam	Exodus 2:1–9, 15:20–21 Numbers 12:1–15, 20:1
Devora	Judges 4–5
Chana	I Samuel 1:1–2:21
Avigail	I Samuel 25
Chulda	II Kings 22:14–20
Esther	The Book of Esther

* According to the Sages, if a prophet is identified with his father's name the father was also a prophet

1 1 It happened in the days of Ahasuerus – that Ahasuerus who reigned over a hundred and twenty-seven provinces from India to Ethiopia.

א וַיְהִי בִּימֵי אֲחַשְׁוֵרוֹשׁ הוּא אֲחַשְׁוֵרוֹשׁ הַמֹּלֵךְ מֵהֹדּוּ וְעַד־כּוּשׁ שֶׁבַע וְעֶשְׂרִים וּמֵאָה מְדִינָה:

2 In those days, when King Ahasuerus occupied the royal throne in the fortress Shushan,

ב בַּיָּמִים הָהֵם כְּשֶׁבֶת הַמֶּלֶךְ אֲחַשְׁוֵרוֹשׁ עַל כִּסֵּא מַלְכוּתוֹ אֲשֶׁר בְּשׁוּשַׁן הַבִּירָה:

3 in the third year of his reign, he gave a banquet for all the officials and courtiers – the administration of Persia and Media, the nobles and the governors of the provinces in his service.

ג בִּשְׁנַת שָׁלוֹשׁ לְמָלְכוֹ עָשָׂה מִשְׁתֶּה לְכָל־שָׂרָיו וַעֲבָדָיו חֵיל פָּרַס וּמָדַי הַפַּרְתְּמִים וְשָׂרֵי הַמְּדִינוֹת לְפָנָיו:

bish-NAT sha-LOSH l'-mol-KHO a-SAH mish-TEH l'-khol sa-RAV va-a-va-DAV KHAYL pa-RAS u-ma-DAI ha-par-t'-MEEM v'-sa-RAY ha-m'-dee-NOT l'-fa-NAV

4 For no fewer than a hundred and eighty days he displayed the vast riches of his kingdom and the splendid glory of his majesty.

ד בְּהַרְאֹתוֹ אֶת־עֹשֶׁר כְּבוֹד מַלְכוּתוֹ וְאֶת־יְקָר תִּפְאֶרֶת גְּדוּלָּתוֹ יָמִים רַבִּים שְׁמוֹנִים וּמְאַת יוֹם:

5 At the end of this period, the king gave a banquet for seven days in the court of the king's palace garden for all the people who lived in the fortress Shushan, high and low alike.

ה וּבִמְלוֹאת הַיָּמִים הָאֵלֶּה עָשָׂה הַמֶּלֶךְ לְכָל־הָעָם הַנִּמְצְאִים בְּשׁוּשַׁן הַבִּירָה לְמִגָּדוֹל וְעַד־קָטָן מִשְׁתֶּה שִׁבְעַת יָמִים בַּחֲצַר גִּנַּת בִּיתַן הַמֶּלֶךְ:

6 [There were hangings of] white cotton and blue wool, caught up by cords of fine linen and purple wool to silver rods and alabaster columns; and there were couches of gold and silver on a pavement of marble, alabaster, mother-of-pearl, and mosaics.

ו חוּר כַּרְפַּס וּתְכֵלֶת אָחוּז בְּחַבְלֵי־בוּץ וְאַרְגָּמָן עַל־גְּלִילֵי כֶסֶף וְעַמּוּדֵי שֵׁשׁ מִטּוֹת זָהָב וָכֶסֶף עַל רִצְפַת בַּהַט־וָשֵׁשׁ וְדַר וְסֹחָרֶת:

7 Royal wine was served in abundance, as befits a king, in golden beakers, beakers of varied design.

ז וְהַשְׁקוֹת בִּכְלֵי זָהָב וְכֵלִים מִכֵּלִים שׁוֹנִים וְיַיִן מַלְכוּת רָב כְּיַד הַמֶּלֶךְ:

8 And the rule for the drinking was, "No restrictions!" For the king had given orders to every palace steward to comply with each man's wishes.

ח וְהַשְּׁתִיָּה כַדָּת אֵין אֹנֵס כִּי־כֵן יִסַּד הַמֶּלֶךְ עַל כָּל־רַב בֵּיתוֹ לַעֲשׂוֹת כִּרְצוֹן אִישׁ־וָאִישׁ:

9 In addition, Queen Vashti gave a banquet for women, in the royal palace of King Ahasuerus.

ט גַּם וַשְׁתִּי הַמַּלְכָּה עָשְׂתָה מִשְׁתֵּה נָשִׁים בֵּית הַמַּלְכוּת אֲשֶׁר לַמֶּלֶךְ אֲחַשְׁוֵרוֹשׁ:

1:3 He gave a banquet What reason was there to celebrate in Ahasuerus's third year? The prophet *Yirmiyahu*, who lived at the end of the first Temple period, prophesied that the Children of Israel would be in exile for seventy years (Jeremiah 29:10). According to the Sages (*Megilla* 11b), Ahasuerus erroneously calculated that these seventy years had elapsed and that *Hashem* had forsaken the Jewish people and the Land of Israel. Not only did he host a celebratory banquet, but the Sages add that he donned the vestments of the High Priest and used captured vessels from the *Beit Hamikdash* to emphasize this point. Punishment was exacted on

Queen Vashti, wife of Ahasuerus and the granddaughter of Nebuchadnezzar, the wicked ruler who had destroyed the Temple. The Sages teach that Vashti convinced her husband not to allow the rebuilding of the *Beit Hamikdash* in *Yerushalayim* during his reign. Therefore, Vashti is punished.

PM Benjamin Netanyahu dines with President Barak Obama at the White House, 2012

10 On the seventh day, when the king was merry with wine, he ordered Mehuman, Bizzetha, Harbona, Bigtha, Abagtha, Zethar, and Carcas, the seven eunuchs in attendance on King Ahasuerus,

י בַּיּוֹם הַשְּׁבִיעִי כְּטוֹב לֵב־הַמֶּלֶךְ בַּיָּיִן אָמַר לִמְהוּמָן בִּזְּתָא חַרְבוֹנָא בִּגְתָא וַאֲבַגְתָא זֵתַר וְכַרְכַּס שִׁבְעַת הַסָּרִיסִים הַמְשָׁרְתִים אֶת־פְּנֵי הַמֶּלֶךְ אֲחַשְׁוֵרוֹשׁ:

11 to bring Queen Vashti before the king wearing a royal diadem, to display her beauty to the peoples and the officials; for she was a beautiful woman.

יא לְהָבִיא אֶת־וַשְׁתִּי הַמַּלְכָּה לִפְנֵי הַמֶּלֶךְ בְּכֶתֶר מַלְכוּת לְהַרְאוֹת הָעַמִּים וְהַשָּׂרִים אֶת־יָפְיָהּ כִּי־טוֹבַת מַרְאֶה הִיא:

12 But Queen Vashti refused to come at the king's command conveyed by the eunuchs. The king was greatly incensed, and his fury burned within him.

יב וַתְּמָאֵן הַמַּלְכָּה וַשְׁתִּי לָבוֹא בִּדְבַר הַמֶּלֶךְ אֲשֶׁר בְּיַד הַסָּרִיסִים וַיִּקְצֹף הַמֶּלֶךְ מְאֹד וַחֲמָתוֹ בָּעֲרָה בוֹ:

13 Then the king consulted the sages learned in procedure. (For it was the royal practice [to turn] to all who were versed in law and precedent.

יג וַיֹּאמֶר הַמֶּלֶךְ לַחֲכָמִים יֹדְעֵי הָעִתִּים כִּי־כֵן דְּבַר הַמֶּלֶךְ לִפְנֵי כָּל־יֹדְעֵי דָּת וָדִין:

14 His closest advisers were Carshena, Shethar, Admatha, Tarshish, Meres, Marsena, and Memucan, the seven ministers of Persia and Media who had access to the royal presence and occupied the first place in the kingdom.)

יד וְהַקָּרֹב אֵלָיו כַּרְשְׁנָא שֵׁתָר אַדְמָתָא תַרְשִׁישׁ מֶרֶס מַרְסְנָא מְמוּכָן שִׁבְעַת שָׂרֵי פָּרַס וּמָדַי רֹאֵי פְּנֵי הַמֶּלֶךְ הַיֹּשְׁבִים רִאשֹׁנָה בַּמַּלְכוּת:

15 "What," [he asked,] "shall be done, according to law, to Queen Vashti for failing to obey the command of King Ahasuerus conveyed by the eunuchs?"

טו כְּדָת מַה־לַּעֲשׂוֹת בַּמַּלְכָּה וַשְׁתִּי עַל אֲשֶׁר לֹא־עָשְׂתָה אֶת־מַאֲמַר הַמֶּלֶךְ אֲחַשְׁוֵרוֹשׁ בְּיַד הַסָּרִיסִים:

16 Thereupon Memucan declared in the presence of the king and the ministers: "Queen Vashti has committed an offense not only against Your Majesty but also against all the officials and against all the peoples in all the provinces of King Ahasuerus.

טז וַיֹּאמֶר מומכן [מְמוּכָן] לִפְנֵי הַמֶּלֶךְ וְהַשָּׂרִים לֹא עַל־הַמֶּלֶךְ לְבַדּוֹ עָוְתָה וַשְׁתִּי הַמַּלְכָּה כִּי עַל־כָּל־הַשָּׂרִים וְעַל־כָּל־הָעַמִּים אֲשֶׁר בְּכָל־מְדִינוֹת הַמֶּלֶךְ אֲחַשְׁוֵרוֹשׁ:

17 For the queen's behavior will make all wives despise their husbands, as they reflect that King Ahasuerus himself ordered Queen Vashti to be brought before him, but she would not come.

יז כִּי־יֵצֵא דְבַר־הַמַּלְכָּה עַל־כָּל־הַנָּשִׁים לְהַבְזוֹת בַּעְלֵיהֶן בְּעֵינֵיהֶן בְּאָמְרָם הַמֶּלֶךְ אֲחַשְׁוֵרוֹשׁ אָמַר לְהָבִיא אֶת־וַשְׁתִּי הַמַּלְכָּה לְפָנָיו וְלֹא־בָאָה:

18 This very day the ladies of Persia and Media, who have heard of the queen's behavior, will cite it to all Your Majesty's officials, and there will be no end of scorn and provocation!

יח וְהַיּוֹם הַזֶּה תֹּאמַרְנָה שָׂרוֹת פָּרַס־וּמָדַי אֲשֶׁר שָׁמְעוּ אֶת־דְּבַר הַמַּלְכָּה לְכֹל שָׂרֵי הַמֶּלֶךְ וּכְדַי בִּזָּיוֹן וָקָצֶף:

19 "If it please Your Majesty, let a royal edict be issued by you, and let it be written into the laws of Persia and Media, so that it cannot be abrogated, that Vashti shall never enter the presence of King Ahasuerus. And let Your Majesty bestow her royal state upon another who is more worthy than she.

יט אִם־עַל־הַמֶּלֶךְ טוֹב יֵצֵא דְבַר־מַלְכוּת מִלְּפָנָיו וְיִכָּתֵב בְּדָתֵי פָרַס־וּמָדַי וְלֹא יַעֲבוֹר אֲשֶׁר לֹא־תָבוֹא וַשְׁתִּי לִפְנֵי הַמֶּלֶךְ אֲחַשְׁוֵרוֹשׁ וּמַלְכוּתָהּ יִתֵּן הַמֶּלֶךְ לִרְעוּתָהּ הַטּוֹבָה מִמֶּנָּה:

²⁰ Then will the judgment executed by Your Majesty resound throughout your realm, vast though it is; and all wives will treat their husbands with respect, high and low alike."

כ וְנִשְׁמַע פִּתְגָם הַמֶּלֶךְ אֲשֶׁר־יַעֲשֶׂה בְּכָל־מַלְכוּתוֹ כִּי רַבָּה הִיא וְכָל־הַנָּשִׁים יִתְּנוּ יְקָר לְבַעְלֵיהֶן לְמִגָּדוֹל וְעַד־קָטָן:

²¹ The proposal was approved by the king and the ministers, and the king did as Memucan proposed.

כא וַיִּיטַב הַדָּבָר בְּעֵינֵי הַמֶּלֶךְ וְהַשָּׂרִים וַיַּעַשׂ הַמֶּלֶךְ כִּדְבַר מְמוּכָן:

²² Dispatches were sent to all the provinces of the king, to every province in its own script and to every nation in its own language, that every man should wield authority in his home and speak the language of his own people.

כב וַיִּשְׁלַח סְפָרִים אֶל־כָּל־מְדִינוֹת הַמֶּלֶךְ אֶל־מְדִינָה וּמְדִינָה כִּכְתָבָהּ וְאֶל־עַם וָעָם כִּלְשׁוֹנוֹ לִהְיוֹת כָּל־אִישׁ שֹׂרֵר בְּבֵיתוֹ וּמְדַבֵּר כִּלְשׁוֹן עַמּוֹ:

2 ¹ Some time afterward, when the anger of King Ahasuerus subsided, he thought of Vashti and what she had done and what had been decreed against her.

ב א אַחַר הַדְּבָרִים הָאֵלֶּה כְּשֹׁךְ חֲמַת הַמֶּלֶךְ אֲחַשְׁוֵרוֹשׁ זָכַר אֶת־וַשְׁתִּי וְאֵת אֲשֶׁר־עָשָׂתָה וְאֵת אֲשֶׁר־נִגְזַר עָלֶיהָ:

² The king's servants who attended him said, "Let beautiful young virgins be sought out for Your Majesty.

ב וַיֹּאמְרוּ נַעֲרֵי־הַמֶּלֶךְ מְשָׁרְתָיו יְבַקְשׁוּ לַמֶּלֶךְ נְעָרוֹת בְּתוּלוֹת טוֹבוֹת מַרְאֶה:

³ Let Your Majesty appoint officers in every province of your realm to assemble all the beautiful young virgins at the fortress Shushan, in the harem under the supervision of Hege, the king's eunuch, guardian of the women. Let them be provided with their cosmetics.

ג וְיַפְקֵד הַמֶּלֶךְ פְּקִידִים בְּכָל־מְדִינוֹת מַלְכוּתוֹ וְיִקְבְּצוּ אֶת־כָּל־נַעֲרָה־בְתוּלָה טוֹבַת מַרְאֶה אֶל־שׁוּשַׁן הַבִּירָה אֶל־בֵּית הַנָּשִׁים אֶל־יַד הֵגֶא סְרִיס הַמֶּלֶךְ שֹׁמֵר הַנָּשִׁים וְנָתוֹן תַּמְרֻקֵיהֶן:

⁴ And let the maiden who pleases Your Majesty be queen instead of Vashti." The proposal pleased the king, and he acted upon it.

ד וְהַנַּעֲרָה אֲשֶׁר תִּיטַב בְּעֵינֵי הַמֶּלֶךְ תִּמְלֹךְ תַּחַת וַשְׁתִּי וַיִּיטַב הַדָּבָר בְּעֵינֵי הַמֶּלֶךְ וַיַּעַשׂ כֵּן:

⁵ In the fortress Shushan lived a *Yehudi* by the name of *Mordechai*, son of *Yair* son of *Shim'i* son of *Keesh*, a Benjaminite.

ה אִישׁ יְהוּדִי הָיָה בְּשׁוּשַׁן הַבִּירָה וּשְׁמוֹ מָרְדֳּכַי בֶּן יָאִיר בֶּן־שִׁמְעִי בֶּן־קִישׁ אִישׁ יְמִינִי:

⁶ [*Keesh*] had been exiled from *Yerushalayim* in the group that was carried into exile along with King *Yechonya* of *Yehuda*, which had been driven into exile by King Nebuchadnezzar of Babylon. –

ו אֲשֶׁר הָגְלָה מִירוּשָׁלַיִם עִם־הַגֹּלָה אֲשֶׁר הָגְלְתָה עִם יְכָנְיָה מֶלֶךְ־יְהוּדָה אֲשֶׁר הֶגְלָה נְבוּכַדְנֶאצַּר מֶלֶךְ בָּבֶל:

*a-SHER hog-LAH mee-ru-sha-LA-im im ha-go-LAH a-SHER
hog-l'-TAH IM y'-khon-YAH ME-lekh y'-hu-DAH a-SHER
heg-LAH n'-vu-khad-ne-TZAR ME-lekh ba-VEL*

2:6 Had been exiled from *Yerushalayim* When chanted aloud in the synagogue on *Purim*, this verse is read in the same solemn tune as *Megillat Eicha*, since it mentions the exile of the Jewish people. The *Vilna Gaon* points out that the verb 'carried away' (ה-ל-ג) is mentioned three times in this verse, alluding to the fact that *Mordechai* was actually carried away from Israel three times. At the end of the first Temple period, the Jews were exiled from the Land of Israel in three stages, and *Mordechai* participated in all three of these. In love with the land, *Mordechai* returned after being forced to leave, was exiled again, and stubbornly returned once more until he was carried away a third time with the remaining Jews following the destruction of the first *Beit Hamikdash*.

Esther

7 He was foster father to *Hadassa* – that is, *Esther* – his uncle's daughter, for she had neither father nor mother. The maiden was shapely and beautiful; and when her father and mother died, *Mordechai* adopted her as his own daughter.

ז וַיְהִי אֹמֵן אֶת־הֲדַסָּה הִיא אֶסְתֵּר בַּת־דֹּדוֹ כִּי אֵין לָהּ אָב וָאֵם וְהַנַּעֲרָה יְפַת־תֹּאַר וְטוֹבַת מַרְאֶה וּבְמוֹת אָבִיהָ וְאִמָּהּ לְקָחָהּ מָרְדֳּכַי לוֹ לְבַת:

8 When the king's order and edict was proclaimed, and when many girls were assembled in the fortress Shushan under the supervision of Hegai, *Esther* too was taken into the king's palace under the supervision of Hegai, guardian of the women.

ח וַיְהִי בְּהִשָּׁמַע דְּבַר־הַמֶּלֶךְ וְדָתוֹ וּבְהִקָּבֵץ נְעָרוֹת רַבּוֹת אֶל־שׁוּשַׁן הַבִּירָה אֶל־יַד הֵגָי וַתִּלָּקַח אֶסְתֵּר אֶל־בֵּית הַמֶּלֶךְ אֶל־יַד הֵגַי שֹׁמֵר הַנָּשִׁים:

9 The girl pleased him and won his favor, and he hastened to furnish her with her cosmetics and her rations, as well as with the seven maids who were her due from the king's palace; and he treated her and her maids with special kindness in the harem.

ט וַתִּיטַב הַנַּעֲרָה בְעֵינָיו וַתִּשָּׂא חֶסֶד לְפָנָיו וַיְבַהֵל אֶת־תַּמְרוּקֶיהָ וְאֶת־מָנוֹתֶהָ לָתֵת לָהּ וְאֵת שֶׁבַע הַנְּעָרוֹת הָרְאֻיוֹת לָתֶת־לָהּ מִבֵּית הַמֶּלֶךְ וַיְשַׁנֶּהָ וְאֶת־נַעֲרוֹתֶיהָ לְטוֹב בֵּית הַנָּשִׁים:

10 *Esther* did not reveal her people or her kindred, for *Mordechai* had told her not to reveal it.

י לֹא־הִגִּידָה אֶסְתֵּר אֶת־עַמָּהּ וְאֶת־מוֹלַדְתָּהּ כִּי מָרְדֳּכַי צִוָּה עָלֶיהָ אֲשֶׁר לֹא־תַגִּיד:

11 Every single day *Mordechai* would walk about in front of the court of the harem, to learn how *Esther* was faring and what was happening to her.

יא וּבְכָל־יוֹם וָיוֹם מָרְדֳּכַי מִתְהַלֵּךְ לִפְנֵי חֲצַר בֵּית־הַנָּשִׁים לָדַעַת אֶת־שְׁלוֹם אֶסְתֵּר וּמַה־יֵּעָשֶׂה בָּהּ:

12 When each girl's turn came to go to King Ahasuerus at the end of the twelve months' treatment prescribed for women (for that was the period spent on beautifying them: six months with oil of myrrh and six months with perfumes and women's cosmetics,

יב וּבְהַגִּיעַ תֹּר נַעֲרָה וְנַעֲרָה לָבוֹא אֶל־הַמֶּלֶךְ אֲחַשְׁוֵרוֹשׁ מִקֵּץ הֱיוֹת לָהּ כְּדָת הַנָּשִׁים שְׁנֵים עָשָׂר חֹדֶשׁ כִּי כֵּן יִמְלְאוּ יְמֵי מְרוּקֵיהֶן שִׁשָּׁה חֳדָשִׁים בְּשֶׁמֶן הַמֹּר וְשִׁשָּׁה חֳדָשִׁים בַּבְּשָׂמִים וּבְתַמְרוּקֵי הַנָּשִׁים:

13 and it was after that that the girl would go to the king), whatever she asked for would be given her to take with her from the harem to the king's palace.

יג וּבָזֶה הַנַּעֲרָה בָּאָה אֶל־הַמֶּלֶךְ אֵת כָּל־אֲשֶׁר תֹּאמַר יִנָּתֵן לָהּ לָבוֹא עִמָּהּ מִבֵּית הַנָּשִׁים עַד־בֵּית הַמֶּלֶךְ:

14 She would go in the evening and leave in the morning for a second harem in charge of Shaashgaz, the king's eunuch, guardian of the concubines. She would not go again to the king unless the king wanted her, when she would be summoned by name.

יד בָּעֶרֶב הִיא בָאָה וּבַבֹּקֶר הִיא שָׁבָה אֶל־בֵּית הַנָּשִׁים שֵׁנִי אֶל־יַד שַׁעֲשְׁגַז סְרִיס הַמֶּלֶךְ שֹׁמֵר הַפִּילַגְשִׁים לֹא־תָבוֹא עוֹד אֶל־הַמֶּלֶךְ כִּי אִם־חָפֵץ בָּהּ הַמֶּלֶךְ וְנִקְרְאָה בְשֵׁם:

15 When the turn came for *Esther* daughter of *Avichayil* – the uncle of *Mordechai*, who had adopted her as his own daughter – to go to the king, she did not ask for anything but what Hegai, the king's eunuch, guardian of the women, advised. Yet *Esther* won the admiration of all who saw her.

טו וּבְהַגִּיעַ תֹּר־אֶסְתֵּר בַּת־אֲבִיחַיִל דֹּד מָרְדֳּכַי אֲשֶׁר לָקַח־לוֹ לְבַת לָבוֹא אֶל־הַמֶּלֶךְ לֹא בִקְשָׁה דָּבָר כִּי אִם אֶת־אֲשֶׁר יֹאמַר הֵגַי סְרִיס־הַמֶּלֶךְ שֹׁמֵר הַנָּשִׁים וַתְּהִי אֶסְתֵּר נֹשֵׂאת חֵן בְּעֵינֵי כָּל־רֹאֶיהָ:

16 *Esther* was taken to King Ahasuerus, in his royal palace, in the tenth month, which is the month of *Tevet*, in the seventh year of his reign.

טז וַתִּלָּקַ֨ח אֶסְתֵּ֜ר אֶל־הַמֶּ֤לֶךְ אֲחַשְׁוֵרוֹשׁ֙ אֶל־בֵּ֣ית מַלְכוּת֔וֹ בַּחֹ֥דֶשׁ הָעֲשִׂירִ֖י הוּא־חֹ֣דֶשׁ טֵבֵ֑ת בִּשְׁנַת־שֶׁ֖בַע לְמַלְכוּתֽוֹ:

17 The king loved *Esther* more than all the other women, and she won his grace and favor more than all the virgins. So he set a royal diadem on her head and made her queen instead of Vashti.

יז וַיֶּאֱהַ֨ב הַמֶּ֤לֶךְ אֶת־אֶסְתֵּר֙ מִכָּל־הַנָּשִׁ֔ים וַתִּשָּׂא־חֵ֥ן וָחֶ֛סֶד לְפָנָ֖יו מִכָּל־הַבְּתוּלֹ֑ת וַיָּ֤שֶׂם כֶּֽתֶר־מַלְכוּת֙ בְּרֹאשָׁ֔הּ וַיַּמְלִיכֶ֖הָ תַּ֥חַת וַשְׁתִּֽי:

18 The king gave a great banquet for all his officials and courtiers, "the banquet of *Esther*." He proclaimed a remission of taxes for the provinces and distributed gifts as befits a king.

יח וַיַּ֨עַשׂ הַמֶּ֜לֶךְ מִשְׁתֶּ֣ה גָד֗וֹל לְכָל־שָׂרָיו֙ וַעֲבָדָ֔יו אֵ֖ת מִשְׁתֵּ֣ה אֶסְתֵּ֑ר וַהֲנָחָ֤ה לַמְּדִינוֹת֙ עָשָׂ֔ה וַיִּתֵּ֥ן מַשְׂאֵ֖ת כְּיַ֥ד הַמֶּֽלֶךְ:

19 When the virgins were assembled a second time, *Mordechai* sat in the palace gate.

יט וּבְהִקָּבֵ֥ץ בְּתוּל֖וֹת שֵׁנִ֑ית וּמָרְדֳּכַ֖י יֹשֵׁ֥ב בְּשַֽׁעַר־הַמֶּֽלֶךְ:

20 But *Esther* still did not reveal her kindred or her people, as *Mordechai* had instructed her; for *Esther* obeyed *Mordechai*'s bidding, as she had done when she was under his tutelage.

כ אֵ֣ין אֶסְתֵּ֗ר מַגֶּ֤דֶת מֽוֹלַדְתָּהּ֙ וְאֶת־עַמָּ֔הּ כַּאֲשֶׁ֛ר צִוָּ֥ה עָלֶ֖יהָ מָרְדֳּכָ֑י וְאֶת־מַאֲמַ֤ר מָרְדֳּכַי֙ אֶסְתֵּ֣ר עֹשָׂ֔ה כַּאֲשֶׁ֛ר הָיְתָ֥ה בְאָמְנָ֖ה אִתּֽוֹ:

21 At that time, when *Mordechai* was sitting in the palace gate, Bigthan and Teresh, two of the king's eunuchs who guarded the threshold, became angry, and plotted to do away with King Ahasuerus.

כא בַּיָּמִ֣ים הָהֵ֗ם וּמָרְדֳּכַ֖י יֹשֵׁ֣ב בְּשַֽׁעַר־הַמֶּ֑לֶךְ קָצַ֣ף בִּגְתָ֣ן וָתֶ֗רֶשׁ שְׁנֵֽי־סָרִיסֵ֤י הַמֶּ֙לֶךְ֙ מִשֹּׁמְרֵ֣י הַסַּ֔ף וַיְבַקְשׁוּ֙ לִשְׁלֹ֣חַ יָ֔ד בַּמֶּ֖לֶךְ אֲחַשְׁוֵֽרֹשׁ:

22 *Mordechai* learned of it and told it to Queen *Esther*, and *Esther* reported it to the king in *Mordechai*'s name.

כב וַיִּוָּדַ֤ע הַדָּבָר֙ לְמָרְדֳּכַ֔י וַיַּגֵּ֖ד לְאֶסְתֵּ֣ר הַמַּלְכָּ֑ה וַתֹּ֧אמֶר אֶסְתֵּ֛ר לַמֶּ֖לֶךְ בְּשֵׁ֥ם מָרְדֳּכָֽי:

23 The matter was investigated and found to be so, and the two were impaled on stakes. This was recorded in the book of annals at the instance of the king.

כג וַיְבֻקַּ֤שׁ הַדָּבָר֙ וַיִּמָּצֵ֔א וַיִּתָּל֥וּ שְׁנֵיהֶ֖ם עַל־עֵ֑ץ וַיִּכָּתֵ֗ב בְּסֵ֛פֶר דִּבְרֵ֥י הַיָּמִ֖ים לִפְנֵ֥י הַמֶּֽלֶךְ:

3 1 Some time afterward, King Ahasuerus promoted Haman son of Hammedatha the Agagite; he advanced him and seated him higher than any of his fellow officials.

ג א אַחַ֣ר ׀ הַדְּבָרִ֣ים הָאֵ֗לֶּה גִּדַּל֩ הַמֶּ֨לֶךְ אֲחַשְׁוֵר֜וֹשׁ אֶת־הָמָ֧ן בֶּֽן־הַמְּדָ֛תָא הָאֲגָגִ֖י וַֽיְנַשְּׂאֵ֑הוּ וַיָּ֙שֶׂם֙ אֶת־כִּסְא֔וֹ מֵעַ֕ל כָּל־הַשָּׂרִ֖ים אֲשֶׁ֥ר אִתּֽוֹ:

2 All the king's courtiers in the palace gate knelt and bowed low to Haman, for such was the king's order concerning him; but *Mordechai* would not kneel or bow low.

ב וְכָל־עַבְדֵ֨י הַמֶּ֜לֶךְ אֲשֶׁר־בְּשַׁ֣עַר הַמֶּ֗לֶךְ כֹּרְעִ֤ים וּמִֽשְׁתַּחֲוִים֙ לְהָמָ֔ן כִּי־כֵ֖ן צִוָּה־ל֣וֹ הַמֶּ֑לֶךְ וּמָ֨רְדֳּכַ֔י לֹ֥א יִכְרַ֖ע וְלֹ֥א יִֽשְׁתַּחֲוֶֽה:

3 Then the king's courtiers who were in the palace gate said to *Mordechai*, "Why do you disobey the king's order?"

ג וַיֹּ֨אמְר֜וּ עַבְדֵ֥י הַמֶּ֛לֶךְ אֲשֶׁר־בְּשַׁ֥עַר הַמֶּ֖לֶךְ לְמָרְדֳּכָ֑י מַדּ֙וּעַ֙ אַתָּ֣ה עוֹבֵ֔ר אֵ֖ת מִצְוַ֥ת הַמֶּֽלֶךְ:

4 When they spoke to him day after day and he would not listen to them, they told Haman, in order to see whether *Mordechai*'s resolve would prevail; for he had explained to them that he was a *Yehudi*.

ד וַיְהִ֗י באמרם [כְּאָמְרָ֤ם] אֵלָיו֙ י֣וֹם וָי֔וֹם וְלֹ֥א שָׁמַ֖ע אֲלֵיהֶ֑ם וַיַּגִּ֣ידוּ לְהָמָ֗ן לִרְאוֹת֙ הֲיַֽעַמְדוּ֙ דִּבְרֵ֣י מָרְדֳּכַ֔י כִּֽי־הִגִּ֥יד לָהֶ֖ם אֲשֶׁר־ה֥וּא יְהוּדִֽי:

5   When Haman saw that *Mordechai* would not kneel or bow low to him, Haman was filled with rage.

ה וַיַּרְא הָמָן כִּי־אֵין מָרְדֳּכַי כֹּרֵעַ וּמִשְׁתַּחֲוֶה לוֹ וַיִּמָּלֵא הָמָן חֵמָה:

6   But he disdained to lay hands on *Mordechai* alone; having been told who *Mordechai*'s people were, Haman plotted to do away with all the *Yehudim*, *Mordechai*'s people, throughout the kingdom of Ahasuerus.

ו וַיִּבֶז בְּעֵינָיו לִשְׁלֹחַ יָד בְּמָרְדֳּכַי לְבַדּוֹ כִּי־הִגִּידוּ לוֹ אֶת־עַם מָרְדֳּכָי וַיְבַקֵּשׁ הָמָן לְהַשְׁמִיד אֶת־כָּל־הַיְּהוּדִים אֲשֶׁר בְּכָל־מַלְכוּת אֲחַשְׁוֵרוֹשׁ עַם מָרְדֳּכָי:

7   In the first month, that is, the month of *Nisan*, in the twelfth year of King Ahasuerus, pur – which means "the lot" – was cast before Haman concerning every day and every month, [until it fell on] the twelfth month, that is, the month of *Adar*.

ז בַּחֹדֶשׁ הָרִאשׁוֹן הוּא־חֹדֶשׁ נִיסָן בִּשְׁנַת שְׁתֵּים עֶשְׂרֵה לַמֶּלֶךְ אֲחַשְׁוֵרוֹשׁ הִפִּיל פּוּר הוּא הַגּוֹרָל לִפְנֵי הָמָן מִיּוֹם לְיוֹם וּמֵחֹדֶשׁ לְחֹדֶשׁ שְׁנֵים־עָשָׂר הוּא־חֹדֶשׁ אֲדָר:

8   Haman then said to King Ahasuerus, "There is a certain people, scattered and dispersed among the other peoples in all the provinces of your realm, whose laws are different from those of any other people and who do not obey the king's laws; and it is not in Your Majesty's interest to tolerate them.

ח וַיֹּאמֶר הָמָן לַמֶּלֶךְ אֲחַשְׁוֵרוֹשׁ יֶשְׁנוֹ עַם־אֶחָד מְפֻזָּר וּמְפֹרָד בֵּין הָעַמִּים בְּכֹל מְדִינוֹת מַלְכוּתֶךָ וְדָתֵיהֶם שֹׁנוֹת מִכָּל־עָם וְאֶת־דָּתֵי הַמֶּלֶךְ אֵינָם עֹשִׂים וְלַמֶּלֶךְ אֵין־שֹׁוֶה לְהַנִּיחָם:

9   If it please Your Majesty, let an edict be drawn for their destruction, and I will pay ten thousand *kikarot* of silver to the stewards for deposit in the royal treasury."

ט אִם־עַל־הַמֶּלֶךְ טוֹב יִכָּתֵב לְאַבְּדָם וַעֲשֶׂרֶת אֲלָפִים כִּכַּר־כֶּסֶף אֶשְׁקוֹל עַל־יְדֵי עֹשֵׂי הַמְּלָאכָה לְהָבִיא אֶל־גִּנְזֵי הַמֶּלֶךְ:

10   Thereupon the king removed his signet ring from his hand and gave it to Haman son of Hammedatha the Agagite, the foe of the *Yehudim*.

י וַיָּסַר הַמֶּלֶךְ אֶת־טַבַּעְתּוֹ מֵעַל יָדוֹ וַיִּתְּנָהּ לְהָמָן בֶּן־הַמְּדָתָא הָאֲגָגִי צֹרֵר הַיְּהוּדִים:

11   And the king said, "The money and the people are yours to do with as you see fit."

יא וַיֹּאמֶר הַמֶּלֶךְ לְהָמָן הַכֶּסֶף נָתוּן לָךְ וְהָעָם לַעֲשׂוֹת בּוֹ כַּטּוֹב בְּעֵינֶיךָ:

12   On the thirteenth day of the first month, the king's scribes were summoned and a decree was issued, as Haman directed, to the king's satraps, to the governors of every province, and to the officials of every people, to every province in its own script and to every people in its own language. The orders were issued in the name of King Ahasuerus and sealed with the king's signet.

יב וַיִּקָּרְאוּ סֹפְרֵי הַמֶּלֶךְ בַּחֹדֶשׁ הָרִאשׁוֹן בִּשְׁלוֹשָׁה עָשָׂר יוֹם בּוֹ וַיִּכָּתֵב כְּכָל־אֲשֶׁר־צִוָּה הָמָן אֶל אֲחַשְׁדַּרְפְּנֵי־הַמֶּלֶךְ וְאֶל־הַפַּחוֹת אֲשֶׁר עַל־מְדִינָה וּמְדִינָה וְאֶל־שָׂרֵי עַם וָעָם מְדִינָה וּמְדִינָה כִּכְתָבָהּ וְעַם וָעָם כִּלְשׁוֹנוֹ בְּשֵׁם הַמֶּלֶךְ אֲחַשְׁוֵרֹשׁ נִכְתָּב וְנֶחְתָּם בְּטַבַּעַת הַמֶּלֶךְ:

13   Accordingly, written instructions were dispatched by couriers to all the king's provinces to destroy, massacre, and exterminate all the *Yehudim*, young

יג וְנִשְׁלוֹחַ סְפָרִים בְּיַד הָרָצִים אֶל־כָּל־מְדִינוֹת הַמֶּלֶךְ לְהַשְׁמִיד לַהֲרֹג וּלְאַבֵּד אֶת־כָּל־הַיְּהוּדִים מִנַּעַר וְעַד־זָקֵן טַף

3:13 To destroy, massacre, and exterminate all the Yehudim Usually, the Torah gives us the reason why an individual, or the nation as a whole, are punished. *Megillat Esther*, however, does not explicitly state what the people did to deserve the threat of annihilation. When viewed in historical context, it becomes clear that the Jews of Shushan were guilty for not having returned to *Eretz Yisrael* even though they had the

and old, children and women, on a single day, on the thirteenth day of the twelfth month – that is, the month of *Adar* – and to plunder their possessions.

וְנָשִׁים בְּיוֹם אֶחָד בִּשְׁלוֹשָׁה עָשָׂר לְחֹדֶשׁ שְׁנֵים־עָשָׂר הוּא־חֹדֶשׁ אֲדָר וּשְׁלָלָם לָבוֹז:

v'-nish-LO-akh s'-fa-REEM b'-YAD ha-ra-TZEEM el kol m'-dee-NOT ha-ME-lekh
l'-hash-MEED la-ha-ROG ul-a-BAYD et kol ha-y'-hu-DEEM mi-NA-ar
v'-AD za-KAYN taf v'-na-SHEEM b'-YOM e-KHAD bish-lo-SHAH a-SAR
l'-KHO-desh sh'-NYM a-SAR hu KHO-desh a-DAR ush-la-LAM la-VOZ

14 The text of the document was to the effect that a law should be proclaimed in every single province; it was to be publicly displayed to all the peoples, so that they might be ready for that day.

יד פַּתְשֶׁגֶן הַכְּתָב לְהִנָּתֵן דָּת בְּכָל־מְדִינָה וּמְדִינָה גָּלוּי לְכָל־הָעַמִּים לִהְיוֹת עֲתִדִים לַיּוֹם הַזֶּה:

15 The couriers went out posthaste on the royal mission, and the decree was proclaimed in the fortress Shushan. The king and Haman sat down to feast, but the city of Shushan was dumfounded.

טו הָרָצִים יָצְאוּ דְחוּפִים בִּדְבַר הַמֶּלֶךְ וְהַדָּת נִתְּנָה בְּשׁוּשַׁן הַבִּירָה וְהַמֶּלֶךְ וְהָמָן יָשְׁבוּ לִשְׁתּוֹת וְהָעִיר שׁוּשָׁן נָבוֹכָה:

4 1 When *Mordechai* learned all that had happened, *Mordechai* tore his clothes and put on sackcloth and ashes. He went through the city, crying out loudly and bitterly,

ד א וּמָרְדֳּכַי יָדַע אֶת־כָּל־אֲשֶׁר נַעֲשָׂה וַיִּקְרַע מָרְדֳּכַי אֶת־בְּגָדָיו וַיִּלְבַּשׁ שַׂק וָאֵפֶר וַיֵּצֵא בְּתוֹךְ הָעִיר וַיִּזְעַק זְעָקָה גְדֹלָה וּמָרָה:

2 until he came in front of the palace gate; for one could not enter the palace gate wearing sackcloth. –

ב וַיָּבוֹא עַד לִפְנֵי שַׁעַר־הַמֶּלֶךְ כִּי אֵין לָבוֹא אֶל־שַׁעַר הַמֶּלֶךְ בִּלְבוּשׁ שָׂק:

3 Also, in every province that the king's command and decree reached, there was great mourning among the *Yehudim*, with fasting, weeping, and wailing, and everybody lay in sackcloth and ashes. –

ג וּבְכָל־מְדִינָה וּמְדִינָה מְקוֹם אֲשֶׁר דְּבַר־הַמֶּלֶךְ וְדָתוֹ מַגִּיעַ אֵבֶל גָּדוֹל לַיְּהוּדִים וְצוֹם וּבְכִי וּמִסְפֵּד שַׂק וָאֵפֶר יֻצַּע לָרַבִּים:

4 When *Esther*'s maidens and eunuchs came and informed her, the queen was greatly agitated. She sent clothing for *Mordechai* to wear, so that he might take off his sackcloth; but he refused.

ד וַתְּבוֹאֶינָה נַעֲרוֹת אֶסְתֵּר וְסָרִיסֶיהָ וַיַּגִּידוּ לָהּ וַתִּתְחַלְחַל הַמַּלְכָּה מְאֹד וַתִּשְׁלַח בְּגָדִים לְהַלְבִּישׁ אֶת־מָרְדֳּכַי וּלְהָסִיר שַׂקּוֹ מֵעָלָיו וְלֹא קִבֵּל:

5 Thereupon *Esther* summoned Hathach, one of the eunuchs whom the king had appointed to serve her, and sent him to *Mordechai* to learn the why and wherefore of it all.

ה וַתִּקְרָא אֶסְתֵּר לַהֲתָךְ מִסָּרִיסֵי הַמֶּלֶךְ אֲשֶׁר הֶעֱמִיד לְפָנֶיהָ וַתְּצַוֵּהוּ עַל־מָרְדֳּכָי לָדַעַת מַה־זֶּה וְעַל־מַה־זֶּה:

6 Hathach went out to *Mordechai* in the city square in front of the palace gate;

ו וַיֵּצֵא הֲתָךְ אֶל־מָרְדֳּכָי אֶל־רְחוֹב הָעִיר אֲשֶׁר לִפְנֵי שַׁעַר־הַמֶּלֶךְ:

A group of students welcome North American immigrants to Israel

opportunity to do so. After the Persian king Cyrus conquered the Babylonians, he allowed the Children of Israel to return to the Land of Israel and begin reconstruction of the *Beit Hamikdash*. However, a mere 42,360 returned to *Yerushalayim* (Ezra 2:64) while close to a million remained in Babylonia. The generation was therefore punished for their lack of enthusiasm towards returning to Israel. This teaches us the importance of making every effort to embrace the land and to physically return to it whenever possible.

7 and *Mordechai* told him all that had happened to him, and all about the money that Haman had offered to pay into the royal treasury for the destruction of the *Yehudim*.

ז וַיַּגֶּד־לוֹ מָרְדֳּכַי אֵת כָּל־אֲשֶׁר קָרָהוּ וְאֵת פָּרָשַׁת הַכֶּסֶף אֲשֶׁר אָמַר הָמָן לִשְׁקוֹל עַל־גִּנְזֵי הַמֶּלֶךְ בַּיְּהוּדִיים [בַּיְּהוּדִים] לְאַבְּדָם:

8 He also gave him the written text of the law that had been proclaimed in Shushan for their destruction. [He bade him] show it to *Esther* and inform her, and charge her to go to the king and to appeal to him and to plead with him for her people.

ח וְאֶת־פַּתְשֶׁגֶן כְּתָב־הַדָּת אֲשֶׁר־נִתַּן בְּשׁוּשָׁן לְהַשְׁמִידָם נָתַן לוֹ לְהַרְאוֹת אֶת־אֶסְתֵּר וּלְהַגִּיד לָהּ וּלְצַוּוֹת עָלֶיהָ לָבוֹא אֶל־הַמֶּלֶךְ לְהִתְחַנֶּן־לוֹ וּלְבַקֵּשׁ מִלְּפָנָיו עַל־עַמָּהּ:

9 When Hathach came and delivered *Mordechai's* message to *Esther*,

ט וַיָּבוֹא הֲתָךְ וַיַּגֵּד לְאֶסְתֵּר אֵת דִּבְרֵי מָרְדֳּכָי:

10 *Esther* told Hathach to take back to *Mordechai* the following reply:

י וַתֹּאמֶר אֶסְתֵּר לַהֲתָךְ וַתְּצַוֵּהוּ אֶל־מָרְדֳּכָי:

11 "All the king's courtiers and the people of the king's provinces know that if any person, man or woman, enters the king's presence in the inner court without having been summoned, there is but one law for him – that he be put to death. Only if the king extends the golden scepter to him may he live. Now I have not been summoned to visit the king for the last thirty days."

יא כָּל־עַבְדֵי הַמֶּלֶךְ וְעַם־מְדִינוֹת הַמֶּלֶךְ יוֹדְעִים אֲשֶׁר כָּל־אִישׁ וְאִשָּׁה אֲשֶׁר יָבוֹא־אֶל־הַמֶּלֶךְ אֶל־הֶחָצֵר הַפְּנִימִית אֲשֶׁר לֹא־יִקָּרֵא אַחַת דָּתוֹ לְהָמִית לְבַד מֵאֲשֶׁר יוֹשִׁיט־לוֹ הַמֶּלֶךְ אֶת־שַׁרְבִיט הַזָּהָב וְחָיָה וַאֲנִי לֹא נִקְרֵאתִי לָבוֹא אֶל־הַמֶּלֶךְ זֶה שְׁלוֹשִׁים יוֹם:

12 When *Mordechai* was told what *Esther* had said,

יב וַיַּגִּידוּ לְמָרְדֳּכָי אֵת דִּבְרֵי אֶסְתֵּר:

13 *Mordechai* had this message delivered to *Esther*: "Do not imagine that you, of all the *Yehudim*, will escape with your life by being in the king's palace.

יג וַיֹּאמֶר מָרְדֳּכַי לְהָשִׁיב אֶל־אֶסְתֵּר אַל־תְּדַמִּי בְנַפְשֵׁךְ לְהִמָּלֵט בֵּית־הַמֶּלֶךְ מִכָּל־הַיְּהוּדִים:

14 On the contrary, if you keep silent in this crisis, relief and deliverance will come to the *Yehudim* from another quarter, while you and your father's house will perish. And who knows, perhaps you have attained to royal position for just such a crisis."

יד כִּי אִם־הַחֲרֵשׁ תַּחֲרִישִׁי בָּעֵת הַזֹּאת רֶוַח וְהַצָּלָה יַעֲמוֹד לַיְּהוּדִים מִמָּקוֹם אַחֵר וְאַתְּ וּבֵית־אָבִיךְ תֹּאבֵדוּ וּמִי יוֹדֵעַ אִם־לְעֵת כָּזֹאת הִגַּעַתְּ לַמַּלְכוּת:

KEE im ha-kha-RAYSH ta-kha-ree-SHEE ba-AYT ha-ZOT RE-vakh
v'-ha-tza-LAH ya-a-MOD la-y'-hu-DEEM mi-ma-KOM a-KHAYR v'-AT u-VAYT
a-VEEKH to-VAY-du u-MEE yo-DAY-a im l'-AYT ka-ZOT hi-GA-at la-mal-KHUT

15 Then *Esther* sent back this answer to *Mordechai*:

טו וַתֹּאמֶר אֶסְתֵּר לְהָשִׁיב אֶל־מָרְדֳּכָי:

4:14 Relief and deliverance will come to the *Yehudim* *Mordechai's* inspiring words move *Esther* to courageously step up and defend her people. *Mordechai* does not say, "If you are silent now, then we are all doomed," because he knows that the God of Israel will never forsake His people. Instead, *Mordechai* empowers *Esther* to take a leading role in the redemption, and not to sit quietly on the sidelines as it unfolds. In every generation there are those who threaten the existence of the Nation of Israel. Ultimately, *Hashem* will defend His people and His land, but is up to each individual to decide if he or she will stand up, as Queen *Esther* did, on behalf of Israel.

Jews and Christians rally for peace in Israel, Trafalgar Square, London

16 "Go, assemble all the *Yehudim* who live in Shushan, and fast in my behalf; do not eat or drink for three days, night or day. I and my maidens will observe the same fast. Then I shall go to the king, though it is contrary to the law; and if I am to perish, I shall perish!"

טז לֵךְ כְּנוֹס אֶת־כָּל־הַיְּהוּדִים הַנִּמְצְאִים בְּשׁוּשָׁן וְצוּמוּ עָלַי וְאַל־תֹּאכְלוּ וְאַל־תִּשְׁתּוּ שְׁלֹשֶׁת יָמִים לַיְלָה וָיוֹם גַּם־אֲנִי וְנַעֲרֹתַי אָצוּם כֵּן וּבְכֵן אָבוֹא אֶל־הַמֶּלֶךְ אֲשֶׁר לֹא־כַדָּת וְכַאֲשֶׁר אָבַדְתִּי אָבָדְתִּי:

17 So *Mordechai* went about [the city] and did just as *Esther* had commanded him.

יז וַיַּעֲבֹר מָרְדֳּכָי וַיַּעַשׂ כְּכֹל אֲשֶׁר־צִוְּתָה עָלָיו אֶסְתֵּר:

5 1 On the third day, *Esther* put on royal apparel and stood in the inner court of the king's palace, facing the king's palace, while the king was sitting on his royal throne in the throne room facing the entrance of the palace.

ה א וַיְהִי בַּיּוֹם הַשְּׁלִישִׁי וַתִּלְבַּשׁ אֶסְתֵּר מַלְכוּת וַתַּעֲמֹד בַּחֲצַר בֵּית־הַמֶּלֶךְ הַפְּנִימִית נֹכַח בֵּית הַמֶּלֶךְ וְהַמֶּלֶךְ יוֹשֵׁב עַל־כִּסֵּא מַלְכוּתוֹ בְּבֵית הַמַּלְכוּת נֹכַח פֶּתַח הַבָּיִת:

2 As soon as the king saw Queen *Esther* standing in the court, she won his favor. The king extended to *Esther* the golden scepter which he had in his hand, and *Esther* approached and touched the tip of the scepter.

ב וַיְהִי כִרְאוֹת הַמֶּלֶךְ אֶת־אֶסְתֵּר הַמַּלְכָּה עֹמֶדֶת בֶּחָצֵר נָשְׂאָה חֵן בְּעֵינָיו וַיּוֹשֶׁט הַמֶּלֶךְ לְאֶסְתֵּר אֶת־שַׁרְבִיט הַזָּהָב אֲשֶׁר בְּיָדוֹ וַתִּקְרַב אֶסְתֵּר וַתִּגַּע בְּרֹאשׁ הַשַּׁרְבִיט:

3 "What troubles you, Queen *Esther*?" the king asked her. "And what is your request? Even to half the kingdom, it shall be granted you."

ג וַיֹּאמֶר לָהּ הַמֶּלֶךְ מַה־לָּךְ אֶסְתֵּר הַמַּלְכָּה וּמַה־בַּקָּשָׁתֵךְ עַד־חֲצִי הַמַּלְכוּת וְיִנָּתֵן לָךְ:

va-YO-mer LAH ha-ME-lekh mah LAKH es-TAYR ha-mal-KAH u-mah ba-ka-sha-TAYKH ad kha-TZEE ha-mal-KHUT v'-yi-na-TAYN LAKH

4 "If it please Your Majesty," *Esther* replied, "let Your Majesty and Haman come today to the feast that I have prepared for him."

ד וַתֹּאמֶר אֶסְתֵּר אִם־עַל־הַמֶּלֶךְ טוֹב יָבוֹא הַמֶּלֶךְ וְהָמָן הַיּוֹם אֶל־הַמִּשְׁתֶּה אֲשֶׁר־עָשִׂיתִי לוֹ:

5 The king commanded, "Tell Haman to hurry and do *Esther*'s bidding." So the king and Haman came to the feast that *Esther* had prepared.

ה וַיֹּאמֶר הַמֶּלֶךְ מַהֲרוּ אֶת־הָמָן לַעֲשׂוֹת אֶת־דְּבַר אֶסְתֵּר וַיָּבֹא הַמֶּלֶךְ וְהָמָן אֶל־הַמִּשְׁתֶּה אֲשֶׁר־עָשְׂתָה אֶסְתֵּר:

6 At the wine feast, the king asked *Esther*, "What is your wish? It shall be granted you. And what is your request? Even to half the kingdom, it shall be fulfilled."

ו וַיֹּאמֶר הַמֶּלֶךְ לְאֶסְתֵּר בְּמִשְׁתֵּה הַיַּיִן מַה־שְּׁאֵלָתֵךְ וְיִנָּתֵן לָךְ וּמַה־בַּקָּשָׁתֵךְ עַד־חֲצִי הַמַּלְכוּת וְתֵעָשׂ:

7 "My wish," replied *Esther*, "my request –

ז וַתַּעַן אֶסְתֵּר וַתֹּאמַר שְׁאֵלָתִי וּבַקָּשָׁתִי:

5:3 Even to half the kingdom When Ahasuerus offered *Esther* up to half of the kingdom, this was not merely an exaggerated show of generosity, but it referred to a specific geographic location. *Rashi* notes that the halfway mark of Ahasuerus' empire was the site of the *Beit Hamikdash*. Ahasuerus tells *Esther* that he is willing to do anything to make her happy, short of allowing the rebuilding of the Temple. Although Cyrus, his predecessor, had allowed the Children of Israel to return to Israel and begin reconstruction of the *Beit Hamikdash*, Ahasuerus was adamantly against it. Ironically, according to Jewish tradition it was his son Darius, born to him by *Esther*, who allowed the construction of the *Beit Hamikdash* to be completed.

The Cyrus cylinder

8 if Your Majesty will do me the favor, if it please Your Majesty to grant my wish and accede to my request – let Your Majesty and Haman come to the feast which I will prepare for them; and tomorrow I will do Your Majesty's bidding."

9 That day Haman went out happy and lighthearted. But when Haman saw *Mordechai* in the palace gate, and *Mordechai* did not rise or even stir on his account, Haman was filled with rage at him.

10 Nevertheless, Haman controlled himself and went home. He sent for his friends and his wife Zeresh,

11 and Haman told them about his great wealth and his many sons, and all about how the king had promoted him and advanced him above the officials and the king's courtiers.

12 "What is more," said Haman, "Queen *Esther* gave a feast, and besides the king she did not have anyone but me. And tomorrow too I am invited by her along with the king.

13 Yet all this means nothing to me every time I see that *Yehudi Mordechai* sitting in the palace gate."

14 Then his wife Zeresh and all his friends said to him, "Let a stake be put up, fifty *amot* high, and in the morning ask the king to have *Mordechai* impaled on it. Then you can go gaily with the king to the feast." The proposal pleased Haman, and he had the stake put up.

6:1 That night, sleep deserted the king, and he ordered the book of records, the annals, to be brought; and it was read to the king.

ח אִם־מָצָ֨אתִי חֵ֜ן בְּעֵינֵ֣י הַמֶּ֗לֶךְ וְאִם־עַל־ הַמֶּ֨לֶךְ֙ ט֔וֹב לָתֵת֙ אֶת־שְׁאֵ֣לָתִ֔י וְלַעֲשׂ֖וֹת אֶת־בַּקָּשָׁתִ֑י יָב֧וֹא הַמֶּ֣לֶךְ וְהָמָ֗ן אֶל־ הַמִּשְׁתֶּה֙ אֲשֶׁ֣ר אֶֽעֱשֶׂ֣ה לָהֶ֔ם וּמָחָ֛ר אֶֽעֱשֶׂ֖ה כִּדְבַ֥ר הַמֶּֽלֶךְ׃

ט וַיֵּצֵ֤א הָמָן֙ בַּיּ֣וֹם הַה֔וּא שָׂמֵ֖חַ וְט֣וֹב לֵ֑ב וְכִרְא֨וֹת הָמָ֜ן אֶֽת־מׇרְדֳּכַ֣י בְּשַׁ֣עַר הַמֶּ֗לֶךְ וְלֹא־קָם֙ וְלֹא־זָ֣ע מִמֶּ֔נּוּ וַיִּמָּלֵ֥א הָמָ֛ן עַֽל־ מׇרְדֳּכַ֖י חֵמָֽה׃

י וַיִּתְאַפַּ֣ק הָמָ֔ן וַיָּב֖וֹא אֶל־בֵּית֑וֹ וַיִּשְׁלַ֥ח וַיָּבֵ֛א אֶת־אֹֽהֲבָ֖יו וְאֶת־זֶ֥רֶשׁ אִשְׁתּֽוֹ׃

יא וַיְסַפֵּ֨ר לָהֶ֥ם הָמָ֛ן אֶת־כְּב֥וֹד עׇשְׁר֖וֹ וְרֹ֣ב בָּנָ֑יו וְאֵת֩ כׇּל־אֲשֶׁ֨ר גִּדְּל֤וֹ הַמֶּ֙לֶךְ֙ וְאֵ֣ת אֲשֶׁ֣ר נִשְּׂא֔וֹ עַל־הַשָּׂרִ֖ים וְעַבְדֵ֥י הַמֶּֽלֶךְ׃

יב וַיֹּ֣אמֶר הָמָ֗ן אַ֣ף לֹא־הֵבִיאָה֩ אֶסְתֵּ֨ר הַמַּלְכָּ֧ה עִם־הַמֶּ֛לֶךְ אֶל־הַמִּשְׁתֶּ֥ה אֲשֶׁר־ עָשָׂ֖תָה כִּ֣י אִם־אוֹתִ֑י וְגַם־לְמָחָ֛ר אֲנִ֥י קָֽרוּא־לָ֖הּ עִם־הַמֶּֽלֶךְ׃

יג וְכׇל־זֶ֕ה אֵינֶ֥נּוּ שֹׁוֶ֖ה לִ֑י בְּכׇל־עֵ֗ת אֲשֶׁ֨ר אֲנִ֤י רֹאֶה֙ אֶת־מׇרְדֳּכַ֣י הַיְּהוּדִ֔י יוֹשֵׁ֖ב בְּשַׁ֥עַר הַמֶּֽלֶךְ׃

יד וַתֹּ֣אמֶר ל֣וֹ זֶ֣רֶשׁ אִשְׁתּ֡וֹ וְכׇל־אֹֽהֲבָ֜יו יַֽעֲשׂוּ־עֵ֗ץ גָּבֹ֣הַּ חֲמִשִּׁ֣ים אַמָּה֮ וּבַבֹּ֣קֶר ׀ אֱמֹ֣ר לַמֶּ֗לֶךְ וְיִתְל֤וּ אֶֽת־מׇרְדֳּכַי֙ עָלָ֔יו וּבֹֽא־עִם־הַמֶּ֥לֶךְ אֶל־הַמִּשְׁתֶּ֖ה שָׂמֵ֑חַ וַיִּיטַ֧ב הַדָּבָ֛ר לִפְנֵ֥י הָמָ֖ן וַיַּ֥עַשׂ הָעֵֽץ׃

ו א בַּלַּ֣יְלָה הַה֔וּא נָדְדָ֖ה שְׁנַ֣ת הַמֶּ֑לֶךְ וַיֹּ֗אמֶר לְהָבִ֞יא אֶת־סֵ֤פֶר הַזִּכְרֹנוֹת֙ דִּבְרֵ֣י הַיָּמִ֔ים וַיִּֽהְי֥וּ נִקְרָאִ֖ים לִפְנֵ֥י הַמֶּֽלֶךְ׃

ba-LAI-lah ha-HU na-d'-DAH sh'-NAT ha-ME-lekh va-YO-mer
l'-ha-VEE et SAY-fer ha-zikh-ro-NOT div-RAY ha-ya-MEEM
va-yih-YU nik-ra-EEM lif-NAY ha-ME-lekh

6:1 That night Upon careful reading of *Megillat Esther*, it becomes clear that "that night" was the second night of *Pesach*. Since Haman's letters had been sent out on the thirteenth day of *Nisan*, and *Esther* called for three days of fasting, the first banquet took place on the sixteenth of *Nissan*. The Talmud (*Megila* 16a) relates that when Haman looked for *Mordechai* in order to lead him around the city, he found the Jewish Sage teaching the laws of the *Omer* offering, which was offered in the Temple on the second day of Passover. When granted permission to rebuild the *Beit Hamikdash* by Cyrus, the Jews did not heed the call, and only a small minority returned to *Yerushalayim*. Hoping to rectify this sin which potentially brought about Haman's decree of annihilation, *Mordechai* was teaching about the Temple and its laws. Though in exile, the Jews have remained connected to *Yerushalayim* and the Holy Temple through the study of *Torah*.

Jerusalem's Tower of David at night

2 There it was found written that *Mordechai* had denounced Bigthana and Teresh, two of the king's eunuchs who guarded the threshold, who had plotted to do away with King Ahasuerus.

ב וַיִּמָּצֵא כָתוּב אֲשֶׁר הִגִּיד מָרְדֳּכַי עַל־בִּגְתָנָא וָתֶרֶשׁ שְׁנֵי סָרִיסֵי הַמֶּלֶךְ מִשֹּׁמְרֵי הַסַּף אֲשֶׁר בִּקְשׁוּ לִשְׁלֹחַ יָד בַּמֶּלֶךְ אֲחַשְׁוֵרוֹשׁ:

3 "What honor or advancement has been conferred on *Mordechai* for this?" the king inquired. "Nothing at all has been done for him," replied the king's servants who were in attendance on him.

ג וַיֹּאמֶר הַמֶּלֶךְ מַה־נַּעֲשָׂה יְקָר וּגְדוּלָּה לְמָרְדֳּכַי עַל־זֶה וַיֹּאמְרוּ נַעֲרֵי הַמֶּלֶךְ מְשָׁרְתָיו לֹא־נַעֲשָׂה עִמּוֹ דָּבָר:

4 "Who is in the court?" the king asked. For Haman had just entered the outer court of the royal palace, to speak to the king about having *Mordechai* impaled on the stake he had prepared for him.

ד וַיֹּאמֶר הַמֶּלֶךְ מִי בֶחָצֵר וְהָמָן בָּא לַחֲצַר בֵּית־הַמֶּלֶךְ הַחִיצוֹנָה לֵאמֹר לַמֶּלֶךְ לִתְלוֹת אֶת־מָרְדֳּכַי עַל־הָעֵץ אֲשֶׁר־הֵכִין לוֹ:

5 "It is Haman standing in the court," the king's servants answered him. "Let him enter," said the king.

ה וַיֹּאמְרוּ נַעֲרֵי הַמֶּלֶךְ אֵלָיו הִנֵּה הָמָן עֹמֵד בֶּחָצֵר וַיֹּאמֶר הַמֶּלֶךְ יָבוֹא:

6 Haman entered, and the king asked him, "What should be done for a man whom the king desires to honor?" Haman said to himself, "Whom would the king desire to honor more than me?"

ו וַיָּבוֹא הָמָן וַיֹּאמֶר לוֹ הַמֶּלֶךְ מַה־לַעֲשׂוֹת בָּאִישׁ אֲשֶׁר הַמֶּלֶךְ חָפֵץ בִּיקָרוֹ וַיֹּאמֶר הָמָן בְּלִבּוֹ לְמִי יַחְפֹּץ הַמֶּלֶךְ לַעֲשׂוֹת יְקָר יוֹתֵר מִמֶּנִּי:

7 So Haman said to the king, "For the man whom the king desires to honor,

ז וַיֹּאמֶר הָמָן אֶל־הַמֶּלֶךְ אִישׁ אֲשֶׁר הַמֶּלֶךְ חָפֵץ בִּיקָרוֹ:

8 let royal garb which the king has worn be brought, and a horse on which the king has ridden and on whose head a royal diadem has been set;

ח יָבִיאוּ לְבוּשׁ מַלְכוּת אֲשֶׁר לָבַשׁ־בּוֹ הַמֶּלֶךְ וְסוּס אֲשֶׁר רָכַב עָלָיו הַמֶּלֶךְ וַאֲשֶׁר נִתַּן כֶּתֶר מַלְכוּת בְּרֹאשׁוֹ:

9 and let the attire and the horse be put in the charge of one of the king's noble courtiers. And let the man whom the king desires to honor be attired and paraded on the horse through the city square, while they proclaim before him: This is what is done for the man whom the king desires to honor!"

ט וְנָתוֹן הַלְּבוּשׁ וְהַסּוּס עַל־יַד־אִישׁ מִשָּׂרֵי הַמֶּלֶךְ הַפַּרְתְּמִים וְהִלְבִּישׁוּ אֶת־הָאִישׁ אֲשֶׁר הַמֶּלֶךְ חָפֵץ בִּיקָרוֹ וְהִרְכִּיבֻהוּ עַל־הַסּוּס בִּרְחוֹב הָעִיר וְקָרְאוּ לְפָנָיו כָּכָה יֵעָשֶׂה לָאִישׁ אֲשֶׁר הַמֶּלֶךְ חָפֵץ בִּיקָרוֹ:

10 "Quick, then!" said the king to Haman. "Get the garb and the horse, as you have said, and do this to *Mordechai* the *Yehudi*, who sits in the king's gate. Omit nothing of all you have proposed."

י וַיֹּאמֶר הַמֶּלֶךְ לְהָמָן מַהֵר קַח אֶת־הַלְּבוּשׁ וְאֶת־הַסּוּס כַּאֲשֶׁר דִּבַּרְתָּ וַעֲשֵׂה־כֵן לְמָרְדֳּכַי הַיְּהוּדִי הַיּוֹשֵׁב בְּשַׁעַר הַמֶּלֶךְ אַל־תַּפֵּל דָּבָר מִכֹּל אֲשֶׁר דִּבַּרְתָּ:

11 So Haman took the garb and the horse and arrayed *Mordechai* and paraded him through the city square; and he proclaimed before him: This is what is done for the man whom the king desires to honor!

יא וַיִּקַּח הָמָן אֶת־הַלְּבוּשׁ וְאֶת־הַסּוּס וַיַּלְבֵּשׁ אֶת־מָרְדֳּכָי וַיַּרְכִּיבֵהוּ בִּרְחוֹב הָעִיר וַיִּקְרָא לְפָנָיו כָּכָה יֵעָשֶׂה לָאִישׁ אֲשֶׁר הַמֶּלֶךְ חָפֵץ בִּיקָרוֹ:

12 Then *Mordechai* returned to the king's gate, while Haman hurried home, his head covered in mourning.

יב וַיָּשָׁב מָרְדֳּכַי אֶל־שַׁעַר הַמֶּלֶךְ וְהָמָן נִדְחַף אֶל־בֵּיתוֹ אָבֵל וַחֲפוּי רֹאשׁ:

Esther

13 There Haman told his wife Zeresh and all his friends everything that had befallen him. His advisers and his wife Zeresh said to him, "If *Mordechai*, before whom you have begun to fall, is of Yehudiish stock, you will not overcome him; you will fall before him to your ruin."

יג וַיְסַפֵּר הָמָן לְזֶרֶשׁ אִשְׁתּוֹ וּלְכָל־אֹהֲבָיו אֵת כָּל־אֲשֶׁר קָרָהוּ וַיֹּאמְרוּ לוֹ חֲכָמָיו וְזֶרֶשׁ אִשְׁתּוֹ אִם מִזֶּרַע הַיְּהוּדִים מָרְדֳּכַי אֲשֶׁר הַחִלּוֹתָ לִנְפֹּל לְפָנָיו לֹא־תוּכַל לוֹ כִּי־נָפוֹל תִּפּוֹל לְפָנָיו:

14 While they were still speaking with him, the king's eunuchs arrived and hurriedly brought Haman to the banquet which *Esther* had prepared.

יד עוֹדָם מְדַבְּרִים עִמּוֹ וְסָרִיסֵי הַמֶּלֶךְ הִגִּיעוּ וַיַּבְהִלוּ לְהָבִיא אֶת־הָמָן אֶל־הַמִּשְׁתֶּה אֲשֶׁר־עָשְׂתָה אֶסְתֵּר:

ז 7 1 So the king and Haman came to feast with Queen *Esther*.

ז א וַיָּבֹא הַמֶּלֶךְ וְהָמָן לִשְׁתּוֹת עִם־אֶסְתֵּר הַמַּלְכָּה:

va-ya-VO ha-ME-lekh v'-ha-MAN lish-TOT im es-TAYR ha-mal-KAH

2 On the second day, the king again asked *Esther* at the wine feast, "What is your wish, Queen *Esther*? It shall be granted you. And what is your request? Even to half the kingdom, it shall be fulfilled."

ב וַיֹּאמֶר הַמֶּלֶךְ לְאֶסְתֵּר גַּם בַּיּוֹם הַשֵּׁנִי בְּמִשְׁתֵּה הַיַּיִן מַה־שְּׁאֵלָתֵךְ אֶסְתֵּר הַמַּלְכָּה וְתִנָּתֵן לָךְ וּמַה־בַּקָּשָׁתֵךְ עַד־חֲצִי הַמַּלְכוּת וְתֵעָשׂ:

3 Queen *Esther* replied: "If Your Majesty will do me the favor, and if it pleases Your Majesty, let my life be granted me as my wish, and my people as my request.

ג וַתַּעַן אֶסְתֵּר הַמַּלְכָּה וַתֹּאמַר אִם־מָצָאתִי חֵן בְּעֵינֶיךָ הַמֶּלֶךְ וְאִם־עַל־הַמֶּלֶךְ טוֹב תִּנָּתֶן־לִי נַפְשִׁי בִּשְׁאֵלָתִי וְעַמִּי בְּבַקָּשָׁתִי:

4 For we have been sold, my people and I, to be destroyed, massacred, and exterminated. Had we only been sold as bondmen and bondwomen, I would have kept silent; for the adversary is not worthy of the king's trouble."

ד כִּי נִמְכַּרְנוּ אֲנִי וְעַמִּי לְהַשְׁמִיד לַהֲרוֹג וּלְאַבֵּד וְאִלּוּ לַעֲבָדִים וְלִשְׁפָחוֹת נִמְכַּרְנוּ הֶחֱרַשְׁתִּי כִּי אֵין הַצָּר שֹׁוֶה בְּנֵזֶק הַמֶּלֶךְ:

5 Thereupon King Ahasuerus demanded of Queen *Esther*, "Who is he and where is he who dared to do this?"

ה וַיֹּאמֶר הַמֶּלֶךְ אֲחַשְׁוֵרוֹשׁ וַיֹּאמֶר לְאֶסְתֵּר הַמַּלְכָּה מִי הוּא זֶה וְאֵי־זֶה הוּא אֲשֶׁר־מְלָאוֹ לִבּוֹ לַעֲשׂוֹת כֵּן:

6 "The adversary and enemy," replied *Esther*, "is this evil Haman!" And Haman cringed in terror before the king and the queen.

ו וַתֹּאמֶר־אֶסְתֵּר אִישׁ צַר וְאוֹיֵב הָמָן הָרָע הַזֶּה וְהָמָן נִבְעַת מִלִּפְנֵי הַמֶּלֶךְ וְהַמַּלְכָּה:

7 The king, in his fury, left the wine feast for the palace garden, while Haman remained to plead with Queen *Esther* for his life; for he saw that the king had resolved to destroy him.

ז וְהַמֶּלֶךְ קָם בַּחֲמָתוֹ מִמִּשְׁתֵּה הַיַּיִן אֶל־גִּנַּת הַבִּיתָן וְהָמָן עָמַד לְבַקֵּשׁ עַל־נַפְשׁוֹ מֵאֶסְתֵּר הַמַּלְכָּה כִּי רָאָה כִּי־כָלְתָה אֵלָיו הָרָעָה מֵאֵת הַמֶּלֶךְ:

7:1 So the king and Haman came to feast Why does *Esther* deem it necessary to invite Haman to her banquet with Ahasuerus? As long as the Jewish people knew that they had *Esther* in the palace, they were counting on her to reverse Haman's evil decree. Yet *Esther* wanted the people themselves to fully repent. Inviting Haman made it appear that she was abandoning her people and aligning with the wicked Haman. At that point, the terrified nation called out to *Hashem* with a new intensity that merited salvation. Throughout the ages, true redemption arrives when we realize that we have no one to rely on aside from God above.

Calling out to *Hashem* at the Western Wall

Esther

8 When the king returned from the palace garden to the banquet room, Haman was lying prostrate on the couch on which *Esther* reclined. "Does he mean," cried the king, "to ravish the queen in my own palace?" No sooner did these words leave the king's lips than Haman's face was covered.

ח וְהַמֶּלֶךְ שָׁב מִגִּנַּת הַבִּיתָן אֶל־בֵּית מִשְׁתֵּה הַיַּיִן וְהָמָן נֹפֵל עַל־הַמִּטָּה אֲשֶׁר אֶסְתֵּר עָלֶיהָ וַיֹּאמֶר הַמֶּלֶךְ הֲגַם לִכְבּוֹשׁ אֶת־הַמַּלְכָּה עִמִּי בַּבָּיִת הַדָּבָר יָצָא מִפִּי הַמֶּלֶךְ וּפְנֵי הָמָן חָפוּ׃

9 Then Harbonahh, one of the eunuchs in attendance on the king, said, "What is more, a stake is standing at Haman's house, fifty *amot* high, which Haman made for *Mordechai* – the man whose words saved the king." "Impale him on it!" the king ordered.

ט וַיֹּאמֶר חַרְבוֹנָה אֶחָד מִן־הַסָּרִיסִים לִפְנֵי הַמֶּלֶךְ גַּם הִנֵּה־הָעֵץ אֲשֶׁר־עָשָׂה הָמָן לְמׇרְדֳּכַי אֲשֶׁר דִּבֶּר־טוֹב עַל־הַמֶּלֶךְ עֹמֵד בְּבֵית הָמָן גָּבֹהַּ חֲמִשִּׁים אַמָּה וַיֹּאמֶר הַמֶּלֶךְ תְּלֻהוּ עָלָיו׃

10 So they impaled Haman on the stake which he had put up for *Mordechai*, and the king's fury abated.

י וַיִּתְלוּ אֶת־הָמָן עַל־הָעֵץ אֲשֶׁר־הֵכִין לְמׇרְדֳּכָי וַחֲמַת הַמֶּלֶךְ שָׁכָכָה׃

8 1 That very day King Ahasuerus gave the property of Haman, the enemy of the *Yehudim*, to Queen *Esther*. *Mordechai* presented himself to the king, for *Esther* had revealed how he was related to her.

ח א בַּיּוֹם הַהוּא נָתַן הַמֶּלֶךְ אֲחַשְׁוֵרוֹשׁ לְאֶסְתֵּר הַמַּלְכָּה אֶת־בֵּית הָמָן צֹרֵר היהודיים [הַיְּהוּדִים] וּמׇרְדֳּכַי בָּא לִפְנֵי הַמֶּלֶךְ כִּי־הִגִּידָה אֶסְתֵּר מַה הוּא־לָהּ׃

2 The king slipped off his ring, which he had taken back from Haman, and gave it to *Mordechai*; and *Esther* put *Mordechai* in charge of Haman's property.

ב וַיָּסַר הַמֶּלֶךְ אֶת־טַבַּעְתּוֹ אֲשֶׁר הֶעֱבִיר מֵהָמָן וַיִּתְּנָהּ לְמׇרְדֳּכָי וַתָּשֶׂם אֶסְתֵּר אֶת־מׇרְדֳּכַי עַל־בֵּית הָמָן׃

3 *Esther* spoke to the king again, falling at his feet and weeping, and beseeching him to avert the evil plotted by Haman the Agagite against the *Yehudim*.

ג וַתּוֹסֶף אֶסְתֵּר וַתְּדַבֵּר לִפְנֵי הַמֶּלֶךְ וַתִּפֹּל לִפְנֵי רַגְלָיו וַתֵּבְךְּ וַתִּתְחַנֶּן־לוֹ לְהַעֲבִיר אֶת־רָעַת הָמָן הָאֲגָגִי וְאֵת מַחֲשַׁבְתּוֹ אֲשֶׁר חָשַׁב עַל־הַיְּהוּדִים׃

4 The king extended the golden scepter to *Esther*, and *Esther* arose and stood before the king.

ד וַיּוֹשֶׁט הַמֶּלֶךְ לְאֶסְתֵּר אֵת שַׁרְבִט הַזָּהָב וַתָּקׇם אֶסְתֵּר וַתַּעֲמֹד לִפְנֵי הַמֶּלֶךְ׃

5 "If it please Your Majesty," she said, "and if I have won your favor and the proposal seems right to Your Majesty, and if I am pleasing to you – let dispatches be written countermanding those which were written by Haman son of Hammedatha the Agagite, embodying his plot to annihilate the *Yehudim* throughout the king's provinces.

ה וַתֹּאמֶר אִם־עַל־הַמֶּלֶךְ טוֹב וְאִם־מָצָאתִי חֵן לְפָנָיו וְכָשֵׁר הַדָּבָר לִפְנֵי הַמֶּלֶךְ וְטוֹבָה אֲנִי בְּעֵינָיו יִכָּתֵב לְהָשִׁיב אֶת־הַסְּפָרִים מַחֲשֶׁבֶת הָמָן בֶּן־הַמְּדָתָא הָאֲגָגִי אֲשֶׁר כָּתַב לְאַבֵּד אֶת־הַיְּהוּדִים אֲשֶׁר בְּכׇל־מְדִינוֹת הַמֶּלֶךְ׃

6 For how can I bear to see the disaster which will befall my people! And how can I bear to see the destruction of my kindred!"

ו כִּי אֵיכָכָה אוּכַל וְרָאִיתִי בָּרָעָה אֲשֶׁר־יִמְצָא אֶת־עַמִּי וְאֵיכָכָה אוּכַל וְרָאִיתִי בְּאׇבְדַן מוֹלַדְתִּי׃

7 Then King Ahasuerus said to Queen *Esther* and *Mordechai* the *Yehudi*, "I have given Haman's property to *Esther*, and he has been impaled on the stake for scheming against the *Yehudim*.

ז וַיֹּאמֶר הַמֶּלֶךְ אֲחַשְׁוֵרֹשׁ לְאֶסְתֵּר הַמַּלְכָּה וּלְמׇרְדֳּכַי הַיְּהוּדִי הִנֵּה בֵית־הָמָן נָתַתִּי לְאֶסְתֵּר וְאֹתוֹ תָּלוּ עַל־הָעֵץ עַל אֲשֶׁר־שָׁלַח יָדוֹ ביהודיים [בַּיְּהוּדִים]׃

8 And you may further write with regard to the *Yehudim* as you see fit. [Write it] in the king's name and seal it with the king's signet, for an edict that has been written in the king's name and sealed with the king's signet may not be revoked."

ח וְאַתֶּם כִּתְבוּ עַל־הַיְּהוּדִים כַּטּוֹב בְּעֵינֵיכֶם בְּשֵׁם הַמֶּלֶךְ וְחִתְמוּ בְּטַבַּעַת הַמֶּלֶךְ כִּי־כְתָב אֲשֶׁר־נִכְתָּב בְּשֵׁם־הַמֶּלֶךְ וְנַחְתּוֹם בְּטַבַּעַת הַמֶּלֶךְ אֵין לְהָשִׁיב:

9 So the king's scribes were summoned at that time, on the twenty-third day of the third month, that is, the month of *Sivan*; and letters were written, at *Mordechai's* dictation, to the *Yehudim* and to the satraps, the governors and the officials of the one hundred and twenty-seven provinces from India to Ethiopia: to every province in its own script and to every people in its own language, and to the *Yehudim* in their own script and language.

ט וַיִּקָּרְאוּ סֹפְרֵי־הַמֶּלֶךְ בָּעֵת־הַהִיא בַּחֹדֶשׁ הַשְּׁלִישִׁי הוּא־חֹדֶשׁ סִיוָן בִּשְׁלוֹשָׁה וְעֶשְׂרִים בּוֹ וַיִּכָּתֵב כְּכָל־אֲשֶׁר־צִוָּה מָרְדְּכַי אֶל־הַיְּהוּדִים וְאֶל הָאֲחַשְׁדַּרְפְּנִים־וְהַפַּחוֹת וְשָׂרֵי הַמְּדִינוֹת אֲשֶׁר מֵהֹדּוּ וְעַד־כּוּשׁ שֶׁבַע וְעֶשְׂרִים וּמֵאָה מְדִינָה מְדִינָה וּמְדִינָה כִּכְתָבָהּ וְעַם וָעָם כִּלְשֹׁנוֹ וְאֶל־הַיְּהוּדִים כִּכְתָבָם וְכִלְשׁוֹנָם:

*va-yi-ka-r'-U so-f'-RAY ha-ME-lekh ba-ayt ha-HEE ba-KHO-desh
ha-sh'-lee-SHEE hu KHO-desh see-VAN bish-lo-SHAH v'-es-REEM BO
va-yi-ka-TAYV k'-khol a-sher tzi-VAH mor-d'-KHAI el ha-y'-hu-DEEM
v'-EL ha-a-khash-dar-p'-NEEM v'-ha-pa-KHOT v'-sa-RAY ha-m'-dee-NOT
a-SHER may-HO-du v'-ad KUSH SHE-va v'-es-REEM u-may-AH
m'-dee-NAH m'-dee-NAH um-dee-NAH kikh-ta-VAH v'-AM va-AM
kil-sho-NO v'-EL ha-y'-hu-DEEM kikh-ta-VAM v'-khil-sho-NAM*

10 He had them written in the name of King Ahasuerus and sealed with the king's signet. Letters were dispatched by mounted couriers, riding steeds used in the king's service, bred of the royal stud,

י וַיִּכְתֹּב בְּשֵׁם הַמֶּלֶךְ אֲחַשְׁוֵרֹשׁ וַיַּחְתֹּם בְּטַבַּעַת הַמֶּלֶךְ וַיִּשְׁלַח סְפָרִים בְּיַד הָרָצִים בַּסּוּסִים רֹכְבֵי הָרֶכֶשׁ הָאֲחַשְׁתְּרָנִים בְּנֵי הָרַמָּכִים:

11 to this effect: The king has permitted the *Yehudim* of every city to assemble and fight for their lives; if any people or province attacks them, they may destroy, massacre, and exterminate its armed force together with women and children, and plunder their possessions –

יא אֲשֶׁר נָתַן הַמֶּלֶךְ לַיְּהוּדִים אֲשֶׁר בְּכָל־עִיר־וָעִיר לְהִקָּהֵל וְלַעֲמֹד עַל־נַפְשָׁם לְהַשְׁמִיד וְלַהֲרֹג וּלְאַבֵּד אֶת־כָּל־חֵיל עַם וּמְדִינָה הַצָּרִים אֹתָם טַף וְנָשִׁים וּשְׁלָלָם לָבוֹז:

12 on a single day in all the provinces of King Ahasuerus, namely, on the thirteenth day of the twelfth month, that is, the month of *Adar*.

יב בְּיוֹם אֶחָד בְּכָל־מְדִינוֹת הַמֶּלֶךְ אֲחַשְׁוֵרוֹשׁ בִּשְׁלוֹשָׁה עָשָׂר לְחֹדֶשׁ שְׁנֵים־עָשָׂר הוּא־חֹדֶשׁ אֲדָר:

Esther

8:9 Of the third month, that is, the month of Sivan This verse refers to the third month of the Jewish calendar, called *Sivan*. Throughout *Megillat Esther*, the Hebrew months are referred to by both number and name. *Ramban* (Exodus 12:2) teaches that originally the months were referred to by numbers, with the first month being the month of the redemption from Egypt, in order to commemorate the Exodus. During the Babylonian exile, however, the Jews adopted the Persian names for the months, which are used to this day. Just as the original numbering of the months included a reference to the Exodus from Egypt, the Persian names recall the return of the Jewish people from the Babylonian exile and the land of the Persians. In this way, all references to the Jewish calendar contain a subtle allusion to the first redemption from exile and the re-entry into the Land of Israel.

Sunset over the Temple Mount in *Yerushalayim*

13 The text of the document was to be issued as a law in every single province: it was to be publicly displayed to all the peoples, so that the *Yehudim* should be ready for that day to avenge themselves on their enemies.

יג פַּתְשֶׁגֶן הַכְּתָב לְהִנָּתֵן דָּת בְּכָל־מְדִינָה וּמְדִינָה גָּלוּי לְכָל־הָעַמִּים וְלִהְיוֹת הַיְּהוּדִיים [הַיְּהוּדִים] עתודים [עֲתִידִים] לַיּוֹם הַזֶּה לְהִנָּקֵם מֵאֹיְבֵיהֶם:

14 The couriers, mounted on royal steeds, went out in urgent haste at the king's command; and the decree was proclaimed in the fortress Shushan.

יד הָרָצִים רֹכְבֵי הָרֶכֶשׁ הָאֲחַשְׁתְּרָנִים יָצְאוּ מְבֹהָלִים וּדְחוּפִים בִּדְבַר הַמֶּלֶךְ וְהַדָּת נִתְּנָה בְּשׁוּשַׁן הַבִּירָה:

15 *Mordechai* left the king's presence in royal robes of blue and white, with a magnificent crown of gold and a mantle of fine linen and purple wool. And the city of Shushan rang with joyous cries.

טו וּמָרְדֳּכַי יָצָא מִלִּפְנֵי הַמֶּלֶךְ בִּלְבוּשׁ מַלְכוּת תְּכֵלֶת וָחוּר וַעֲטֶרֶת זָהָב גְּדוֹלָה וְתַכְרִיךְ בּוּץ וְאַרְגָּמָן וְהָעִיר שׁוּשָׁן צָהֲלָה וְשָׂמֵחָה:

16 The *Yehudim* enjoyed light and gladness, happiness and honor.

טז לַיְּהוּדִים הָיְתָה אוֹרָה וְשִׂמְחָה וְשָׂשֹׂן וִיקָר:

17 And in every province and in every city, when the king's command and decree arrived, there was gladness and joy among the *Yehudim*, a feast and a holiday. And many of the people of the land professed to be *Yehudim*, for the fear of the *Yehudim* had fallen upon them.

יז וּבְכָל־מְדִינָה וּמְדִינָה וּבְכָל־עִיר וָעִיר מְקוֹם אֲשֶׁר דְּבַר־הַמֶּלֶךְ וְדָתוֹ מַגִּיעַ שִׂמְחָה וְשָׂשׂוֹן לַיְּהוּדִים מִשְׁתֶּה וְיוֹם טוֹב וְרַבִּים מֵעַמֵּי הָאָרֶץ מִתְיַהֲדִים כִּי־נָפַל פַּחַד־הַיְּהוּדִים עֲלֵיהֶם:

9 1 And so, on the thirteenth day of the twelfth month – that is, the month of *Adar* – when the king's command and decree were to be executed, the very day on which the enemies of the *Yehudim* had expected to get them in their power, the opposite happened, and the *Yehudim* got their enemies in their power.

ט א וּבִשְׁנֵים עָשָׂר חֹדֶשׁ הוּא־חֹדֶשׁ אֲדָר בִּשְׁלוֹשָׁה עָשָׂר יוֹם בּוֹ אֲשֶׁר הִגִּיעַ דְּבַר־הַמֶּלֶךְ וְדָתוֹ לְהֵעָשׂוֹת בַּיּוֹם אֲשֶׁר שִׂבְּרוּ אֹיְבֵי הַיְּהוּדִים לִשְׁלוֹט בָּהֶם וְנַהֲפוֹךְ הוּא אֲשֶׁר יִשְׁלְטוּ הַיְּהוּדִים הֵמָּה בְּשֹׂנְאֵיהֶם:

2 Throughout the provinces of King Ahasuerus, the *Yehudim* mustered in their cities to attack those who sought their hurt; and no one could withstand them, for the fear of them had fallen upon all the peoples.

ב נִקְהֲלוּ הַיְּהוּדִים בְּעָרֵיהֶם בְּכָל־מְדִינוֹת הַמֶּלֶךְ אֲחַשְׁוֵרוֹשׁ לִשְׁלֹחַ יָד בִּמְבַקְשֵׁי רָעָתָם וְאִישׁ לֹא־עָמַד לִפְנֵיהֶם כִּי־נָפַל פַּחְדָּם עַל־כָּל־הָעַמִּים:

3 Indeed, all the officials of the provinces – the satraps, the governors, and the king's stewards – showed deference to the *Yehudim*, because the fear of *Mordechai* had fallen upon them.

ג וְכָל־שָׂרֵי הַמְּדִינוֹת וְהָאֲחַשְׁדַּרְפְּנִים וְהַפַּחוֹת וְעֹשֵׂי הַמְּלָאכָה אֲשֶׁר לַמֶּלֶךְ מְנַשְּׂאִים אֶת־הַיְּהוּדִים כִּי־נָפַל פַּחַד־מָרְדֳּכַי עֲלֵיהֶם:

4 For *Mordechai* was now powerful in the royal palace, and his fame was spreading through all the provinces; the man *Mordechai* was growing ever more powerful.

ד כִּי־גָדוֹל מָרְדֳּכַי בְּבֵית הַמֶּלֶךְ וְשָׁמְעוֹ הוֹלֵךְ בְּכָל־הַמְּדִינוֹת כִּי־הָאִישׁ מָרְדֳּכַי הוֹלֵךְ וְגָדוֹל:

5 So the *Yehudim* struck at their enemies with the sword, slaying and destroying; they wreaked their will upon their enemies.

ה וַיַּכּוּ הַיְּהוּדִים בְּכָל־אֹיְבֵיהֶם מַכַּת־חֶרֶב וְהֶרֶג וְאַבְדָן וַיַּעֲשׂוּ בְשֹׂנְאֵיהֶם כִּרְצוֹנָם:

6 In the fortress Shushan the *Yehudim* killed a total of five hundred men.

ו וּבְשׁוּשַׁן הַבִּירָה הָרְגוּ הַיְּהוּדִים וְאַבֵּד חֲמֵשׁ מֵאוֹת אִישׁ:

7 They also killed* Parshandatha, Dalphon, Aspatha,

ז וְאֵת פַּרְשַׁנְדָּתָא וְאֵת דַּלְפוֹן וְאֵת אַסְפָּתָא:

8 Poratha, Adalia, Aridatha,

ח וְאֵת פּוֹרָתָא וְאֵת אֲדַלְיָא וְאֵת אֲרִידָתָא:

9 Parmashta, Arisai, Aridai, and Vaizatha,

ט וְאֵת פַּרְמַשְׁתָּא וְאֵת אֲרִיסַי וְאֵת אֲרִדַי וְאֵת וַיְזָתָא:

10 the ten sons of Haman son of Hammedatha, the foe of the *Yehudim*. But they did not lay hands on the spoil.

י עֲשֶׂרֶת בְּנֵי הָמָן בֶּן־הַמְּדָתָא צֹרֵר הַיְּהוּדִים הָרָגוּ וּבַבִּזָּה לֹא שָׁלְחוּ אֶת־יָדָם:

11 When the number of those slain in the fortress Shushan was reported on that same day to the king,

יא בַּיּוֹם הַהוּא בָּא מִסְפַּר הַהֲרוּגִים בְּשׁוּשַׁן הַבִּירָה לִפְנֵי הַמֶּלֶךְ:

12 the king said to Queen *Esther*, "In the fortress Shushan alone the *Yehudim* have killed a total of five hundred men, as well as the ten sons of Haman. What then must they have done in the provinces of the realm! What is your wish now? It shall be granted you. And what else is your request? It shall be fulfilled."

יב וַיֹּאמֶר הַמֶּלֶךְ לְאֶסְתֵּר הַמַּלְכָּה בְּשׁוּשַׁן הַבִּירָה הָרְגוּ הַיְּהוּדִים וְאַבֵּד חֲמֵשׁ מֵאוֹת אִישׁ וְאֵת עֲשֶׂרֶת בְּנֵי־הָמָן בִּשְׁאָר מְדִינוֹת הַמֶּלֶךְ מֶה עָשׂוּ וּמַה־שְּׁאֵלָתֵךְ וְיִנָּתֵן לָךְ וּמַה־בַּקָּשָׁתֵךְ עוֹד וְתֵעָשׂ:

13 "If it please Your Majesty," *Esther* replied, "let the *Yehudim* in Shushan be permitted to act tomorrow also as they did today; and let Haman's ten sons be impaled on the stake."

יג וַתֹּאמֶר אֶסְתֵּר אִם־עַל־הַמֶּלֶךְ טוֹב יִנָּתֵן גַּם־מָחָר לַיְּהוּדִים אֲשֶׁר בְּשׁוּשַׁן לַעֲשׂוֹת כְּדָת הַיּוֹם וְאֵת עֲשֶׂרֶת בְּנֵי־הָמָן יִתְלוּ עַל־הָעֵץ:

14 The king ordered that this should be done, and the decree was proclaimed in Shushan. Haman's ten sons were impaled:

יד וַיֹּאמֶר הַמֶּלֶךְ לְהֵעָשׂוֹת כֵּן וַתִּנָּתֵן דָּת בְּשׁוּשָׁן וְאֵת עֲשֶׂרֶת בְּנֵי־הָמָן תָּלוּ:

15 and the *Yehudim* in Shushan mustered again on the fourteenth day of *Adar* and slew three hundred men in Shushan. But they did not lay hands on the spoil.

טו וַיִּקָּהֲלוּ הַיְּהוּדִיים [הַיְּהוּדִים] אֲשֶׁר־בְּשׁוּשָׁן גַּם בְּיוֹם אַרְבָּעָה עָשָׂר לְחֹדֶשׁ אֲדָר וַיַּהַרְגוּ בְשׁוּשָׁן שְׁלֹשׁ מֵאוֹת אִישׁ וּבַבִּזָּה לֹא שָׁלְחוּ אֶת־יָדָם:

16 The rest of the *Yehudim*, those in the king's provinces, likewise mustered and fought for their lives. They disposed of their enemies, killing seventy-five thousand of their foes; but they did not lay hands on the spoil.

טז וּשְׁאָר הַיְּהוּדִים אֲשֶׁר בִּמְדִינוֹת הַמֶּלֶךְ נִקְהֲלוּ וְעָמֹד עַל־נַפְשָׁם וְנוֹחַ מֵאֹיְבֵיהֶם וְהָרֹג בְּשֹׂנְאֵיהֶם חֲמִשָּׁה וְשִׁבְעִים אָלֶף וּבַבִּזָּה לֹא שָׁלְחוּ אֶת־יָדָם:

17 That was on the thirteenth day of the month of *Adar*; and they rested on the fourteenth day and made it a day of feasting and merrymaking.

יז בְּיוֹם־שְׁלֹשָׁה עָשָׂר לְחֹדֶשׁ אֲדָר וְנוֹחַ בְּאַרְבָּעָה עָשָׂר בּוֹ וְעָשֹׂה אֹתוֹ יוֹם מִשְׁתֶּה וְשִׂמְחָה:

---

* "They also killed" moved up from verse 10 for greater clarity

¹⁸ But the *Yehudim* in Shushan mustered on both the thirteenth and fourteenth days, and so rested on the fifteenth, and made it a day of feasting and merrymaking.)

יח וְהַיְּהוּדִים [וְהַיְּהוּדִים] אֲשֶׁר־בְּשׁוּשָׁן נִקְהֲלוּ בִּשְׁלֹשָׁה עָשָׂר בּוֹ וּבְאַרְבָּעָה עָשָׂר בּוֹ וְנוֹחַ בַּחֲמִשָּׁה עָשָׂר בּוֹ וְעָשֹׂה אֹתוֹ יוֹם מִשְׁתֶּה וְשִׂמְחָה:

¹⁹ That is why village *Yehudim*, who live in unwalled towns, observe the fourteenth day of the month of *Adar* and make it a day of merrymaking and feasting, and as a holiday and an occasion for sending gifts to one another.

יט עַל־כֵּן הַיְּהוּדִים הַפְּרוֹזִים [הַפְּרָזִים] הַיֹּשְׁבִים בְּעָרֵי הַפְּרָזוֹת עֹשִׂים אֵת יוֹם אַרְבָּעָה עָשָׂר לְחֹדֶשׁ אֲדָר שִׂמְחָה וּמִשְׁתֶּה וְיוֹם טוֹב וּמִשְׁלוֹחַ מָנוֹת אִישׁ לְרֵעֵהוּ:

²⁰ *Mordechai* recorded these events. And he sent dispatches to all the *Yehudim* throughout the provinces of King Ahasuerus, near and far,

כ וַיִּכְתֹּב מָרְדֳּכַי אֶת־הַדְּבָרִים הָאֵלֶּה וַיִּשְׁלַח סְפָרִים אֶל־כָּל־הַיְּהוּדִים אֲשֶׁר בְּכָל־מְדִינוֹת הַמֶּלֶךְ אֲחַשְׁוֵרוֹשׁ הַקְּרוֹבִים וְהָרְחוֹקִים:

²¹ charging them to observe the fourteenth and fifteenth days of *Adar*, every year –

כא לְקַיֵּם עֲלֵיהֶם לִהְיוֹת עֹשִׂים אֵת יוֹם אַרְבָּעָה עָשָׂר לְחֹדֶשׁ אֲדָר וְאֵת יוֹם־חֲמִשָּׁה עָשָׂר בּוֹ בְּכָל־שָׁנָה וְשָׁנָה:

l'-ka-YAYM a-lay-HEM lih-YOT o-SEEM AYT YOM ar-ba-AH a-SAR l'-KHO-desh a-DAR v'-AYT yom kha-mi-SHAH a-SAR BO b'-khol sha-NAH v'-sha-NAH

²² the same days on which the *Yehudim* enjoyed relief from their foes and the same month which had been transformed for them from one of grief and mourning to one of festive joy. They were to observe them as days of feasting and merrymaking, and as an occasion for sending gifts to one another and presents to the poor.

כב כַּיָּמִים אֲשֶׁר־נָחוּ בָהֶם הַיְּהוּדִים מֵאוֹיְבֵיהֶם וְהַחֹדֶשׁ אֲשֶׁר נֶהְפַּךְ לָהֶם מִיָּגוֹן לְשִׂמְחָה וּמֵאֵבֶל לְיוֹם טוֹב לַעֲשׂוֹת אוֹתָם יְמֵי מִשְׁתֶּה וְשִׂמְחָה וּמִשְׁלוֹחַ מָנוֹת אִישׁ לְרֵעֵהוּ וּמַתָּנוֹת לָאֶבְיוֹנִים:

²³ The *Yehudim* accordingly assumed as an obligation that which they had begun to practice and which *Mordechai* prescribed for them.

כג וְקִבֵּל הַיְּהוּדִים אֵת אֲשֶׁר־הֵחֵלּוּ לַעֲשׂוֹת וְאֵת אֲשֶׁר־כָּתַב מָרְדֳּכַי אֲלֵיהֶם:

²⁴ For Haman son of Hammedatha the Agagite, the foe of all the *Yehudim*, had plotted to destroy the *Yehudim*, and had cast pur – that is, the lot – with intent to crush and exterminate them.

כד כִּי הָמָן בֶּן־הַמְּדָתָא הָאֲגָגִי צֹרֵר כָּל־הַיְּהוּדִים חָשַׁב עַל־הַיְּהוּדִים לְאַבְּדָם וְהִפִּל פּוּר הוּא הַגּוֹרָל לְהֻמָּם וּלְאַבְּדָם:

 9:21 To observe the fourteenth and fifteenth days of *Adar* *Purim* is the only Jewish holiday that is observed on two different days, depending on one's location. The residents of cities that were walled at the time that the Jewish people entered the Land of Israel with *Yehoshua* celebrate on the fifteenth of *Adar*, while the rest of the world celebrates on the fourteenth. Practically, the only city that celebrates Purim on the fifteenth of *Adar* is *Yerushalayim*. In establishing the holiday of *Purim*, *Esther* wanted to guarantee that the lesson of *Purim* would not be forgotten. In her time, the Children of Israel had forsaken *Yerushalayim* when they feasted at a party celebrating its destruction. Celebrating in *Yerushalayim* on a different day highlights its special status and its eternal connection to the People of Israel.

Celebrating *Purim* in *Yerushalayim*

25 But when [*Esther*] came before the king, he commanded: "With the promulgation of this decree, let the evil plot, which he devised against the *Yehudim*, recoil on his own head!" So they impaled him and his sons on the stake.

26 For that reason these days were named *Purim*, after pur. In view, then, of all the instructions in the said letter and of what they had experienced in that matter and what had befallen them,

27 the *Yehudim* undertook and irrevocably obligated themselves and their descendants, and all who might join them, to observe these two days in the manner prescribed and at the proper time each year.

28 Consequently, these days are recalled and observed in every generation: by every family, every province, and every city. And these days of *Purim* shall never cease among the *Yehudim*, and the memory of them shall never perish among their descendants.

29 Then Queen *Esther* daughter of *Avichayil* wrote a second letter of *Purim* for the purpose of confirming with full authority the aforementioned one of *Mordechai* the *Yehudi*.

30 Dispatches were sent to all the *Yehudim* in the hundred and twenty-seven provinces of the realm of Ahasuerus with an ordinance of "equity and honesty:"

31 These days of *Purim* shall be observed at their proper time, as *Mordechai* the *Yehudi* – and now Queen *Esther* – has obligated them to do, and just as they have assumed for themselves and their descendants the obligation of the fasts with their lamentations.

32 And *Esther*'s ordinance validating these observances of *Purim* was recorded in a scroll.

10 1 King Ahasuerus imposed tribute on the mainland and the islands.

2 All his mighty and powerful acts, and a full account of the greatness to which the king advanced *Mordechai*, are recorded in the Annals of the Kings of Media and Persia.

כה וּבְבֹאָהּ לִפְנֵי הַמֶּלֶךְ אָמַר עִם־הַסֵּפֶר יָשׁוּב מַחֲשַׁבְתּוֹ הָרָעָה אֲשֶׁר־חָשַׁב עַל־הַיְּהוּדִים עַל־רֹאשׁוֹ וְתָלוּ אֹתוֹ וְאֶת־בָּנָיו עַל־הָעֵץ:

כו עַל־כֵּן קָרְאוּ לַיָּמִים הָאֵלֶּה פוּרִים עַל־שֵׁם הַפּוּר עַל־כֵּן עַל־כָּל־דִּבְרֵי הָאִגֶּרֶת הַזֹּאת וּמָה־רָאוּ עַל־כָּכָה וּמָה הִגִּיעַ אֲלֵיהֶם:

כז קִיְּמוּ וְקִבֵּל [וְקִבְּלוּ] הַיְּהוּדִים עֲלֵיהֶם וְעַל־זַרְעָם וְעַל כָּל־הַנִּלְוִים עֲלֵיהֶם וְלֹא יַעֲבוֹר לִהְיוֹת עֹשִׂים אֵת שְׁנֵי הַיָּמִים הָאֵלֶּה כִּכְתָבָם וְכִזְמַנָּם בְּכָל־שָׁנָה וְשָׁנָה:

כח וְהַיָּמִים הָאֵלֶּה נִזְכָּרִים וְנַעֲשִׂים בְּכָל־דּוֹר וָדוֹר מִשְׁפָּחָה וּמִשְׁפָּחָה מְדִינָה וּמְדִינָה וְעִיר וָעִיר וִימֵי הַפּוּרִים הָאֵלֶּה לֹא יַעַבְרוּ מִתּוֹךְ הַיְּהוּדִים וְזִכְרָם לֹא־יָסוּף מִזַּרְעָם:

כט וַתִּכְתֹּב אֶסְתֵּר הַמַּלְכָּה בַת־אֲבִיחַיִל וּמָרְדֳּכַי הַיְּהוּדִי אֶת־כָּל־תֹּקֶף לְקַיֵּם אֵת אִגֶּרֶת הַפּוּרִים הַזֹּאת הַשֵּׁנִית:

ל וַיִּשְׁלַח סְפָרִים אֶל־כָּל־הַיְּהוּדִים אֶל־שֶׁבַע וְעֶשְׂרִים וּמֵאָה מְדִינָה מַלְכוּת אֲחַשְׁוֵרוֹשׁ דִּבְרֵי שָׁלוֹם וֶאֱמֶת:

לא לְקַיֵּם אֶת־יְמֵי הַפֻּרִים הָאֵלֶּה בִּזְמַנֵּיהֶם כַּאֲשֶׁר קִיַּם עֲלֵיהֶם מָרְדֳּכַי הַיְּהוּדִי וְאֶסְתֵּר הַמַּלְכָּה וְכַאֲשֶׁר קִיְּמוּ עַל־נַפְשָׁם וְעַל־זַרְעָם דִּבְרֵי הַצֹּמוֹת וְזַעֲקָתָם:

לב וּמַאֲמַר אֶסְתֵּר קִיַּם דִּבְרֵי הַפֻּרִים הָאֵלֶּה וְנִכְתָּב בַּסֵּפֶר:

י א וַיָּשֶׂם הַמֶּלֶךְ אחשרש [אֲחַשְׁוֵרוֹשׁ] מַס עַל־הָאָרֶץ וְאִיֵּי הַיָּם:

ב וְכָל־מַעֲשֵׂה תָקְפּוֹ וּגְבוּרָתוֹ וּפָרָשַׁת גְּדֻלַּת מָרְדֳּכַי אֲשֶׁר גִּדְּלוֹ הַמֶּלֶךְ הֲלוֹא־הֵם כְּתוּבִים עַל־סֵפֶר דִּבְרֵי הַיָּמִים לְמַלְכֵי מָדַי וּפָרָס:

³ For *Mordechai* the *Yehudi* ranked next to King Ahasuerus and was highly regarded by the *Yehudim* and popular with the multitude of his brethren; he sought the good of his people and interceded for the welfare of all his kindred.

גְּ כִּי מָרְדְּכַי הַיְּהוּדִי מִשְׁנֶה לַמֶּלֶךְ
אֲחַשְׁוֵרוֹשׁ וְגָדוֹל לַיְּהוּדִים וְרָצוּי לְרֹב
אֶחָיו דֹּרֵשׁ טוֹב לְעַמּוֹ וְדֹבֵר שָׁלוֹם
לְכָל־זַרְעוֹ:

KEE mor-d'-KHAI ha-y'-hu-DEE mish-NEH la-ME-lekh
a-khash-vay-ROSH v'-ga-DOL la-y'-hu-DEEM v'-ra-TZUY l'-ROV
e-KHAV do-RAYSH TOV l'-a-MO v'-do-VAYR sha-LOM l'-khol zar-O

10:3 For *Mordechai* the *Yehudi* ranked next to King Ahasuerus According to one opinion among the Sages, this verse describes two stages of *Mordechai's* life following the *Purim* miracle. He was "next to King Ahasuerus" until Darius, son of *Esther* and Ahasuerus, allowed the rebuilding of the *Beit Hamikdash*. At that point, he stepped down from his governmental position and became "highly regarded by the *Yehudim*," returning to the Land of Israel and assuming responsibility for the offerings in the *Beit Hamikdash* (see *Mishna Shekalim* 5:1). *Mordechai* did not let honor and fame stand in the way of his principles. Dismissing the glory, he jumped at the first opportunity to serve his people in *Eretz Yisrael*.

Walls of the Old City of *Yerushalayim*

List of Transliterated Words in *The Israel Bible*

The following is a list of nouns which have been transliterated into Hebrew in the English translation and commentary of *The Israel Bible*:

Hebrew Name	English Name	Pronunciation	Hebrew
Achan	Achan	a-KHAN	עָכָן
Achav	Ahab	akh-AV	אַחְאָב
Achaz	Ahaz	a-KHAZ	אָחָז
Achazyahu	Ahaziah	a-khaz-YA-hu	אֲחַזְיָהוּ
Achiezer	Ahiezer	a-khee-E-zer	אֲחִיעֶזֶר
Achihud	Ahihud	a-khee-HUD	אֲחִיהוּד
Achikam	Ahikam	a-khee-KAM	אֲחִיקָם
Achilud	Ahilud	a-khee-LUD	אֲחִילוּד
Achimelech	Ahimelech	a-khee-ME-lekh	אֲחִימֶלֶךְ
Achira	Ahira	a-khee-RA	אֲחִירַע
Achisamach	Ahisamach	a-khee-sa-MAKH	אֲחִיסָמָךְ
Achitofel	Ahithophel	a-khee-TO-fel	אֲחִיתֹפֶל
Achituv	Ahitub	a-khee-TUV	אֲחִיטוּב
Achiya	Ahijah	a-khi-YAH	אֲחִיָּה
Adam	Adam	a-DAM	אָדָם
Adar	Adar	a-DAR	אֲדָר
Adoniyahu	Adonijah	a-do-ni-YA-hu	אֲדֹנִיָּהוּ
Adulam	Adullam	a-du-LAM	עֲדֻלָּם
Agur	Agur	a-GUR	אָגוּר
Aharon	Aaron	a-ha-RON	אַהֲרֹן
Amasa	Amasa	a-ma-SA	עֲמָשָׂא
Amatzya	Amaziah	a-matz-YAH	אֲמַצְיָה
Amen	Amen	a-MAYN	אָמֵן
Amiel	Ammiel	a-mee-AYL	עַמִּיאֵל
Aminadav	Amminadab	a-mee-na-DAV	עַמִּינָדָב
Amitai	Amittai	a-mi-TAI	אֲמִתַּי
Amnon	Amnon	am-NON	אַמְנֹן

Hebrew Name	English Name	Pronunciation	Hebrew
Amon	Amon	a-MON	אָמוֹן
Amos	Amos	a-MOS	עָמוֹס
Amotz	Amoz	a-MOTZ	אָמוֹץ
Amram	Amram	am-RAM	עַמְרָם
Anatot	Anathoth	a-na-TOT	עֲנָתוֹת
Aron	Ark	a-RON	אָרוֹן
Aron HaBrit	Ark of the Covenant	a-RON ha-b'-REET	אָרוֹן הַבְּרִית
Arpachshad	Arpachshad	ar-pakh-SHAD	אַרְפַּכְשָׁד
Asa	Asa	a-SA	אָסָא
Asael	Asahel	a-sah-AYL	עֲשָׂהאֵל
Asaf	Asaph	a-SAF	אָסָף
Ashdod	Ashdod	ash-DOD	אַשְׁדּוֹד
Asher	Asher	a-SHAYR	אָשֵׁר
Ashkelon	Ashkelon	ash-k'-LON	אַשְׁקְלוֹן
Atalya	Athaliah	a-tal-YAH	עֲתַלְיָה
Avdon	Abdon	av-DON	עַבְדּוֹן
Avichayil	Abihail	a-vee-KHA-yil	אֲבִיחַיִל
Avidan	Abidan	a-vee-DAN	אֲבִידָן
Avigail	Abigail	a-vee-GA-yil	אֲבִיגַיִל
Avihu	Abihu	a-vee-HU	אֲבִיהוּא
Avimelech	Abimelech	a-vee-ME-lekh	אֲבִימָלֶךְ
Avinadav	Abinadab	a-vee-na-DAV	אֲבִינָדָב
Aviram	Abiram	a-vee-RAM	אֲבִירָם
Avishai	Abishai	a-vee-SHAI	אֲבִישַׁי
Aviya	Abijah	a-vi-YAH	אֲבִיָּה
Aviyam	Abijam	a-vi-YAM	אֲבִיָּם
Avner	Abner	av-NAYR	אַבְנֵר
Avraham	Abraham	av-ra-HAM	אַבְרָהָם
Avram	Abram	av-RAM	אַבְרָם
Avshalom	Absalom	av-sha-LOM	אַבְשָׁלוֹם
Azarya	Azariah	a-zar-YAH	עֲזַרְיָה
Azeika	Azekah	a-zay-KAH	עֲזֵקָה
Azza	Gaza	a-ZAH	עַזָּה

Hebrew Name	English Name	Pronunciation	Hebrew
B'nei Yisrael	The Children of Israel	b'-NAY yis-ra-AYL	בְּנֵי יִשְׂרָאֵל
Barak	Barak	ba-rakh-AYL	בָּרָק
Baruch	Baruch	ba-RUKH	בָּרוּךְ
Barzilai	Barzillai	bar-zi-LAI	בַּרְזִלַּי
Basha	Baasa	ba-SHA	בַּעְשָׁא
Batsheva	Bath-sheba	bat-SHE-va	בַּת־שֶׁבַע
Be'er Sheva	Beer-sheba	b'-AYR SHE-va	בְּאֵר שֶׁבַע
Be'eri	Beeri	b'-ay-REE	בְּאֵרִי
Beit Aven	Beth-aven	bayt A-ven	בֵּית אָוֶן
Beit El	Beth-el	bayt el	בֵּית אֵל
Beit Hamikdash	Temple	bayt ha-mik-DASH	בֵּית הַמִּקְדָּשׁ
Beit Lechem	Beth-lehem	bayt LE-khem	בֵּית לֶחֶם
Beit Shean	Beth-shean	bayt sh'-AN	בֵּית שְׁאָן
Beit Shemesh	Beth-shemesh	bayt SHE-mesh	בֵּית שָׁמֶשׁ
Berechya	Berechiah	be-rekh-YAH	בֶּרֶכְיָה
Betzalel	Bezalel	b'-tzal-AYL	בְּצַלְאֵל
Bilha	Bilhah	bil-HAH	בִּלְהָה
Binyamin	Benjamin	bin-ya-MIN	בִּנְיָמִין
Boaz	Boaz	BO-az	בֹּעַז
Buki	Bukki	bu-KEE	בֻּקִּי
Buzi	Buzi	bu-ZEE	בּוּזִי
Carmel	Carmel	kar-MEL	כַּרְמֶל
Chachalya	Hacaliah	kha-khal-YAH	חֲכַלְיָה
Chagai	Haggai	kha-GAI	חַגַּי
Chana	Hannah	kha-NAH	חַנָּה
Chanamel	Hanamel	kha-nam-AYL	חֲנַמְאֵל
Chanani	Hanani	kha-NA-nee	חֲנָנִי
Chananya	Hananiah	kha-nan-YAH	חֲנַנְיָה
Chaniel	Hanniel	kha-nee-AYL	חַנִּיאֵל
Chanoch	Enoch	kha-NOKH	חֲנוֹךְ
Chava	Eve	kha-VAH	חַוָּה
Chavakuk	Habakkuk	kha-va-KUK	חֲבַקּוּק
Chermon	Hermon	kher-MON	חֶרְמוֹן

Hebrew Name	English Name	Pronunciation	Hebrew
Chetzron	Hezron	khetz-RON	חֶצְרוֹן
Chever	Heber	KHE-ver	חֶבֶר
Chevron	Hebron	khev-RON	חֶבְרוֹן
Chilkiyahu	Hilkiah	khil-ki-YA-hu	חִלְקִיָּהוּ
Chizkiyahu	Hezekiah	khiz-ki-YA-hu	חִזְקִיָּהוּ
Chofni	Hophni	khof-NEE	חָפְנִי
Chogla	Hoglah	khog-LAH	חָגְלָה
Chulda	Hulda	khul-DAH	חֻלְדָּה
Chur	Hur	Khur	חוּר
Dan	Dan	Dan	דָּן
Daniel	Daniel	da-ni-YAYL	דָּנִיֵּאל
Datan	Dathan	da-TAN	דָּתָן
David	David	da-VID	דָּוִד
Devora	Deborah	d'-vo-RAH	דְּבוֹרָה
Dina	Dinah	DEE-nah	דִּינָה
Doeg Ha'adomi	Doeg the Edomite	do-AYG ha-a-do-MEE	דּוֹאֵג הָאֲדֹמִי
Efraim	Ephraim	ef-RA-yim	אֶפְרַיִם
Efrat	Ephrat	ef-RAT	אֶפְרָתָה
Efrat	Ephrathah	ef-RA-tah	אֶפְרָתָה
Ehud	Ehud	ay-HUD	אֵהוּד
Eila	Elah	AY-lah	אֵלָה
Eilon	Elon	ay-LON	אֵילוֹן
Ein Gedi	En-gedi	ayn GE-dee	עֵין גֶּדִי
Elazar	Eleazar	el-a-ZAR	אֶלְעָזָר
Elchanan	Elhanan	el-kha-NAN	אֶלְחָנָן
Eli	Eli	ay-LEE	עֵלִי
Eliav	Eliab	e-lee-AV	אֱלִיאָב
Elidad	Elidad	e-lee-DAD	אֱלִידָד
Eliezer	Eliezer	e-lee-E-zer	אֱלִיעֶזֶר
Elimelech	Elimelech	e-lee-ME-lekh	אֱלִימָלֶךְ
Elisha	Elisha	e-lee-SHA	אֱלִישָׁע
Elishama	Elishama	e-lee-sha-MA	אֱלִישָׁמָע
Elisheva	Elisheba	e-lee-SHE-va	אֱלִישֶׁבַע

Hebrew Name	English Name	Pronunciation	Hebrew
Elitzafan	Eli-zaphan	e-lee-tza-FAN	אֱלִיצָפָן
Elitzur	Elizur	e-lee-TZUR	אֱלִיצוּר
Eliyahu	Elijah	ay-li-YA-hu	אֵלִיָּהוּ
Elkana	Elkanah	el-ka-NAH	אֶלְקָנָה
Elyasaf	Eliasaph	el-ya-SAF	אֶלְיָסָף
Elyashiv	Eliashib	el-ya-SHEEV	אֶלְיָשִׁיב
Enosh	Enosh	e-NOSH	אֱנוֹשׁ
Er	Er	ayr	עֵר
Eshtaol	Eshtaol	esh-ta-OL	אֶשְׁתָּאֹל
Esther	Esther	es-TAYR	אֶסְתֵּר
Eved Melech	Ebed-melech	E-ved ME-lekh	עֶבֶד־מֶלֶךְ
Even Ha-Ezer	Eben-Ezer	E-ven ha-E-zer	אֶבֶן הָעֵזֶר
Ever	Eber	AY-ver	עֵבֶר
Evyatar	Abiathar	ev-ya-TAR	אֶבְיָתָר
Ezra	Ezra	ez-RA	עֶזְרָא
Gad	Gad	gad	גָּד
Gadi	Gaddi	ga-DEE	גַּדִּי
Gadiel	Gaddiel	ga-dee-AYL	גַּדִּיאֵל
Gamliel	Gamaliel	gam-lee-AYL	גַּמְלִיאֵל
Gedalia	Gedaliah	g'-dal-YA (hu)	גְּדַלְיָהוּ
Gedera	Gederah	g'-day-RAH	גְּדֵרָה
Gershom	Gershom	gay-r'-SHOM	גֵּרְשֹׁום
Gershon	Gershon	gay-r'-SHON	גֵּרְשׁוֹן
Geshem	Geshem	GE-shem	גֶּשֶׁם
Geuel	Geuel	g'-u-AYL	גְּאוּאֵל
Gidon	Gideon	gid-ON	גִּדְעוֹן
Gilad	Gilead	gil-AD	גִּלְעָד
Gilgal	Gilgal	gil-GAL	גִּלְגָּל
Giva	Gibeah	giv-AH	גִּבְעָה
Givon	Gibeon	giv-ON	גִּבְעוֹן
Hadassa	Hadassah	ha-da-SAH	הֲדַסָּה
Har Eival	Mount Ebal	ay-VAL	הַר עֵיבָל
Har Gerizim	Mount Gerizim	g'-ri-ZEEM	הַר גְּרִזִים

Hebrew Name	English Name	Pronunciation	Hebrew
Har HaBayit	Temple Mount	har ha-BA-yit	הַר הַבַּיִת
Har HaZeitim	the Mount of Olives	har ha-zay-TEEM	הַר הַזֵּיתִים
Hashem	Lord/God		
Hayman	Heman	hay-MAN	הֵימָן
Hoshea	Hosea	ho-SHAY-a	הוֹשֵׁעַ
Ido	Iddo	i-DO	עִדּוֹ
Imanu-El	Immanuel	i-MA-nu ayl	עִמָּנוּ אֵל
Ish-boshet	Ish-bosheth	eesh BO-shet	אִישׁ־בֹּשֶׁת
Itamar	Ithamar	ee-ta-MAR	אִיתָמָר
Itiel	Ithiel	ee-tee-AYL	אִיתִיאֵל
Ivtzan	Ibzan	iv-TZAN	אִבְצָן
Iyov	Job	i-YOV	אִיּוֹב
Kadmiel	Kadmiel	kad-mee-AYL	קַדְמִיאֵל
Kalev	Caleb	ka-LAYV	כָּלֵב
Keesh	Kish	keesh	קִישׁ
Kehat	Kohath	k'-HAT	קְהָת
Keinan	Kenan	kay-NAN	קֵינָן
Kemuel	Kemuel	k'-mu-AYL	קְמוּאֵל
Keruvim	Cherubim	k'-ru-VEEM	כְּרוּבִים
Kilyon	Chilion	kil-YON	כִּלְיוֹן
Kiryat Arba	Kiriath-arba	keer-YAT AR-bah	קִרְיַת אַרְבַּע
Kiryat Sefer	Kiriath-sepher	keer-YAT SAY-fer	קִרְיַת־סֵפֶר
Kiryat Ye'arim	Kiriath-jearim	keer-YAT y'-a-REEM	קִרְיַת יְעָרִים
Kislev	Chislev	kis-LAYV	כִּסְלֵו
Kohanim	Priests	ko-ha-NEEM	כֹּהֲנִים
Kohelet	Koheleth	ko-HE-let	קֹהֶלֶת
Kohen	Priest	ko-HAYN	כֹּהֵן
Kohen Gadol	High Priest	ko-HAYN ga-DOL	כֹּהֵן גָּדוֹל
Korach	Korah	KO-rakh	קֹרַח
Kushi	Cushi	ku-SHEE	כּוּשִׁי
Lachish	Lachish	la-KHEESH	לָכִישׁ
Leah	Leah	lay-AH	לֵאָה
Lemech	Lamech	LE-mekh	לֶמֶךְ

Hebrew Name	English Name	Pronunciation	Hebrew
Lemuel	Lemuel	l'-mu-AYL	לְמוּאֵל
Levi	Levi	lay-VEE	לֵוִי
Leviim	Levites	l'-vee-IM	לְוִיִם
Machla	Mahlah	makh-LAH	מַחְלָה
Machlon	Mahlon	makh-LON	מַחְלוֹן
Machseya	Mahseiah	makh-say-YAH	מַחְסֵיָה
Malachi	Malachi	mal-a-KHEE	מַלְאָכִי
Manoach	Manoah	ma-NO-akh	מָנוֹחַ
Mashiach	Messiah	ma-SHEE-akh	מָשִׁיחַ
Mefiboshet	Mephibosheth	m'-fee-VO-shet	מְפִיבֹשֶׁת
Mehalalel	Mahalalel	ma-ha-lal-AYL	מַהֲלַלְאֵל
Menachem	Menahem	m'-na-KHAYM	מְנַחֵם
Menashe	Menasseh	m'-na-SHEH	מְנַשֶּׁה
Menorah	Candlestick	m'-no-RAH	מְנֹרָה
Merari	Merari	m'-ra-REE	מְרָרִי
Metushelach	Methusaleh	m'-tu-SHE-lakh	מְתוּשָׁלַח
Micha	Micah	mee-KHAH	מִיכָה
Michael	Michael	mee-kha-AYL	מִיכָאֵל
Michaihu	Micaiah	mee-KHAI-hu	מִיכָיְהוּ
Michal	Michal	mee-KHAL	מִיכַל
Milka	Milcah	mil-KAH	מִלְכָּה
Miriam	Miriam	mir-YAM	מִרְיָם
Mishael	Mishael	mee-sha-AYL	מִישָׁאֵל
Mishkan	Tabernacle	mish-KAN	מִשְׁכַּן
Mitzpa	Mizpah	mitz-PAH	מִצְפָּה
Mizbayach	Altar	miz-BAY-akh	מִזְבֵּחַ
Mordechai	Mordecai	mor-d'-KHAI	מָרְדְּכַי
Moriah	Moriah	mo-ri-YAH	מוֹרִיָה
Moshe	Moses	mo-SHEH	מֹשֶׁה
Nachbi	Nahbi	nakh-BEE	נַחְבִּי
Nachor	Nahor	na-KHOR	נָחוֹר
Nachshon	Nahshon	nakh-SHON	נַחְשׁוֹן
Nachum	Nahum	na-KHUM	נַחוּם

Hebrew Name	English Name	Pronunciation	Hebrew
Nadav	Nadab	na-DAV	נָדָב
Naftali	Naphtali	naf-ta-LEE	נַפְתָּלִי
Naomi	Naomi	na-o-MEE	נָעֳמִי
Natan	Nathan	na-TAN	נָתָן
Naval	Nabal	na-VAL	נָבָל
Navi	Prophet	na-VEE	נָבִיא
Navot	Naboth	na-VAL	נָבָל
Nechemya	Nehemiah	n'-khem-YAH	נְחֶמְיָה
Negev	Negeb	NE-gev	נֶגֶב
Nerya	Neriah	nay-ri-YAH	נֵרִיָּה
Netanel	Nethanel	n'-tan-AYL	נְתַנְאֵל
Neviah	Prophetess	n'-vee-AH	נְבִיאָה
Neviim	Prophets	n'-vee-EEM	נְבִיאִים
Nisan	Nisan	nee-SAN	נִיסָן
Noa	Noah	no-AH	נֹעָה
Noach	Noah	NO-akh	נֹחַ
Nov	Nob	nov	נֹב
Nun	Nun	nun	נוּן
Oded	Oded	o-DAYD	עוֹדֵד
Ohola	Oholah	a-ho-LAH	אָהֳלָה
Oholiav	Oholiab	o-ha-lee-AV	אָהֳלִיאָב
Oholiva	Oholibah	a-ho-lee-VAH	אָהֳלִיבָה
Omri	Omri	om-REE	עָמְרִי
Onan	Onan	o-NAN	אוֹנָן
Otniel	Othniel	ot-nee-AYL	עָתְנִיאֵל
Ovadya	Obadiah	o-vad-YAH	עֹבַדְיָה
Oved	Obed	o-VAYD	עוֹבֵד
Oved Edom	Obed Edom	o-VAYD e-DOM	עוֹבֵד אֱדֹם
Pagiel	Pagiel	pag-ee-AYL	פַּגְעִיאֵל
Palti	Palti	pal-TEE	פַּלְטִי
Paltiel	Paltiel	pal-tee-AYL	פַּלְטִיאֵל
Pekach	Pekah	PE-kakh	פֶּקַח
Pedael	Pedahel	p'-da-AYL	פְּדַהְאֵל

Hebrew Name	English Name	Pronunciation	Hebrew
Pekachya	Pekahiah	p'-kakh-YAH	פְּקַחְיָה
Peleg	Peleg	PE-leg	פֶּלֶג
Penina	Peninnah	p'-ni-NAH	פְּנִנָּה
Peretz	Perez	PE-retz	פֶּרֶץ
Petuel	Pethuel	p'-tu-AYL	פְּתוּאֵל
Pinchas	Phinehas	peen-KHAS	פִּינְחָס
Rachel	Rachel	ra-KHAYL	רָחֵל
Ram	Ram	ram	רָם
Rama	Ramah	ra-MAH	רָמָה
Re'u	Reu	r'-U	רְעוּ
Rechovam	Rehoboam	r'-khav-AM	רְחַבְעָם
Reuven	Reuben	r'-u-VAYN	רְאוּבֵן
Rivka	Rebecca	riv-KAH	רִבְקָה
Rut	Ruth	rut	רוּת
Salma	Salmon/Salmah	sal-MAH	שַׂלְמָה
Salmon	Salmon	sal-MON	שַׂלְמוֹן
Sara	Sarah	sa-RAH	שָׂרָה
Sarai	Sarai	sa-RAI	שָׂרַי
Selah	Selah	SE-lah	סֶלָה
Seraya	Seraiah	s'-ra-YAH	שְׂרָיָה
Serug	Serug	s'-RUG	שְׂרוּג
Setur	Sethur	s'-TUR	סְתוּר
Shaarayim	Shaaraim	sha-a-RA-yim	שַׁעֲרַיִם
Shabbat	Sabbath	sha-BAT	שַׁבַּת
Shabbatot	Sabbaths	sha-ba-TOT	שַׁבָּתוֹת
Shafan	Shaphan	sha-FAN	שָׁפָן
Shafat	Shaphat	sha-FAT	שָׁפָט
Shalem	Salem	sha-LAYM	שָׁלֵם
Shalum	Shallum	sha-LUM	שַׁלּוּם
Shamgar	Shamgar	sham-GAR	שַׁמְגַּר
Shamua	Shammua	sha-MU-a	שַׁמּוּעַ
Shaul	Saul	sha-UL	שָׁאוּל
Shealtiel	Shealtiel	sh'-al-tee-AYL	שְׁאַלְתִּיאֵל

Hebrew Name	English Name	Pronunciation	Hebrew
Shear Yashuv	Shear-Jashub	sh'-AR ya-SHUV	שְׁאָר יָשׁוּב
Shechanya	Shecaniah	sh'-khan-YAH	שְׁכַנְיָה
Shechem	Shechem	sh'-KHEM	שְׁכֶם
Sheila	Shelah	shay-LAH	שֵׁלָה
Shelach	Shelah	SHE-lakh	שָׁלַח
Shelumiel	Shelumiel	sh'-lu-mee-AYL	שְׁלֻמִיאֵל
Shem	Shem	Shaym	שֵׁם
Shemaya	Shemaiah	sh'-ma-YAH	שְׁמַעְיָה
Sheshbatzar	Sheshbazzar	shaysh-ba-TZAR	שֵׁשְׁבַּצַּר
Shet	Seth	Shayt	שֵׁת
Shevat	Shebat	sh'-VAT	שְׁבָט
Shilo	Shiloh	shi-LOH	שִׁלֹה
Shim'i	Shimei	shim-EE	שִׁמְעִי
Shimon	Simeon	shim-ON	שִׁמְעוֹן
Shimshon	Samson	shim-SHON	שִׁמְשׁוֹן
Shlomo	Solomon	sh'-lo-MOH	שְׁלֹמֹה
Shmuel	Samuel	sh'-mu-AYL	שְׁמוּאֵל
Shofar	Horn	sho-FAR	שׁוֹפָר
Shofarot	Horns	sho-fa-ROT	שׁוֹפָרוֹת
Shomron	Samaria	sho-m'-RON	שֹׁמְרוֹן
Sivan	Sivan	see-VAN	סִיוָן
Tamar	Tamar	ta-MAR	תָּמָר
Tanakh	Hebrew Bible	ta-NAKH	תָּנָ"ךְ
Tapuach	Tappuah	ta-PU-akh	תַּפּוּחַ
Tavor	Tabor	ta-VOR	תָּבוֹר
Tekoa	Tekoa	t'-KO-a	תְּקוֹעַה
Terach	Terah	TE-rakh	תֶּרַח
Teveria	Tiberias	t'-ver-YAH	טְבֶרְיָה
Tevet	Tebeth	tay-VAYT	טֵבֵת
Tirtza	Tirzah	tir-TZAH	תִּרְצָה
Tola	Tola	to-LA	תּוֹלָע
Tzadok	Zadok	tza-DOK	צָדוֹק
Tzefanya	Zephaniah	tz'-fan-YAH	צְפַנְיָה

Hebrew Name	English Name	Pronunciation	Hebrew
Tzelofchad	Zelophehad	tz'-lo-f-KHAD	צְלָפְחָד
Tzeruya	Zeruiah	tz'-ru-YAH	צְרוּיָה
Tzfat	Safed	tz'-FAT	צְפַת
Tzidkiyahu	Zedekiah	tzid-ki-YA-hu	צִדְקִיָּהוּ
Tziklag	Ziklag	tzi-k'-LAG	צִקְלַג
Tzion	Zion	tzi-YON	צִיּוֹן
Tzipora	Zipporah	tzi-po-RAH	צִפֹּרָה
Tzora	Zorah	tzor-AH	צָרְעָה
Tzuriel	Zuriel	tzu-ree-AYL	צוּרִיאֵל
Ukal	Ucal	u-KAL	אֻכָל
Uri	Uri	u-REE	אוּרִי
Uriya	Uriah	u-ri-YAH	אוּרִיָּה
Utz	Uz	Utz	עוּץ
Uzziyahu	Uzziah	u-zi-YA-hu	עֻזִּיָּהוּ
Yaakov	Jacob	ya-a-KOV	יַעֲקֹב
Yachaziel	Jahaziel	ya-kha-zee-AYL	יַחֲזִיאֵל
Yael	Jael	ya-AYL	יָעֵל
Yaffo	Joppa/Jaffa	ya-FO	יָפוֹ
Yair	Jair	ya-EER	יָאִיר
Yakeh	Jakeh	ya-KEH	יָקֶה
Yarden	Jordan	yar-DAYN	יַרְדֵּן
Yarmut	Jarmuth	yar-MUT	יַרְמוּת
Yechezkel	Ezekiel	y'-khez-KAYL	יְחֶזְקָאל
Yechiel	Jehiel	y'-khee-AYL	יְחִיאֵל
Yechonya	Jeconiah	y'-khon-YAH	יְכָנְיָה
Yedutun	Jeduthun	y'-du-TUN	יְדוּתוּן
Yehoachaz	Jehoahaz	y'-ho-a-KHAZ	יְהוֹאָחָז
Yehoash	Jehoash	y'-ho-ASH	יְהוֹאָשׁ
Yehochanan	Jehohanan	y'-ho-kha-NAN	יְהוֹחָנָן
Yehonatan	Jonathan	y'-ho-na-TAN	יְהוֹנָתָן
Yehoram	Jehoram	y'-ho-RAM	יְהוֹרָם
Yehoshafat	Jehoshaphat	y'-ho-sha-FAT	יְהוֹשָׁפָט
Yehoshavat	Jehoshabeath	y'-ho-shav-AT	יְהוֹשַׁבְעַת

Hebrew Name	English Name	Pronunciation	Hebrew
Yehosheva	Jehosheba	y-ho-SHE-va	יְהוֹשֶׁבַע
Yehoshua	Joshua	y'-ho-SHU-a	יְהוֹשֻׁעַ
Yehotzadak	Jehozadak	y'-ho-tza-DAK	יְהוֹצָדָק
Yehoyachin	Jehoiachin	y'-ho-ya-KHEEN	יְהוֹיָכִין
Yehoyada	Jehoiada	y'-ho-ya-DA	יְהוֹיָדָע
Yehoyakim	Jehoiakim	y'-ho-ya-KEEM	יְהוֹיָקִים
Yehu	Jehu	yay-HU	יֵהוּא
Yehuda	Judah	y'-hu-DAH	יְהוּדָה
Yehudi	Jew	y'-hu-DEE	יְהוּדִי
Yehudim	Jews	y'-hu-DEEM	יְהוּדִים
Yered	Jared	YE-red	יֶרֶד
Yericho	Jericho	y'-ree-KHO	יְרִיחוֹ
Yerovam	Jeroboam	ya-rov-AM	יָרָבְעָם
Yerubaal	Jerubbaal	y'-ru-BA-al	יְרֻבַּעַל
Yerushalayim	Jerusalem	y'-ru-sha-LA-yim	יְרוּשָׁלַיִם
Yeshayahu	Isaiah	y'-sha-YA-hu	יְשַׁעְיָהוּ
Yeshua	Jeshua	yay-SHU-a	יֵשׁוּעַ
Yiftach	Jephthah	yif-TAKH	יִפְתָּח
Yigal	Igal	yig-AL	יִגְאָל
Yirmiyahu	Jeremiah	yir-m'-YA-hu	יִרְמְיָהוּ
Yishai	Jesse	yi-SHAI	יִשַׁי
Yisrael	Israel	yis-ra-AYL	יִשְׂרָאֵל
Yissachar	Issachar	yi-sa-KHAR	יִשָּׂשׂכָר
Yitzchak	Issac	yitz-KHAK	יִצְחָק
Yizrael	Jezreel	yiz-r'-EL	יִזְרְעֵאל
Yoash	Joash	yo-ASH	יוֹאָשׁ
Yoav	Joab	yo-AV	יוֹאָב
Yochanan	Johanan	yo-kha-NAN	יוֹחָנָן
Yocheved	Jochebed	yo-KHE-ved	יוֹכֶבֶד
Yoel	Joel	yo-AYL	יוֹאֵל
Yona	Jonah	yo-NAH	יוֹנָה
Yonadav	Jonadab	yo-na-DAV	יוֹנָדָב
Yonatan	Jonathan	yo-na-TAN	יוֹנָתָן

Hebrew Name	English Name	Pronunciation	Hebrew
Yoram	Joram	yo-RAM	יוֹרָם
Yosef	Joseph	yo-SAYF	יוֹסֵף
Yoshiyahu	Josiah	yo-shi-YA-hu	יֹאשִׁיָּהוּ
Yotam	Jotham	yo-TAM	יוֹתָם
Yotzadak	Jozadak	yo-tza-DAK	יוֹצָדָק
Yozavad	Jozabad	yo-za-VAD	יוֹזָבָד
Zanoach	Zanoah	za-NO-akh	זָנוֹחַ
Zecharya	Zechariah	z'-khar-YAH	זְכַרְיָה
Zerach	Zerah	ZE-rakh	זֶרַח
Zerubavel	Zerubbabel	z'-ru-ba-VEL	זְרֻבָּבֶל
Zevulun	Zebulun	z'-vu-LUN	זְבוּלֻן
Zilpa	Zilpah	zil-PAH	זִלְפָּה
Zimri	Zimri	zim-REE	זִמְרִי

Jewish Holidays

Hebrew Name	English Name	Pronunciation	Hebrew
Chanukah	Hanukkah	kha-nu-KAH	חֲנוּכָּה
Pesach	Passover	PE-sakh	פֶּסַח
Purim	Purim	pu-REEM	פּוּרִים
Rosh Hashana	Jewish New Year	rosh ha-sha-NAH	רֹאשׁ הַשָּׁנָה
Shavuot	Feast of Weeks	sha-vu-OT	שָׁבוּעוֹת
Shemini Atzeret	Eight Day of Assembly	sh'-mee-NEE a-TZE-ret	שְׁמִינִי עֲצֶרֶת
Sukkot	Feast of Tabernacles	su-KOT	סֻכּוֹת
Yom Kippur	Day of Atonement	yom kee-PUR	יוֹם כִּיפּוּר

Biblical Measurements

Hebrew Name	English Name	Pronunciation	Hebrew
Amah	Cubit	a-MAH	אַמָּה
Amot	Cubits	a-MOT	אַמּוֹת
Bat	Bath	bat	בַּת
Batim	Baths	ba-TEEM	בַּתִּים
Beka	half-shekel	BE-ka	בֶּקַע
Chomarim	Homers	kho-ma-REEM	חֳמָרִים
Chomer	Homer	KHO-mer	חֹמֶר
Efah	Ephah	ay-FAH	אֵיפָה
Geira	Gerah	gay-RAH	גֵּרָה

Hebrew Name	English Name	Pronunciation	Hebrew
Gomed	Gomed	GO- med	גֹּמֶד
Hin	Hin	heen	הִין
Kav	kab	kav	קַב
Kesita	kesitah	k'-see-TAH	קְשִׂיטָה
Kikar	talent	ki-KAR	כִּכָּר
Kikarim	talents	ki-ka-RIM	כִּכָּרִים
Kor	kor	kor	כֹּר
Letek	lethech	LE-tek	לֶתֶךְ
Log	Log	log	לֹג
Maneh	Mina	ma-NEH	מָנֶה
Manim	Minas	ma-NEEM	מָנִים
Omer	Omer	O-mer	עֹמֶר
Pim	Pim	peem	פִּים
Se'ah	Seah	say-AH	סְאָה
Se'eem	Seahs	s'-EEM	סְאִים
Shekalim	Shekels	sh'-ka-LEEM	שְׁקָלִים
Shekel	Shekel	SHE-kel	שֶׁקֶל
Tefach	Handbreadth	TE-fakh	טֶפַח
Zeret	Span	ZE-ret	זֶרֶת

Photo Credits

Song of Songs
1:14 Einat Anker, 2:13 Avi Ohayon Government Press Office (Israel), 3:10 Stefano Rocca/Shutterstock.com, 4:13 Moshe Milner Government Press Office (Israel), 6:4 John Theodor/Shutterstock.com, 7:8 Oleg Zalavsky/Shutterstock.com, 8:14 SJ Travel Photo and Video/Shutterstock.com

Ruth
1:5 Courtesy of Israel365, 1:16 Courtesy of Israel365, 2:4 AP Photo/Clara Amit, courtesy of the Israel Antiquities Authority, 2:17 Yaakov Gefen, Government Press Office (Israel), 2:23 John Theodor/Shutterstock.com, 3:9 len4ik/Shutterstock.com, 4:22 Lenar Musin/Shutterstock.com

Lamentations
1:2 Chaim, Wikimedia Commons, 1:16 Amos Ben Gershom, Government Press Office (Israel), 2:1 John Theodor/Shutterstock.com, 2:15 John Theodor/Shutterstock.com, 3:8 Oleg Ivanov IL/Shutterstock.com, 3:31 Protasov AN/Shutterstock.com, 3:58 By Melery821976 – Own work, CC BY-SA 4.0, https://commons.wikimedia.org/w/index.php?curid=107017921, 4:15 Bukvoed, Wikimedia Commons, 4:19 Avishai Teicher, Wikimedia Commons, 5:18 Rudy Balasko/Shutterstock.com, 5:21 Mark Neyman, Government Press Office (Israel)

Ecclesiastes
1:1 posztos/Shutterstock.com, 2:5 Asia Krivenko/Shutterstock.com, 3:5 Denis Kabanov/Shutterstock.com, 4:1 Liron-Afuta/Shutterstock.com, 5:9 ArtMari/Shutterstock.com, 6:2 Okrasiuk/Shutterstock.com, 7:11 Irit Gamlai, Wikimedia Commons, 8:6 Mark Neyman, Government Press Office (Israel), 9:8 elbud/Shutterstock.com, 10:19 Dmitry Pistrov/Shutterstock.com, 11:9 vblinov/Shutterstock.com, 12:9 Oren Ravid/Shutterstock.com

Esther
1:3 Amos Ben Gershom, Government Press Office (Israel), 2:6 John Theodor/Shutterstock.com, 3:13 By Eic413 (talk) – Own work (Original text: I created this work entirely by myself.), Public Domain, https://commons.wikimedia.org/w/index.php?curid=22600955, 4:14 STAN HONDA/AFP/Getty Images, 5:3 Prioryman, CC BY-SA 3.0 <https://creativecommons.org/licenses/by-sa/3.0>, via Wikimedia Commons, 6:1 Alexey Stiop/Shutterstock.com, 7:1 Yuri Yavnik/Shutterstock.com, 8:9 John Theodor/Shutterstock.com, 9:21 Mark Neyman, Government Press Office (Israel), 10:3 John Theodor/Shutterstock.com

Map of Modern-Day Israel and its Neighbors

The following is a map of modern-day Israel and the surrounding countries

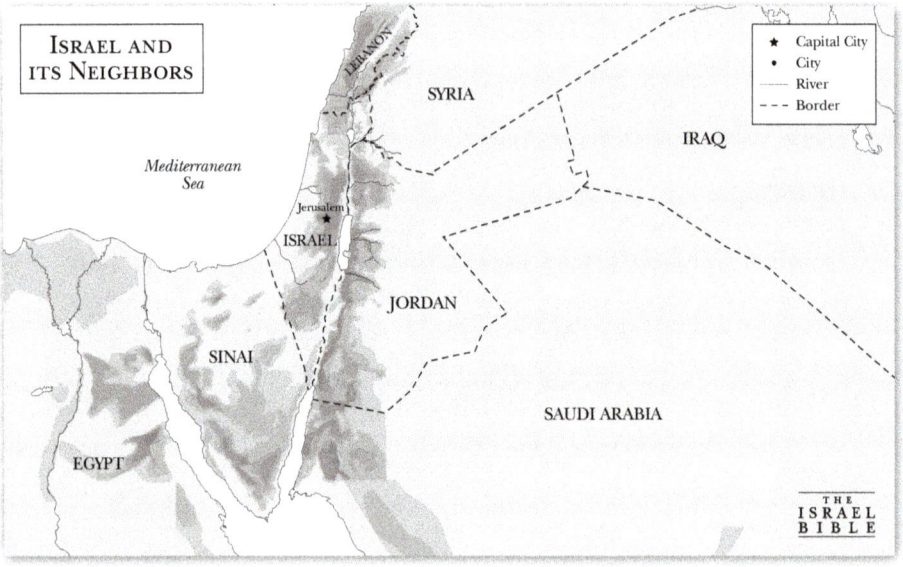

NOTES

NOTES

NOTES

NOTES

NOTES

For more inspiring commentary,
interactive maps, educational videos,
vivid photographs and more,
please visit our website

www.TheIsraelBible.com

THE
ISRAEL
BIBLE